•

•

•

more praise for IT AIN'T EASY:

"There have been many tales of talented eccentrics
along the rock 'n' roll highway. But *It Ain't Easy* digs well below
the surface to offer an affectionate, warts-and-all
portrait of the erudite dandy with the big baritone who
mentored Rod the Mod and Captain Fantastic and forever
reigns as the towering king of British blues."

NICHOLAS JENNINGS, author of *Before the Gold Rush*

"To understand the music of Elton John, Rod Stewart,
Eric Clapton and even the Beatles, you have to first understand
Long John Baldry's contribution to British pop.
Paul Myers's biography vividly captures John's charm and
humour and the colourful times in which he lived."

LARRY LEBLANC, *Billboard*

•

•

•

paul myers · · ·

LONG
JOHN
BALDRY

ain't easy

and the
BIRTH
of the
BRITISH
BLUES

GREYSTONE BOOKS
Douglas & McIntyre Publishing Group
Vancouver/Toronto/Berkeley

Greystone Books
A division of Douglas & McIntyre Ltd.
2323 Quebec Street, Suite 201
Vancouver, British Columbia · Canada v5T 4s7
www.greystonebooks.com

Library and Archives Canada Cataloguing in Publication
Myers, Paul, 1960–
It ain't easy : Long John Baldry and the birth
of the British blues / Paul Myers.

Includes index.

ISBN 978-1-55365-200-7

1. Baldry, Long John. 2. Singers—England—Biography.
3. Blues musicians—England—Biography. 4. Singers—Canada—Biography.
5. Blues musicians—Canada—Biography. 1. Title.
ML420.B178M98 2007   782.421643'092   C2007-903888-3

Editing by Barbara Pulling
Copy editing by Iva Cheung
Cover and text design by Peter Cocking
Cover photograph courtesy EMI Archives
Printed and bound in Canada by Friesens
Printed on acid-free paper that is forest friendly (100% post-consumer
recycled paper) and has been processed chlorine free.
Distributed in the U.S. by Publishers Group West

Lyrics from "A Thrill's a Thrill" by Barbra Amesbury,
© 1975 Amesbury Music. Used by permission.
Lyrics from "A Life of Blues" by John Baldry, Jimmy Horowitz,
and John King, © 1987 BMAR (copyright controlled).

Every reasonable effort has been made to locate and acknowledge the owners
of copyright for the photographs reproduced in this volume. The author
and the publisher would welcome any information regarding errors or omissions.

We gratefully acknowledge the financial support of the Canada Council for the
Arts, the British Columbia Arts Council, the Province of British Columbia through
the Book Publishing Tax Credit, and the Government of Canada through the Book
Publishing Industry Development Program (BPIDP) for our publishing activities.

To my parents, Eric and Bunny Myers,

who left England for North America in the late

1950s and gave me the life I have today.

And to my wife, Liza, who makes that life way

more interesting.

"The Blues are the true facts of life
expressed in words and song,
inspiration, feeling, and understanding."

WILLIE DIXON

(1915–92)

"Without music, life would be a mistake."

FRIEDRICH NIETZSCHE

(1844–1900)

contents

introduction: **the joint's jumpin'**

"The Thames is liquid history."
John Burns (1858–1943)

IN TWICKENHAM, ENGLAND, at the point
where the mighty, muddy Thames snakes
through the southwest London borough of Richmond, sits a
humble isthmus known as Eel Pie Island. Local history boasts
that Henry VIII once made regular junkets there to partake
of the eel pies. As time and the river flowed, however, Eel Pie
Island would become known for other delights.

By 1964 a musical revolution was fulminating in the ballroom of the Eel Pie Island Hotel. Maybe it was a reaction to the
postwar greyness of British life, or maybe it was just something
in the water, but the joint was, as they say, jumpin'.

For the young hipsters of the early '60s "Eelpisland" was
a magical place, if one your parents warned you about. Surprise raids by the local constabulary were routine. The sprung
dance floor in the hotel ballroom had been ideal for the jumping,

jiving and wailing of the "trad jazz" boom of the '50s, but as the next decade kicked into gear, a new breed of R&B-styled groups arrived on the scene.

On an evening in January 1964 the sweaty club walls reverberated with the distinctly bluesy songs of Lead Belly, Muddy Waters and Big Bill Broonzy. And yet the six-foot-seven gentleman wailing into the microphone could not have been more distinctly British. As a compère he was witty and assured, with a posh yet gravelly voice that suggested Noel Coward doing a comic impression of Winston Churchill. When he opened his mouth to sing, however, he was channelling the voice of a black sharecropper, transforming the island on the Thames into a paddle-wheeled riverboat on the Mississippi. Ladies and gentlemen, meet Long John Baldry.

Already a local legend, Baldry had only just taken over Cyril Davies R&B All Stars. Davies himself had died the night before. In tribute, and in defiance, Baldry led Davies's band through a blistering set, his gruff baritone cutting across the swampy din like a machete.

A shy, mop-haired teenager with a lager in his hand and a blues harp in his back pocket stood in the audience, swaggering to the music pealing from the stage. After the show the pleasantly buzzed young man, ears ringing and head spinning, shuffled over the footbridge to Twickenham Railway Station for the train back to the city. A little while later, as Baldry approached the platform to wait for the same train, his ears picked up the sound of the boy wailing the blues on his harmonica. A hasty introduction was made and, within a week, young Rod Stewart had joined Long John Baldry's band on the way to launching his historic career. Like many before and after him, he would have Baldry to thank.

For the charismatic, enigmatic Long John, it was merely one night in a roller-coaster career filled with giddy highs and crashing lows. Over the next four decades Baldry's muse would take him halfway around the world on a remarkable journey. Just who was this theatrical English dandy with a voice like a Mississippi delta gravel road? And more importantly, why did he sing the blues?

born in the blitz

JOHN WILLIAM BALDRY, the first of three children born to Margaret Louisa Baldry and London police constable James William Baldry, arrived on January 12, 1941, into a disquieted world. Hitler's relentless London night-bombing campaign, Blitzkrieg, was already in full swing. Baldry's parents had married in 1938, and in the winter of 1940, Margaret Louisa dropped a bombshell of her own: she was going to have a baby. According to family lore Officer Baldry, not especially thrilled by the news, demanded of his wife, "What did you let yourself get pregnant for?"

Before the Blitz began, the Baldrys had been living in Poplar, in East London's depressed Docklands, an area on which today sits the chrome-and-marble development known as Canary Wharf. "Jimbo" Baldry had reluctantly accepted a posting in the rundown precinct, and the young couple did their best to build a cozy nest in less than ideal circumstances. Hitler's army was on the march throughout Eastern Europe, however, prompting Officer Baldry to heed Winston Churchill's call to help "fight them on the beaches." He enlisted in the army.

Alone and with child Mrs. Baldry did what many women in her situation were doing: she headed for the countryside, far from the gunsights of the Luftwaffe. Travelling by British Rail, she set off for North Hamptonshire, where she hoped to deliver her baby in relative safety. As the train pulled into East Haddon, she was already going into labour. Nonetheless, wartime transportation shortages forced her to undertake a harrowing nine-mile walk to the Tudor-style stately home, Haddon Hall, which had been converted into a makeshift maternity ward. Remarkably, she made it in time.

Only six pounds at birth, baby John William was otherwise healthy. What stood out to all in the delivery room, though, was the child's *length:* he was a full twenty-seven inches.

"Apparently," says John's sister, Margaret, today, "they delivered his head and his shoulders first, but then his legs just went on for ever and ever. The midwife was said to have remarked, 'Oh my God, this is a *Long John* coming out here.'"

"The average baby is maybe twenty-one, twenty-two inches," John Baldry himself would boast to an interviewer later in life, "so I held some kind of a record in that hospital. Apparently I was quite an ugly sight, because I was totally purple in colour and covered in a white downy hair all over. Not just on my head but all over my body. I looked for all the world like a baboon or a mandrill. They said I looked more apelike than anything."

As was the custom, Baldry's proud mother remained at the maternity home for a couple of weeks after delivering. At least at Haddon Hall, the young mother could enjoy a proper hot bath; back home in Poplar, washing was done at the sink to save on fuel rations. When it was time to leave, Mrs. Baldry took young John back to the city, relocating to 68 Rowe Lane in Kingsbury, North London.

Baldry's sister, who was born four years later, remembers how their mother often told stories of how she became malnourished as she gave over her own food rations to her ravenous newborn son.

"Protein was limited," Baldry's sister recalls. "You were allowed one egg or an ounce of butter a week. Sugar and sweets were rationed, too. During the week we had bread and jam, but no butter. On Sunday we would have what was called a 'knife-and-fork tea.' It was the only time we ever tasted real butter. Unless you made it yourself bread was also rationed, as well as heating fuel and paper."

By all accounts little Long John was a healthy, happy—and increasingly chatty—baby, apparently conducting conversations by the time he was barely a year old. "Most babies of that age," his sister says, "will say the occasional word, but he was actually joining words together in full sentences."

The war raged on, and although Jim Baldry spent little time at home, one of his brief visits produced another child. At the tail end of 1943, amid nightly bombing raids that were now threatening even Kingsbury, John's brother, Roger, another tall baby, was born in the house at Rowe Lane.

Young John Baldry developed a lasting bond with his mother during these war years. Typically, during bombing raids, children were shepherded away from their parents in the name of safety. Mrs. Baldry, however, never allowed her children to be separated from her. Whenever the bombs got too close for comfort, she would flee, with John and Roger in tow, to her sister's place in Somerset.

Vancouver-based documentary filmmaker Nick Orchard conducted a series of revealing interviews with Long John Baldry between 2000 and 2001. In one of these conversations Baldry described for Orchard's camera a bombing raid in which Kingsbury suffered a direct hit.

"They say that in times of emergency and disaster, your memory is somewhat sharpened. So as a four-year-old kid, I can remember all that stuff vividly. It was a hairy time. We were actually at our house when the house next door got hit. It just took the house bang, right out. I didn't actually see it go up, but several hours afterwards you could see the rubble and the smoke and steam and whatever else coming out of it. Yet funnily enough, the surrounding houses weren't damaged too much. Then a little bit further down that street there were a couple that were taken out at random, almost like when a tornado hits. There is still an enormous crater across the street [from the former Baldry home], which has never been developed. It's very weird. It's just undergrowth and bushes and trees there where a house was taken out."

On April 9, 1945, just as the war was ending, Baldry's sister, Margaret, yet another tall child, was born. The family was billeted at the time in the northwest beachside town of New Brighton, near Wallasey, just a ferry across the Mersey River from Liverpool. It was a time of displacement for the Baldrys, who had joined other British families wandering nomadically across the land in busses, trains and automobiles. Liverpool, though, was not exactly the safest place to be. The ship-building industrial port was a prime Nazi target, as Baldry later told Orchard.

"It was a case of out of the frying pan into the fire," Baldry recalled, "because Liverpool was the main entry from the States and all the North Atlantic convoys. They wanted to knock it out by any means. By April 1945 there was no Luftwaffe left, but they were still sending over those damn v1s and, right at the end, v2s. The v1, which was like a small airplane with the rocket engine mounted on the top, could be especially frightening. I remember dashing to get to the shelters and out of the way, because they weren't just sending one or two over. They were sending fleets of these damn things. They would make a sort of buzzing sound, then they'd make a flapping noise and cut out. Then they would just drop down."

The German v1 technology, though somewhat imprecise, nonetheless left a lot of what is euphemistically called "collateral damage." But what the people really feared were the v2 rockets, with their improved accuracy. Luckily, Baldry recalled, the war ended shortly after the first v2 attacks began.

Although the children were never separated from their mother, for the first five years of his life John Baldry rarely saw his father. Nonetheless, according to his sister, Margaret, young John was a happy child and was doted upon by no fewer than five aunties.

"John was the first grandchild born," says Margaret, "and my father had five sisters, so John had a lot of attendants."

Young John also spent a fair amount of time with his grandparents, William and Ellen Baldry, in the Edgware area known as Burnt Oak. "I can remember sitting on my grandfather's knee in the kitchen and him teaching me to read from the newspaper," Baldry later recalled with fondness. "Within quite a short time, I was a very proficient reader, and almost to the age of four, I could read books and newspapers and everything else."

All of Britain rejoiced when, on September 2, 1945, the war that had devastated the tiny island was officially pronounced over. Baldry would later say that seeing the joy on his mother's face when she heard the news was his most cherished childhood memory. Jim Baldry, however, was forced to stay on in Germany during the postwar period, investigating Hitler's concentration camps and eventually prosecuting Nazi war criminals at Nuremberg.

"That was a particularly cold winter in Europe," Baldry later told Nick Orchard. "Dad had had to stay over there because he was part of this special investigation bureau attached to the armed forces... but he [also] dealt with a lot of... undercover sort of stuff. I guess it was all linked up to his past as a police-man. Dad ended up being billeted in one of the best places of all: the Krupps mansion, on the Unter den Linden, in Berlin."

It wasn't until Christmas 1947, upon his father's return from Berlin, that John, now approaching his seventh birthday, could start to really get to know his father. Jim Baldry's stories of Germany and its rich cultural history had a deep influence upon his oldest son. The senior Baldry also derived great pleasure from telling young John how he had evicted the Krupps family, who had made their fortune from war profiteering.

"My dad felt a bit of justification in shoving them out into the street," Baldry told Orchard, "with a tin cup, a spoon and a blanket. They were Hitler's original allies, the businessmen of the Ruhr, and they had led the movement to re-arm Germany."

Jim Baldry and his team had also helped themselves to the spoils of war. "A lot of that went on, I'm sure," Baldry told Orchard. "It wasn't just the Germans that went around looting. The Allies did as much as they did stealing things."

Significantly, Jim Baldry had liberated a quality German phonograph and stacks of twelve-inch Deutsche Grammophon and Telefunken classical 78s to play on it. These recordings would have a profound impact on young Baldry as he discovered his father's passion for classical music. Hearing the Berlin Symphony Orchestra performing Beethoven, Bach, Strauss and Verdi, he was hooked by the music's power.

An advanced child by the age of seven, John had already developed a case of wanderlust. He would frequently lead his siblings, three-year-old Margaret and five-year-old Roger, miles away from home, on foot, on unsupervised outings. He was also developing an interest in the arts, the cinema in particular, sometimes persuading his brother and sister to watch the same film three or four times over. Over the next few years, John, as the eldest, would constantly play the role of ringleader. His naturally adventurous nature often tended towards misadventure and, one time, very nearly got his younger brother killed. The three children had been given half a crown (two and sixpence) and sent off to the toy store on Edgware Road. John carried all the coins and saw to it that they were spent to his liking. The boys bought tin trains, but John forced Margaret to buy a book, which he quickly snapped up and began to read for himself.

"We were standing at the traffic lights," Margaret recalls, "and John was deeply into reading *Babes in the Wood*. The next thing we know, this little old lady is asking us, 'Was that little boy with you?'"

Roger had been struck by a car and dragged some three hundred yards. Margaret says today, "I remember going down the road and seeing him lying there in the gutter, unconscious, and asking if he was dead." Roger was not dead, but he was badly injured, and the three Baldry children were shaken by the incident.

Edgware Road was quite close to the police precinct where their father was now stationed. Jim Baldry had been transferred there from Kingsbury in 1949. Speaking to Nick Orchard, John Baldry recalled being "terribly upset" about being uprooted. "I think everything means that much more to you at the age of eight or nine," he said, "maybe more than it would later in life. I felt awful being dragged out of my environment."

In Edgware, Baldry attended the unpromisingly named Downer Grammar School, a "mind-shatteringly modern... example of postwar architecture and modern education." Along with his early exposure to classical music, John had for some time been curious about English folk music, epitomized by musicians like Percy Grainger and Roger Quilter. At the age of eight, he joined the choir at St. Lawrence's Church. Margaret Baldry says that although their parents weren't particularly religious, all three children were "chucked off three times on a Sunday" to St. Lawrence's.

"We spent a lot of time playing in the graveyard there," Margaret adds mischievously. "John would get us to gather all the flowers off people's graves and take them home for my mum."

Margaret still recalls the thrill of her brother's ethereal voice resonating in St. Lawrence's rafters. It was quite moving for a four-year-old girl. "In his choir robes," she recalls, "I actually thought he was an angel. I still get that sensation to this day of almost wanting to cry."

By his own admission, Baldry had "a glorious soprano voice" at the time. Puberty came early to him, however. Shortly after his tenth birthday John Baldry's voice broke, and his choir days were over. Luckily, he was about to become consumed by the primal, tribal sound that would define the rest of his life: the blues.

The Baldrys had acquired their first television set in 1949. One night the family gathered around the telly to watch a BBC magazine program called *Kaleidoscope*, hosted by Ronnie Waldman. Among the evening's entertainers were a spooky dance troupe, dressed head to toe in black bodysuits with bone structures painted onto them in white fluorescent paint. Under ultra-violet light, the dancers appeared to be reanimated skeletons. Visually, the effect was mesmerizing, but what really moved John Baldry was the exotic-sounding, harmonica-flavoured music behind the dancers: "Silver Fox Chase" by the American blues duo Sonny Terry and Brownie McGhee.

Charles Chilton's BBC documentaries employed American folk and blues songs, and John had seen a few children's television shows that used the folk songs of Woody Guthrie, but the "Silver Fox Chase" segment was the first time Baldry really *heard* and *felt* the blues. Although he still didn't know what to call it, this fascinating music spoke to him like no music had in the past. He learned the musical genre's name when he purchased a

Big Bill Broonzy recording, on the Disques Vogue label, in 1953. From the moment he heard Broonzy's music, Baldry was hooked on the blues, voraciously devouring records by Jimmy Witherspoon, Mahalia Jackson and Muddy Waters.

While attending Harrow School—which, as he liked to point out, Sir Winston Churchill had also attended—Baldry spent many hours in the nearby Harrow market. It boasted one of the finest used record shops in all of London. A young man on a mission, Baldry snapped up discs like Big Bill Broonzy's "Blues in 1890" and "Honey Bee" by Muddy Waters.

"There were mainly 78s," Baldry recalled to Nick Orchard, "but we were just starting to get the stereophonic LP in about 1956. I remember buying my first Chris Barber recording, *Chris Barber and His Jazz Band*, along with a Mahalia Jackson EP called *In the Upper Room*, in that market."

Despite these musical distractions, Baldry was a keen student and got on well with his teachers who, by and large, encouraged his artistic side.

"They were great people," Baldry remembered. "When you think of English teachers, you think of them as being particularly severe, nasty individuals. But I learned a hell of a lot, especially from my art teacher, Oliver Lippett."

While Mr. Lippett nurtured Baldry's visual-arts side—even by this age, he had demonstrated enough facility with drawing that he could well have pursued a career in design—Baldry would credit his music teacher, Mr. Evans, with nurturing his already blossoming love of music. Beyond the basic academic requirements of classical studies, Mr. Evans shared a fondness for jazz, folk and blues. Baldry was encouraged to start up a Jazz and Blues Appreciation Society—which included a fellow school chum named Charlie Watts—of which Mr. Evans and Mr. Lippett became members.

"We all put in a sixpence each to have a fund," Baldry told Orchard, "and we'd buy a record each week. We'd play it once, twice and sometimes three times, and then analyze it and give our opinions on it. Looking back now, it was probably very silly. It's strange when you think we were twelve-year-old English kids discussing all this like history professors, almost."

Britain, in 1953, was abuzz with news of the impending coronation of Queen Elizabeth II. For the first time since the miserable days of the war, Britons everywhere emerged from a kind of hibernation.

"The whole of London was adorned with lights and decorations," Margaret Baldry remembers. "They put on street parties for the children, and where we lived there was a big fancy costume pageant."

John had decided to go the dress-up event as the Roman emperor Nero, assigning his sister to the role of his slave. "He got himself done up in a white sheet," Margaret recalls, "with ribbons and bits and pieces, and we made him a crown out of leaves and followed along with this chariot the boys had made. He would command us, 'Faster, slaves, faster!'"

Roger Baldry, though only a little shorter than John, says it wasn't hard to look up to his older brother in those days.

"He had a good brain," says Roger, "was very clever with words, and a brilliant mimic. It was fortunate that John would make people laugh, as he was sometimes the target of bullying by local ruffians and, on a few occasions, would require rescuing from them. The bullying would probably have been worse had he not been able to spread his humour, which was quite disarming for the bullies."

At home, John frequently used his quick wits to evade the strict discipline of their father. "Dad thought slapping the kids about was the right thing to do," says Margaret. "I can remember being lined up in the kitchen and my father asking, 'Did you do it?' We'd all stick with each other on occasions like that."

Since John could charm his way out of trouble, though, the worst punishments were often dealt to her and Roger.

"John used to say he felt quite guilty that Roger and I, particularly Roger, used to come in for a lot of punishment over the most stupid, stupid things. It might just be that, you know, your face didn't look clean that day. But John was just sort of affable and he'd say [to our father], 'Oh, I'm sorry,' then go and do whatever it was he was gonna do."

As he got deeper into the Jazz and Blues Appreciation Society at school, John felt that he required an instrument of his own. He got off to a false start when he acquired a decidedly unbluesy tenor banjo for ten shillings, the proceeds from selling some prized belongings.

"He sold a chess set that my parents had bought him," remembers Margaret, "along with his huge postage stamp collection." Young John practised diligently on the noisy banjo in a park behind St. Lawrence's Church.

"It was an old banjo," says Roger Baldry, "which had only one or two strings left on it. I think it was some time before he could afford a full set of strings, but that didn't deter him from plink, plink, plinking away, driving everyone mad."

Like many boys his age, Baldry was taken with the so-called skiffle craze of the day, championed by Lonnie Donegan, a featured soloist in Chris Barber's jazz band. Soon he had put together his own skiffle group with a few of his like-minded schoolmates. Among the most influential of Donegan's recordings was his interpretation of Lead Belly's "Rock Island Line." Years later, Baldry explained the effect Lead Belly's music had on him in an interview with his friend Holger Petersen.

"Lonnie chose the 'Rock Island Line' as one side," Baldry recalled, "and 'John Henry' on the back. And when I saw the name [Huddie] 'Ledbetter' [Lead Belly's legal name] there, I thought, 'Hmm, let's find out more about this man.'"

A neighbourhood artist named Graham Bradbury, an early musical mentor, introduced John to the original Lead Belly recordings upon which Donegan had based his version. According to Baldry's sister, Margaret, their parents disapproved of Bradbury because he had long hair and wore corduroy trousers.

"Graham lived two doors down," says Margaret, "and he was quite a bit older than John. John was in awe of him because he was an artist. Graham said, 'Come down to my house, and I'll show you what proper music is.'"

Baldry had soon amassed a collection of vinyl Lead Belly discs that included the 1953 recordings made by Frederic Ramsey Jr. for the Folkways label, which he kept in mint condition. Listening to Lead Belly's big-handed guitar playing convinced him, however, that his banjo was ill suited to the blues.

"It would have sounded daft," Baldry told Nick Orchard. "I didn't really like it as an instrument. Although later on, I did keep a banjo, tuned to guitar tuning, to play with Dixieland bands."

Fifteen pounds bought the young Baldry a prewar, arched-top Harmony jazz guitar, with what is referred to as an "F hole" cut into it.

"When I got my first guitar," he later told Holger Petersen, "I rapidly started to learn, parrot fashion, because there was no one to teach you. They made them so they had a nice pokey sound for jazz and dance bands in pre-amplified days."

At first, Baldry carted around his new guitar, on bikes and trains, in nothing more than a canvas sack. Then one day, walking through Hanover Square, he noticed a handsome guitar case out by the dustbins of a prestigious music store. He entered the shop to ask if he could have it. Not only was he welcome to the case, they told him, but he could also help himself to the battered instrument inside it.

"It turned out," Baldry told Orchard, "that it was a Maccaferri guitar manufactured by Mario Maccaferri, who worked for the Selmer Company in Paris. It was the same kind of guitar that

Django Reinhardt played, with the 'D' sound hole, the square cutaway and a series of chambers inside, immaculately made of wood, rather like an old acoustic gramophone from the '20s with the big horns and such. It really was an amazing instrument."

Amazing as it was, the battered guitar was in desperate need of repair. Baldry consulted luthier Emil Grimshaw of Grimshaw and Sons in Golden Square. In Grimshaw's learned opinion, the instrument was beyond repair. He had long been fascinated by Maccaferri's designs, however, so he offered John a deal. If Baldry would allow him to take the whole thing apart, to use as an educational specimen, Grimshaw would build Baldry a replica of it, at a reasonable price.

"This guitar had cost me nothing," Baldry recalled, "so I said okay, and he constructed it. Although it did end up costing me eighty pounds, which was a fair amount back then."

By now, Baldry was a habitué of the Edgware Jazz Club and, much to his father's dismay, West End clubs such as the Flamingo. Soon he began to try his hand at actually playing on their stages.

"They were sort of coffee bars," Margaret recalled, "and Dad was continually going round to [drag] John out of these places where there were all these cobwebs and filth."

At sixteen, Baldry left school and for a time attended the Hornsey College of Art, in Highgate. Before long he felt the urge to go out into the world, and he took a day job at the Central Arts Studio. In a 1968 interview, Baldry's mother recalled her initial dismay at her son's decision.

"I was very disappointed," she confessed. "He was one of those boys who are really brilliant at school. He didn't have to swot-up on anything in the evening like most kids, and when it came to exams, he just sailed through them. We thought, at the time, that it was a terrible waste that such a wonderful brain was going to be thrown away."

Jim Baldry, for his part, felt that a stint in the army would be just the thing for a rake and rambling boy like his eldest son.

"When John left school," John's sister, Margaret, recalls, "my father said, 'Oh, he'll be in the army soon. They'll make a proper man out of him.' John had received his conscription papers, because everyone had to do national service. One day, Dad heard on the radio that they had abolished the conscription program beginning with people born after December 1940. So John, born in January of 1941, had missed it by twelve days. My father was almost in tears."

John, however, had already decided that he'd rather go to prison as a conscientious objector. "With his pacifist leanings," notes Roger Baldry today, "he would have undoubtedly evaded the call-up."

With the draft now a moot point, Baldry continued his dual career as a full-time graphic artist by day and an aspiring guitarist and singer by night. On the road and in the local clubs, he met and shared bills with scores of like-minded blues travellers and frequently found his way onto the British airwaves. The schedule was demanding—after certain out-of-town performances in Manchester or Liverpool he would have to travel all night to make it back to his day job at nine in the morning—but somehow he muddled through.

"To an extent I was able to do it at nineteen," he recalled in an interview. "I seemed to have an enormous amount of energy." But by the spring of 1960, after three years of moonlighting, his punishing schedule had brought him to a breaking point.

"I had made my debut on British television and on BBC Radio in about 1957," Baldry later told Nick Orchard, "so I'd been singing on the radio and television for quite a while before I just decided I had to drop one of my activities. I gave up the art studio, because by that time people had begun to know of me."

Baldry was also increasingly certain about his true vocation in life. He had always stood out in a crowd for his height, and now he was gaining recognition for his music. He'd been born in the Blitz, but he would soon launch a musical assault of his own, taking London and the U.K. by storm.

"I had already established quite a reputation and a name for myself," he later recalled. "People would say, 'Oh, that's Long John Baldry, the kid who does the blues.'"

have guitar, will travel

AT THE AGE OF nineteen, John Baldry left the nine-to-five grind to devote himself to a full-time career in music. Although his height made him seem a likely candidate to follow his father into the constabulary, his brother, Roger—who did join the force—doesn't recall any pressure for John to do the same.

"Quite the contrary," says Roger Baldry today, "as the hours were long, the conditions and the pay were poor. My annual salary on joining in 1963 was roughly the same as John's then weekly income. So I don't think Father disapproved. We all considered John to be rather alternative, though, particularly for the 1950s. He wore an unconventional hairstyle—no 'short back and sides' for him—and unusual clothes, like a duffle coat."

By this time, too, Baldry's parents had come to appreciate their son's exceptional talent, as Mrs. Baldry revealed in the 1968 interview. "I remember the first time I'd seen him doing folk music," she said. "Just to sit there and see the way he was able to sway the audience was really wonderful."

Since his public performance debut, on a "skiffle" bill with Ken Colyer at the Acton Town Hall in 1956, Baldry had become eager to make a living solely from music. Frequently, this meant performing for change from passersby on the sidewalks of London. The establishment saw busking as an affront to decency, but as Baldry explained in 2001, the managers of certain types of venues, such as the National Film Theatre on the South Bank, actively encouraged street performers outside their doors.

"[They] loved having us around the place," Baldry told Nick Orchard, "playing for the crowds who were lining up to go in."

One night, Baldry recalled, Vittorio De Sica, the Italian director of *The Bicycle Thief*, put a whole "tenner" into Baldry's hat as he left the National cinema. "Ten pounds was a lot of money in 1957," Baldry reminded Orchard, "probably like a thousand pounds today."

Busking is now a part of everyday life in London, with licensed entertainers appearing in the tunnels at most major stops on the Tube. In the late '50s, however, it was a dodgy business likely to get you nicked by the local police. On "Conditional Discharge," the spoken-word opener from his 1971 album, *It Ain't Easy*, Baldry—accompanied by a rollicking boogie-woogie piano riff—recounted the time he was busted for busking in Wardour Place, Soho. Standing on the spot where he had been arrested decades earlier, Baldry recreated the event for Orchard's cameras in 2000.

"I was an innocent sixteen-year-old youth," he explained, consciously mirroring the lyrics of the song, "just standing there, playing guitar. This policeman dragged me and my guitar off, with my hatful of pennies, for causing a public disturbance. It wasn't a case of being clapped in irons; I just had my collar felt very gently. He said, 'Will you walk with me, young man?' Then he walked me all the way back to Marlborough Street Magistrates Court, where they gave me a year's conditional discharge."

On the recording, which presages one of his better-known songs, "Don't Try to Lay No Boogie Woogie on the King of Rock 'n' Roll," Baldry performs a series of comedic voice characterizations, such as the judge tripping over the term "boo-gee woo-gee" and the fastidious arresting officer reading from his notebook. While these characters were reminiscent of the authority figures lampooned in the humour of *The Goon Show*'s Peter Sellers and Spike Milligan, Baldry did not have to look far afield for the inspiration for his "policeman" character. He had grown up with him.

"The copper in the intro to 'Boogie Woogie' really is my father," confirms John's sister, Margaret. "I mean, it actually *is* my father's voice."

Margaret recalls John's arrest from the home-front perspective. As the family was sitting in their front room one evening, Officer Baldry received a call from a fellow policeman to say that his eldest boy had been hauled in for busking. Rather than going down to the station to pick him up, Jim Baldry suggested that a night in jail might be just the thing to smarten up his wayward son.

"My father was beside himself," says Margaret. "He just saw John as being a wastrel, never knuckling down and getting a proper job. It was an embarrassment to know that your son had been arrested, and for singing and begging, no less. It just wasn't right for my father. He was very proper and concerned about what the neighbours thought of him. He mellowed as he got older, and we could laugh at those things, but back then it was very important to him."

The incident did nothing to deter John Baldry from his calling. He continued to live with his family, but by the late '50s he had become a fixture—inside and outside London's music venues—on a local scene that included Davy Graham, Robin Hall, Jimmie MacGregor and Steve Benbow. He sat in frequently with the leading lights of the old-guard, trad jazz scene, including Humphrey Lyttleton and the three Bs: Kenny Ball, Acker Bilk and Chris Barber.

Barber specialized in New Orleans–flavoured jazz, but he kept an ear to the ground for new variations. As such, he is rightly credited for both the birth of the "skiffle" craze and the arrival of genuine American blues on British shores.

"By the late 1940s," Barber explains today, "there were a lot of amateur bands doing a kind of New Orleans revival. Some of us, however, were very conscious of the fact that we wanted to be a part of the jazz life, not just outsiders imitating part of it. Around 1952, Lonnie Donegan had joined my amateur band on banjo and vocals. We would do what I would call '20s skiffle stuff. We actually had the original Paramount recording from 1929 called 'Hometown Skiffle,' which had the first use of the name 'skiffle' that I've ever come across."

In a 1983 interview with Canadian journalist Richard Crouse, Baldry explained how he navigated the music scene at the time. "I split my performances," he said, "between doing a few blues tunes, just me and my guitar, and then I'd be up with [Chris Barber's] band, doing 'When the Saints Go Marchin' In' and all those songs associated with New Orleans. It was a means to an end, but I wasn't head over heels in love with that music."

Significantly, Baldry also crossed paths with the influential American folksinger Ramblin' Jack Elliott. A wandering troubadour most famously associated with Woody Guthrie and, later, Bob Dylan, Elliott had been travelling to England since 1955.

"The first week we were in England," Elliott recalls today, "I got to play at a concert with Lonnie Donegan at the Royal Festival Hall. Lonnie had a very good skiffle group, which was actually a part of Chris Barber's Jazz Band."

With his genuine American twang, Ramblin' Jack Elliott was a hit with Barber and Donegan's Yank-centric audience.

"They just flipped," says Elliott. "It was the first time I'd ever seen a crowd react like that. A week later, we played at the Blues and Barrelhouse Club, upstairs at Charrington's Roundhouse Pub."

Unbeknownst to Elliott, John Baldry, by then a regular performer at the Thursday night sessions, was also in attendance that evening. It would not be until a year later, when the two were double-billed on a show at the Troubadour, that they would actually meet.

"He was like a puppy dog," says Elliott, recalling the teenage Baldry. "I liked him a lot. He was only seventeen years old, but even then he was just this very pleasant kid, long and tall, with a very engaging smile. My wife and I were both very fond of him, and during that whole time we were in London, we spent a lot of time in some great Indian restaurants with him. He was a very likeable chap. He kind of specialized in Lead Belly and did a lot of his songs, like 'Black Girl' and 'Midnight Special.' I think we did a couple of those songs together at one time."

The Roundhouse, located to this day at the corner of Brewer and Wardour streets in Soho, remains a crucial landmark in the histories of both Long John Baldry and the British Blues movement. It was upstairs in that purple-brick Victorian establishment that Baldry had first met two musicians who would play a key role in his transition from part-time musician to professional.

Guitarist Alexis Korner and harmonica player Cyril Davies were unlikely partners as hosts of the Roundhouse Blues and Barrelhouse Club. Korner had been a member of Chris Barber's trad jazz band before striking out on his own to play blues material in clubs and coffee bars. Davies had started "blues and skiffle" nights at the Roundhouse, with former partner Bob Watson, back in 1952. By 1955, Davies had enlisted Korner to help him launch what British rock historian Pete Frame called "the firstest and bestest skiffle club" in Britain.

When they weren't at each other's throats, Korner and Davies—along with Chris Barber—played a major role in tracking down and bringing to England the most influential American blues acts of their generation, including Sonny Terry and Brownie McGhee, Memphis Slim, Big Bill Broonzy and Muddy Waters.

"We agreed on the blues," Korner admitted to Pete Frame, "but disagreed about almost everything else."

Chris Barber recalls today how a significant ruling by the Musicians Union created an environment in which homegrown British players were allowed to work with visiting American artists.

"Broonzy had been over in 1951, and he was brought back again in '54," says Barber, "and that time they got my band to play with him. The Musicians Union had banned any American musicians playing in Britain because the American Federation of Musicians had banned British musicians from playing in America. They [the AFM] had pulled the plug on some concerts done by some British dance bands or stage bands around 1939. We discovered, however, that the Musicians Union, in Britain *or* America, didn't consider singers accompanying themselves as musicians. This one smart agent had worked out how to fool the union into thinking they had scored a great point off us all and done something. In reality, *he* scored the point. Basically, the deal was that any concert played by an American band in Britain was matched by a British band in America. It wouldn't happen, but they would say it happened. Broonzy could come in because he was a singer and accompanied himself, and we immediately booked a tour beginning in '57. We had Big Bill with former gospel singer Brother John Sellers, and then we brought in Sister Rosetta Tharpe in November of '57 and again in '58. We brought Sonny Terry and Brownie McGhee over, because they had done some kind of folky, bluesy stuff for Folkways. As this happened, a lot of the jazz groups came in from America authorized by the union under this 'nudge, nudge, wink, wink' exchange deal. The union didn't realize they were being fooled."

From about 1958 until early 1960, Korner and Davies also routinely hired John Baldry, at ten shillings a night, to play at their Thursday series. "Ten shillings is basically about a dollar. But, again, back then that was a lot of money," Baldry told Nick Orchard, perhaps exaggerating just a little when he added, "You could go out for the evening, get wined and dined, maybe even pick up a whore, for ten shillings."

Baldry would perform short solo sets on his acoustic guitar, or play as part of a duo with guitarist Geoff Bradford or even a trio if piano man Keith Scott was handy. Bradford, a nascent member of the Rolling Stones, was enthralled by the authenticity of Baldry's solo sets at the Roundhouse.

"He used to sing unaccompanied," Bradford recalls today. "He was quite exceptional. He understood the music and had that quality in the voice that everyone else was striving for at the time. He didn't have a London accent, well, it was kind of a *cultivated* accent, which he retained until he sang. But then he automatically changed to a Mississippi Delta accent."

When he wasn't playing on the Roundhouse's stage, Baldry could frequently be found among the audience. Decades later, Baldry sat in the club once again, with Nick Orchard, and recalled watching Korner and Davies in action.

"Oh, yes," Baldry told Orchard, "I was the ultimate enthusiast. Alex played mandolin, sometimes guitar. Cyril was on guitar then, and Ken Colyer's brother, Bill, was playing washboard. Very often, there was a young lady called Lisa Turner playing five-string banjo. Alex was very influential, but even Cyril and Alex would agree that Ken Colyer was the man who started it all. He was really the catalyst for all things blues in this country. Great cornet player and trumpet player, in the New Orleans style, but he moonlighted as a folky, bluesy singer with a voice somewhat like Jack Teagarden. A lot of people found him an irascible bugger and very stubborn, but he also had a lot of warmth and charm about him. I was very proud to have known him. He ran Studio 51, which was also known as the Ken Colyer Club. In 1957 that was the tail end of the whole skiffle movement in England, which, in British terms, was like a continuation of country blues and acts like Gus Cannon's jug band or the Memphis Jug Band. Lonnie also played guitar and banjo in the Ken Colyer Skiffle Group. They had Alex, again, on mandolin, Ken played guitar, Chris Barber played the bass and Ken's brother Bill Colyer played the washboard. Sometimes, Beryl Brydon played washboard, as she did on Lonnie Donegan's 'Rock Island Line,' which he had so much success with."

Aside from their fondness for skiffle, Korner and Davies's deeply felt love of the blues and jazz proved to be extremely contagious. "I think that's how Alexis touched me," Baldry explained, "and Mick, Brian and Keith from the Stones and others. It was that pioneering spirit. It set our little corner of the world ablaze in the early '60s."

Baldry elaborated on this "little corner of the world" in a 1996 interview with Stony Plain Records president Holger Petersen.

"It was very, very odd," Baldry recalled, "because many of the students in art colleges scattered around London were very enamoured of the music of Big Bill Broonzy, Muddy Waters and other blues artists. None of us knew each other at that particular time, but we came together in the seeds of a movement. Eric Clapton, I had met in '59 or '60. I was playing in a folk club in Richmond, which is to the west of London, and he came down to see me."

Eric Clapton says now that Baldry was something of an iconic figure to him. "I suppose because he was very tall and thin, and played twelve-string guitar," he explains. "Plus, he was one of the few people playing a lot of the bluesy kind of stuff. I saw a lot of him around those days."

With no disrespect to the later electric, full-band material, Clapton says, it was Baldry's earlier, folkier blues that spoke to him the loudest. "I've gotta say," Clapton declares, "my earliest impression of John was that he was actually more powerful to me when he was on his own, just playing acoustic. And John was probably one of the only guys who was *solely* a blues musician, to begin with anyway. He was very interested in Muddy Waters and Lead Belly, but he really grasped the whole genre. I think, in a way, he was kind of a musicologist. He was studied, a scholar. He knew what was going on."

Besides sets at the Crawdaddy Club in Richmond, Clapton remembers watching Baldry play as an interval act between big band sets down at Eel Pie Island.

"They had Chris Barber or Ken Colyer in one room," Clapton says, "and then there was another room given over to more intimate stuff. John would be there when he was playing unamplified guitar, without a microphone."

"You had to rely on your own projection, vocally, to carry to an audience," Baldry would tell Nick Orchard in recalling those days. "So that may have a lot to do with the way I sing, because obviously you've got to put out for the audience to hear what you do."

Clapton was also taken with Baldry's between-song banter. "He was just an incredible man," he says, "with a kind of a droll English accent. If he was holding court talking to a group of people, he could be quite cutting and very funny, with a good grasp of irony and all that kind of thing. But when he played, he became a different person altogether."

Although Baldry admitted that he was merely copying American "black music," the sight of a white Englishman playing the blues confirmed for a young Eric Clapton that it could be done.

"I had already decided what I liked and what I was going to do," Clapton says today, "but seeing him, I think, compounded that for me. What it was probably coming down to was that most of the white guys that were playing the guitar and singing in this country were more headed towards being rock, pop or skiffle musicians, you know?"

Geoff Bradford notes that, in its infancy, the blues cult was limited to a small number of listeners and an even smaller number of players. "There were only about fifteen or twenty players involved, in the whole of England," he recalls. "This was long before John Mayall came down from Manchester, and when I see these TV programs about how the blues started with him and Clapton, I think to myself, my God, why can't they do some research?"

John Mayall concurs. "Before I came down to London from Manchester to form the Bluesbreakers," Mayall recalls today, "Long John was a distinguished figurehead for such pioneering bands as Cyril Davies's All Stars and Alexis Korner's Blues Incorporated. He ranks as an important link between the trad jazz movement and the birth of the British Blues."

Although Baldry had few peers at the time, particularly among acoustic blues guitarists, he paid tribute to a few notable influences, like Rory and Alex McEwan, brothers from the Scottish brewing family. "They were great players in that Blind Gary Davis style they called the 'Piedmont Blues Rag,'" Baldry told Holger Petersen. "I guess, if I became any good or proficient on twelve-string guitar, it was really the influence of Rory McEwan." Baldry also credited the German promotion team of Horst Lippmann and Fritz Rau, who were responsible for bringing many genuine blues artists to Europe.

All of these live shows greatly inspired the teenage Baldry, but imported records remained a major influence. Habitually raiding Doug Dobell's record shop on Charing Cross Road,

Baldry spent a fortune he didn't have on obscure audio delights. From jamming along with the records, he soon knew all the riffs by heart, a skill that stood him in good stead when he was later called upon to accompany many of these same artists.

Periodically, Baldry would drop in at the 100 Club, Humphrey Lyttleton's music venue at 100 Oxford Street, where piano player and manager George Webb regularly booked greats such as Champion Jack Dupree, Memphis Slim, Speckled Red and Roosevelt Sykes. Baldry would sit in and "noodle" behind the likes of Sykes, the first blues pianist he played guitar for on a regular basis.

"Not that I was that good," he later admitted to Holger Petersen, "but when Roosevelt came over for the first time, doing a club tour, Alex was not available, so they asked me if I'd sit in. I, of course, said I'd be delighted to."

Piano players toured frequently, as they were easy to book and most venues had a house piano. "As long as there's a piano there," Baldry told Petersen, "you can shove him on without any kind of accompaniment. Very often, the great blues and boogie-woogie piano players were their own drummers, you know. Their left hand would be very percussive so you wouldn't even need drums."

Of course, the quality between one house piano and the next was wildly inconsistent, and there was no guarantee that the piano provided would even be tuned. As Baldry remembers, most times they were not. Still, as a self-described "journeyman guitar player," he quickly got to know most of the piano men, particularly Memphis Slim, composer of the popular blues number "Every Day I Have the Blues."

Memphis Slim was accompanied on a 1959 tour of Europe by renowned Chicago blues songwriter Willie Dixon. Besides being an early mentor to Baldry, Dixon would become a lifelong friend.

"Willie came over to Europe to tour with Memphis Slim as a double act," Baldry told Holger Petersen. "I'd known Slim from a couple of years before when he first came to England. They established a base at the Trois Mailletz in Paris, where Slim played for many, many years. Willie and I became very good friends from that time onwards, and I saw quite a lot of him in England, because he would organize all the international blues package tours for Lippman and Rau. Willie was their American booking agent, their man in Chicago. They would have about fifteen legendary artists all on the same bill. For many of us, in England, it was our first opportunity to see people like Sonny Boy Williamson, also known as Rice Miller, and to see John Lee Hooker. Those tours went on for about ten years, maybe more. Willie would always be over for these shows in one capacity or another, playing or organizing things. So I saw a lot of Willie in the '60s right through to the '70s."

Most American blues artists, particularly the black ones, were happy to skip across the Atlantic to Europe, where audiences treated them with respect and lined up to hear their music—something they were not getting back home in the States.

"All this was going on in England," Baldry told Nick Orchard, "before American people were even aware that they had this music on their doorstep. Americans didn't want to listen to that black music, oh no! White people, with a few exceptions, didn't take the time to realize what wonderful, beautiful poetry was there in jazz and blues music. There had been that forced division for so long between whites and blacks in society."

The young Baldry, already keenly sensitive to civil rights issues, felt lucky to be honing his craft with the best of them. He roamed the country—"have guitar, will travel"—like a cowboy with his trusty twelve-string by his side. "It was like being a pioneer in the Old West," he remembered. "Totally in love with it all, totally enthusiastic about it all, just wanting it to go on for ever and ever."

Baldry's tours took him far from London and frequently to Liverpool. For his Liverpool debut in 1957, he played a "folkie" acoustic show at Sampson and Barlows Grill on London Road, and around this time he often appeared with a vocal group called the Thameside Four.

In 1958, Baldry toured the country with Ramblin' Jack Elliott, often playing in "soft-seater" halls that were a welcome respite from the usual cramped nightclubs. The poster for their show at the Mechanics' Institute in Bradford boasted that Elliott was continuing Woody Guthrie's folk legacy while Baldry was proclaimed "the greatest white twelve-string guitar player in the world."

Years later, Baldry told Holger Petersen that this was probably "stretching it quite a bit." However, he said, "I was probably the only twelve-string player they could think of at the time. When I was very young, I was actually quite an accomplished player. Sadly, there's not much around on tape. Possibly BBC Radio has some stuff."

Baldry's fondness for the twelve-string guitar stemmed directly from his love of Lead Belly, whose music just sounded better, he felt, over twelve resonant strings. "There was a fellow that I met around '56 or '57 named Pete Watson," he told Holger Petersen, "who was the ultimate Lead Belly fan. But he was doing all the Lead Belly tunes on six-string, when of course, you know, Lead Belly's material just lends itself so well to the twelve-string."

In 1957, Baldry came across a cabinet-maker named Anthony Zemaitis who built him his first custom-made twelve-string guitar, free of charge. Zemaitis had never built guitars at that point, but he would subsequently go on to become one of the best-known luthiers in the world and, before his death in 2002, to make custom guitars for the likes of Ronnie Wood, Keith Richards, Donovan, George Harrison and Eric Clapton.

Baldry liked to say that he had been Zemaitis's "guinea pig." The two had met in late 1956, at the Gyre and Gimbel, near Charing Cross tube station. It was a favourite watering hole of Baldry's and quite close to the Chelsea woodworking studio where Zemaitis made top-quality cabinets, some of which are in Windsor Castle's permanent collection today. Zemaitis's expert touch with furniture was evident in the crafting of his first guitar.

"It really was an amazing-sounding instrument," Baldry would recall in later years. "Oh my lord, it was my constant companion. I played that damn thing almost every waking moment for I think about eighteen months."

Sadly, this prized guitar was damaged on a weekend trip to the seaside resort town of Brighton, fifty miles south of London. A favourite getaway for London's youth in the '50s, Brighton was later the scene of violent clashes between Mods and Rockers—famously observed by the Who's Pete Townshend in *Quadrophenia*. In Baldry's day, things there were far less frantic. Hundreds of London weekenders would board the "milk train" out of the city. Although it stopped at every station between London Bridge and Brighton, one couldn't argue with the incredibly cheap fare.

"It was like two shillings, or two and sixpence a turn," Baldry told Nick Orchard, "which even in the late '50s was a considerable deal. Then, once we'd got to Brighton, all the guitar players would get their guitars out."

One very hot day in the summer of 1957, Baldry took his prized Zemaitis guitar down to Brighton. "I remember thinking, 'Oh my God, I don't want the guitar to be in this direct sunlight,'" he recalled in an interview with Petersen. "I'd forgotten where I'd put my case, so I wrapped it up in a towel, there by my side, so it wouldn't get too much direct sun. Then some fool came running along, jumped over me, landed, didn't see the guitar there and crashed. The guitar ended up as matchwood. The guy was distraught... *crying* with remorse."

Baldry consoled himself with the fact that the damaged guitar had cost him nothing. But then it dawned on him that he no longer had a guitar at all. He took the pile of kindling, optimistically, back to Zemaitis, but the instrument was beyond repair. Zemaitis agreed to build a newer, better guitar for Baldry, but this time said he'd have to charge a nominal fee.

"He charged me fifteen pounds or something," Baldry remembered, "but it was a much bigger guitar. I think that on the second one, he had figured out the strutting, which is the internal mechanics of acoustic guitar. He had figured out what to do with the strutting so he could have a fixed bridge instead of an adjustable bridge."

Sadly, Baldry's second Zemaitis guitar was stolen in Trafalgar Square when he took it along to an anti-apartheid rally outside the South African embassy. "It was the night after the Sharpeville Massacre," Baldry told Holger Petersen. "I think two hundred and something people had been shot down. We were protesting outside South Africa House. In fact, I was marching round and round this bloody embassy for three whole days."

Distracted by his anger, Baldry left his guitar unattended for a moment. When he returned, it was gone. "I left it standing in a corner," he recalled, "while I was busy protesting, and somebody made off with it."

Although Baldry would have Zemaitis build him other guitars over the years, he never got over the loss of the first two. But just as London in 1960 was a time of loss, it was also a time of growth and change. As typified by the anti-apartheid protest, revolution was in the air, and the next decade would witness a social and sexual revolution unlike any in history. For Baldry and his Lead Belly–worshipping clique, the seeds of a musical revolution had been sown upstairs at the Roundhouse. As punk was to the corporate rock of the 1970s and grunge to late '80s "hair metal," Baldry's late-'50s blues movement represented a backlash against the watered-down pop music of American imports like Doris Day and Pat Boone and their British equivalents.

In the introduction to his 1997 book *The Beatles and Some Other Guys*, rock historian Pete Frame describes eloquently the postwar British mood. "I had grown up," Frame wrote, "during a time when everything in austere ration-booked, bomb-cratered Britain seemed to be dull and grimy and grey—while everything American was utterly wonderful. We had Morris Minors in black or drab olive green; they had huge-finned Cadillacs in duo-tone colour combinations of salmon and charcoal, or turquoise and ivory—with enough chrome to blind you at two miles. We had terraced houses, encased in smoke and fog; they had elegant timbered bungalows with neat suburban lawns, kept green by underground sprinklers. We had boring old film stars like Kenneth More and John Mills; they had Marlon Brando and James Dean. We had Diana Dors; they had Marilyn Monroe. We had ersatz rock 'n' rollers like Tommy Steele and Terry Dene; they had Jerry Lee Lewis and Chuck Berry."

The young Baldry himself observed the greyness of London. Yet looking around the Roundhouse with Nick Orchard years later, he recalled, "In here there was a sparkle... There was flock wallpaper on the walls, which was very popular back in the '50s and '60s in England—especially in a room that might have had a higher ceiling than normal—and very heavy drapes. There was a table by the door, and the people used to pay two and sixpence to come in and sit on the linoleum floor, which must have been very cold."

Across town, Chris Barber and Harold Pendleton, who ran the National Jazz Federation, had begun presenting jazz shows in 1958 at the original Marquee Club, which had occupied the space below the Academy Cinema at 165 Oxford Street in Oxford Circus. A year earlier, the two had also set the wheels in motion for the blues revolution, bringing over artists like Muddy Waters and Otis Spann to play.

"We had brought in the Modern Jazz Quartet in December '57," recalls Barber today. "Their leader, John Lewis, asked me, 'What else are you doing?' So I said, 'We've got Sonny and Brownie coming in May.' He said, 'Well, that's good, but you've got to have Muddy Waters; he is the nearest to the real thing that exists!'" When Waters finally made it over the next year, Baldry, Korner and Davies were among the aficionados crowding the club along with Ramblin' Jack Elliott, who still remembers Muddy's electrifying effect on the young British audience.

"I was sitting on the floor in the first row," Elliott recalls, laughing, "right there, about three feet away from him, close as you could be. When he was singing, 'I'm a *maaaan*,' the sweat came right off his brow and onto my face. These English kids were just so wacky about him. Oh yeah, it was like a feeding frenzy, you know?"

Baldry later lamented to Holger Petersen that certain U.K. critics had savaged Waters for abandoning his earlier acoustic blues and going electric. "Poor Muddy really did get a hammering in the press," Baldry recalled. "They said, 'We don't want any of this rock 'n' roll music here.' Because, to their ears, at that time, it was loudly overamplified."

Baldry and his fellow blues enthusiasts were greatly impressed by the power of Waters's electric sound and took little notice of the reviewers. Waters, in contrast, apparently took the criticism to heart, and upon his return to the Marquee some years later, he brought only an acoustic guitar.

"It was music under a folk banner," Baldry told Petersen, "and to me it was very strange. The Muddy records that I'd fallen in love with in '54 or thereabouts were the heavily amplified stuff. Eventually, we became the first bunch of white people to start electric blues bands, right after Muddy came over to England. We said, 'Oh, that's it! We want to make a band like that!' It had been a germ of an idea between Cyril, Alexis and myself, but it didn't actually happen until 1962. We thought, we really want to try and do this music electronically. So we hid away our acoustic guitars and turned up the juice."

As the '50s closed out, Baldry would continue to play anytime and anywhere, including on numerous television and radio shows such as the BBC's *Easy Beat*. For the most part, however, it was still "have guitar, will travel," which meant striking out on a tour of Denmark as lead guitarist for the Bob Cort Skiffle Group in November 1960. Upon his return to London, Baldry would finally get to "turn up the juice" with Cyril and Alexis. With the '60s upon him, Long John Baldry was about to be rewarded for all his hard work and the dues he'd paid.

r&b from the marquee

ALTHOUGH THE blues and R&B were clearly
in his future, the young John Baldry con-
tinued to dabble in other musical styles. He even held down a
job, for a time, as the singer for Liverpool-based trad jazz cornet player Ken Sims's Vintage Jazz Band. As a result, Baldry frequently found himself in the north of England, performing in
the ballrooms of New Brighton, at the Chester Jazz Club or as a
regular headliner at Liverpool's in-crowd club, the Cavern. Evening and afternoon performances there also featured a scruffy
beat combo called the Beatles, whom Baldry had befriended
in Germany while both acts were booked into Hamburg's Star
Club. In 1961, the Beatles were strictly a northern phenomenon.
Baldry would cross paths with them whenever he was in "the
Pool," whether with Sims or moonlighting with Terry Lightfoot's
jazz band. Their mutual friendship would continue to thrive
long after Beatlemania swept Britain and then the world.

One of Baldry's most high-profile engagements in 1961 was
a television appearance on *The Acker Bilk Show*. Bilk was one

of trad jazz's most enduring bandleaders, as immortalized in Richard Lester's 1962 jukebox film *It's Trad, Dad!* Bilk, like Chris Barber, was from the old guard but was also hip enough to recognize the tribal beat of blues and R&B as the future sound of London. As 1961 began, Bilk toured the U.K. on the back of his massive number-one hit "Stranger on the Shore." Just as Barber's sets had featured a skiffle segment, Bilk hired Alexis Korner to put together a compact R&B combo to join him on tour. Bilk's timing couldn't have been better. According to self-confessed "blues freak" Giorgio Gomelsky, the nascent R&B scene was about to eclipse trad jazz, both critically and commercially. Gomelsky was a fast-talking European huckster who had come to London from Germany, where he had been working for promoters Horst Lippman and Fritz Rau. Gomelsky's father was from Georgia and his mother from Monte Carlo, and he recalls that many of the xenophobic Brits on the Soho scene looked down on him for being a "continental."

"I worked my ass off," he says today, "but you can imagine with my accent and everything, they were taking the mickey out of me ferociously in England. 'Who is this frog?' They called me frog because they eat frogs on the continent. I was smoking Gauloises, infesting their tidy little pubs with French cigarette smoke!"

Gomelsky would later go on to manage the early Rolling Stones, the Yardbirds and Steampacket, but in 1961 he was just another independent promoter trying to influence what he saw as a staid British music scene.

"At the very beginning," he recalls, "there were perhaps forty people in the whole of London who were following the blues, but the skiffle craze was over and done with, and trad was on its way out, having been diluted with all of these commercialized versions. Commercial music had taken the upper hand, and there was nothing going on. That's when the blues came. We thought, yes, let's go back to the roots and start again."

Gomelsky says he noticed Baldry "awkwardly attempting to insert himself" into the rather exclusive world of young English blues enthusiasts. But he liked the young upstart, and although he felt Baldry was a "charmingly aggressive" person, Gomelsky appreciated Baldry's sense of humour about it all.

"All the young up-and-coming artists felt they should be getting more opportunities," says Gomelsky, "and he, too, made himself a bit of a nuisance, bending everyone's ear. But he was a good singer, he had this nice, deep baritone voice, and he could growl and do the Louis Armstrong thing. He was a white Negro."

Baldry stood out, Gomelsky says, not only for his remarkable height but also for his guardedly flamboyant mannerisms. Although he had dabbled with a few girlfriends, it was an open secret that Baldry was gay. The early '60s was a time of liberation on many fronts, but being gay was still not something one talked about in public conversation. In fact, until 1967, it was against British law. So while Baldry rarely hid his orientation, he didn't advertise it either.

According to Gomelsky, musicians and music people didn't care that much either way. "Sure, he had little gestures that indicated a kind of a gay thing, but in those days nobody [on the scene] gave a hoot about people's sexuality."

Eric Clapton had identified Baldry as a dandy in the blues underworld, although he admits that, at first, he didn't add up the obvious clues. "He was very elegant and incredibly flamboyant," says Clapton, "combined with this highly acute sense of humour. I think I found out much later that he was gay. I think when I was very young, in the early days, I didn't really know what 'gay' meant anyway."

Clapton *had* noticed, however, a potentially gloomy side to Baldry.

"There was a darkness to him, too, that I didn't really get to know very well," Clapton says today. "I just could sense that the guy was troubled, you know? I'm not sure, at that stage of his life, if he had really come to terms with his sexuality. It was much more open in the '70s and everything, once he had kind of come out, although I don't know if he ever came out publicly. But he was definitely out on a personal level."

Chris Barber noted what he called Baldry's "camp" behaviour, confirming Gomelsky's assertion that it actually mattered very little to those in the entertainment industry. "Show business has been full of camp people for years," says Barber today. "Loads of people were camp. On the other hand, [Baldry] was a bit more outrageous than most. But he was talented, and you have to accept that talented people sometimes are a little bit eccentric."

Barber had also heard whispers—from other musicians and promoters—of Baldry's "bitchiness" and unmanageable mood swings, possibly fuelled by his partiality to strong drink. Gomelsky acknowledges that although he never witnessed this side personally, Baldry could very often be "his own worst enemy." Gomelsky insists, however, that it never got in the way of Baldry's personal dealings. "He wasn't, you know, catty. His being a gay person was not in the way of anything. Not psychologically, not artistically, not in terms of comradeship or anything like that. It wasn't an issue."

Anyone who witnessed Baldry's performances noted that any effeminate airs ceased the minute he took to the stage, channelling the decidedly macho strains of the Delta blues. Gomelsky says the blues gave Baldry a focus for his deep baritone voice. "John had initially been on the fringes of the traditional jazz scene," he says. "But when the blues began to appear on the horizon, he turned out to be quite a good singer."

Chris Barber says Baldry knew that there was a right way and a wrong way to interpret the blues.

"If you're going to sing Mississippi Delta songs," says Barber, "you have to respect the authentic sound of the words. You're not just imitating a guy from Mississippi, you're singing within the historical parameters of the music. On the other hand, John was an Englishman between songs, well spoken and academic sounding, like an English public school boy saying, 'How *are you*, dear boy?' It wasn't phony, though. It's a matter of fellow feeling for other sufferers. You can have feeling for people without undergoing what they've gone through, and anybody who didn't have an understanding about it wouldn't even bother to sing it."

In 1962, Horst Lippman and Fritz Rau enlisted Willie Dixon to help put together the first of several annual American Folk Blues Festival tours of Britain. The inaugural bill included John Lee Hooker, T-Bone Walker and Memphis Slim. Subsequent tours included the return of Muddy Waters, along with Otis Spann, Howlin' Wolf, Hubert Sumlin, Buddy Guy and Sonny Boy Williamson. Baldry, Korner and Davies were faithful attendees at these shows, hoping to pick up tips from the masters. So fond were his memories of the concerts that Baldry kept a mint collection of Lippman and Rau's elaborate tour posters, wherever he lived, for the rest of his life.

"The first one that Cyril, Alex and I went to, Muddy and Otis were there," Baldry told Holger Petersen. "Sunnyland Slim, Memphis Slim, Victoria Spivey, Joe Williams—poor Joe Williams, of course, not the Basie Joe Williams. Howlin' Wolf came over a little later on to do a club tour, and, of course, my band was very privileged to accompany them on that tour. For me, to be able to get right up close and watch Wolf nightly was an amazing thing to see."

Sometimes the action got a little too close for comfort, as it did one evening in the lobby of the Bloomsbury Hotel after Barber had brought Little Walter over to play some shows.

"It was a very good, older kind of hotel, and many of the blues singers and jazz people would stay there," Baldry recalled to Holger Petersen. "Sonny Boy Williamson and Little Walter started getting at it, in public, right there in the lobby. I couldn't believe it. It had started out as an argument between them, each saying, 'I'm the greatest harmonica player who ever was.' And of course Walter, you know, *could* make a claim like that. But Sonny Boy wasn't gonna take that, so they started standing up and screaming and shouting. Walter pulled out a cutthroat razor, so Sonny Boy pulled out his own huge switchblade knife. It was kind of like a thing out of *Crocodile Dundee,* except it wasn't a comedy. I was never quite so frightened, quaking in my boots."

With their blues apprenticeships well underway, Baldry and associates got their own project together in March 1962, when Korner launched Blues Incorporated, with Davies on harmonica and Baldry as the featured vocalist. They announced their presence on the scene with a residency at the newly christened Ealing Jazz Club.

"The club," Baldry wrote in a 1989 essay from his personal collection, "ran only on Thursday nights in a dark and damp—actually 'awash' would be a more apt description—basement below the ABC Tea Rooms in Ealing Broadway. It was handily situated directly opposite the Underground station. I say *handily* because very few of us owned or could drive automobiles back then, so all travel was undertaken by means of public transport."

Fellow musician and blues enthusiast Art Wood, recently deceased older brother of guitarist Ron Wood, had told them about the former trad hangout, nicknamed "The Moist Hoist." Giorgio Gomelsky says that the cellar atmosphere was evocative of the underground jazz clubs of Paris, particularly after the war.

"A lot of the trad jazz things took on the Parisian cellar kind of phenomenon," Gomelsky recalls. "In Liverpool they had the Cavern, which was a cellar. In Germany there was nothing else, because the towns were razed [during the war]. In London, of course, there weren't that many cellars around, so they would assemble in the back of pubs or in rooms upstairs, like at the Roundhouse."

The previous year, however, Korner and Davies had been cast out of the Roundhouse, for playing too loud. Once they could, in Baldry's words, "turn up the juice," Blues Incorporated became, according to Richard Williams of the *Guardian*, "a virtual finishing school for the whole [blues and R&B] movement."

Blues Incorporated's inaugural lineup had Korner on guitar and Davies on harmonica and vocals. Andy Hoogenboom played the stand-up bass. Charlie Watts, Baldry's old school chum and a former member of his Jazz and Blues Appreciation Society, played the drums. The two had continued to be nodding acquaintances on the scene, and Baldry had been at art college with Watts's wife, Shirley.

"It was an amazing band," Watts once said of Blues Incorporated, "but a total cacophony of sound... a cross between R&B and Charlie Mingus, which was what Alexis wanted."

The band also included saxophone player Dick Heckstall-Smith, a trad jazzer and self-confessed "bopper" whom Baldry had met while moonlighting in the jazz world. Korner had come across Heckstall-Smith in February of 1962 during an impromptu jazz-versus-blues jam down at the Troubadour. In his memoir *Blowing the Blues*, Heckstall-Smith recalled being charmed by Korner's defiance in standing up to a room full of jazzers and playing blues in their faces. One by one, Heckstall-Smith recalled, the bandstand had cleared out until it was reduced to just him and Korner.

"None of the other hornmen seemed at all blues-inclined," wrote Heckstall-Smith. "Not so with me, however, and the two of us ended up playing blues together. He said he was thinking of starting up a Chicago-style blues band later that year, with brass in it... would I be interested? I said 'Yes.'"

Korner called later to request Heckstall-Smith's presence at a rehearsal he was arranging at the Roundhouse.

"I showed up at seven on the day we'd arranged," Heckstall-Smith wrote, "and got my horn out. The drummer arrived, and we introduced ourselves: 'Watts,' he said, 'Charlie Watts. But I'm not much good, I'm afraid.' At ten to eight the clattery pub-room double doors were flung open and a burly balding figure in a dirty raincoat pushed in, holding an old and very bulging briefcase. Ignoring the good-natured shouts of 'Hullo Cyril!' he made his way straight to the decrepit upright piano in the corner of the room and upended his briefcase over the top of it. An enormous amount of harmonicas flowed out, rather like liquid, and he cursed roundly and obscenely. That was my introduction to Cyril Davies, panel-beater, the first fully-fledged genius I ever worked with on a regular basis."

In addition to Baldry, the band would sometimes feature vocalists such as a young Mick Jagger—who had first read about the Ealing Jazz Club in *Melody Maker*—and Paul Jones, later of Manfred Mann. Occasionally, Art Wood also sat in with the band, as did the curiously named Hogsnort Rupert—whose appellation, Baldry later told Holger Petersen, "may have had something to do with his exceptionally large nose."

Regarded as the band's permanent singer, Baldry said the title fell to him because he was the only one who considered himself a professional. "I was the only one who ever actually got paid," he later admitted to Petersen. "The rest of them just did it for a pint of beer or for the love of it all."

On piano was Keith Scott, an old acquaintance of Baldry's, whom he referred to as "the Bean" due to "the unique shape of his cranium." Scott had been making a name for himself in small duos with Alexis and Cyril and with guitarist Geoff Bradford.

Blues Incorporated, the self-styled "first white electric blues group in the world," began packing clubs all over the London area. Heckstall-Smith's memoir describes, in vivid detail, one of Blues Incorporated's Ealing Club residencies.

"One of the strongest elements in this amalgam," Heckstall-Smith wrote, "is remembering the heat, sweat and overcrowded-ness... It seemed to be perpetually full, erupting lava-like with screeching, raving, compressed underground life—like a lot of good clubs I guess. But it also had something that the discreet, horn-rimmed, note-taking, unsmiling jazz clubs in town lacked: *enthusiasm.*"

Ads in *Melody Maker* alerted hep cats to the cool new sounds on, or under, the street, and crowds congregated with ever-increasing frequency. The Ealing Jazz Club was one of the coolest places in London to hang out, and its policy of encouraging young players to get up on the bandstand, a holdover from the jazz tradition, gave new musicians a chance to announce themselves. Future Rolling Stone Brian Jones became an ardent admirer of Davies's harmonica technique and was a constant visitor to Korner's house, where he would borrow or listen to selections from Korner's sizable collection of vintage blue records. Jones also borrowed Baldry's albums; his failure to return many of them would cause a major falling-out between them.

By April, the humid Ealing basement had become a hothouse for young blues talent. Regulars included Ginger Baker and Jack Bruce, who would later enlist in Blues Incorporated on their way to joining the Graham Bond Organization and then forming Cream with Eric Clapton, another habitué of the club. Besides Mick Jagger and Brian Jones, future bandmates Bill Wyman and Keith Richards were also frequent visitors to the subterranean club.

"By that time," Richards explained to *Rolling Stone* magazine's Robert Greenfield in 1971, "the initial wham had gone out of rock 'n' roll. England itself was turning on to its own breed of rock 'n' rollers... Cliff Richard... Adam Faith, Billy Fury... Then suddenly in '62, just when we were getting together, we read this little thing about a rhythm and blues club starting in Ealing. Everybody must have been trying to get one together."

The basement was so damp that Davies had put a sheet over the bandstand, hoping to prevent condensation from dripping directly onto the musicians. It proved of no avail, however, and moisture continued to bleed straight through the sheet onto the amplifiers and microphones, presenting an electrocution hazard. The prospect of death by electric shock was no deterrent for Mick Jagger, who would get up on that dangerous stage whenever he could. Korner soon enlisted him to handle the increasing volume of requests for Chuck Berry and Bo Diddley songs.

Baldry wrote about his first meeting with Jagger in the aforementioned 1989 essay. "My first visual impression of Mick was that he was all ears and lips, and oh so skinny. Funnily, over the years his ears seem to have shrunk to normal proportions, and the lips, while still notoriously gigantic, have deflated from dirigible size to the more accessible thickness of a pair of meaty kielbasas. Also, it did not go unnoticed that Mick had the ability to make young girls rotate."

Just as Baldry compared Jagger to "a medieval rendering of hobgoblin or a praying mantis with lips," he considered Richards "a dark serious elf... already on the way to being one slick guitar player."

In his *Rolling Stone* interview with Greenfield, Keith Richards remarked that everyone in his new group had been inspired by the tireless enthusiasm of Alexis Korner. "Alexis made the breakthrough," Richards said, "... at the Ealing Club. Then he moved on to the Marquee, and R&B started to become the thing. Alexis was packin' 'em in, man. Jus' playing blues. Workers and art students, kids who couldn't make the ballrooms with supposedly long hair... you gravitated to places where you wouldn't get hassled."

The music press, eager to find the next big thing, seized upon the energy of the emerging R&B scene. In the hipper London jazz clubs, blues and R&B acts were now eclipsing the trad jazzers. Naturally, there was some resistance from some members of the old guard. Harold Pendleton, for one, was not convinced that the new R&B music was entirely appropriate for the Marquee's jazz audience. Giorgio Gomelsky, already on the bandwagon, recalls hounding his friend to change his policy.

"I had a big mouth," says Gomelsky today, "and I said, 'You've got to have some blues.' He said, 'What, that rock 'n' roll?'"

Barber got it, though, having booked American blues bands into England in the first place.

"Chris wasn't prejudiced," says Gomelsky. "My argument was always with Harold. And of course, Long John was on my side because I was arguing so that he and Alexis could get gigs at the Marquee. Then finally it happened. Harold gave a Thursday night to Alexis. Then everybody used to show up there and sit in with him."

Baldry also wrote, in his 1989 essay, about the move to the Marquee. "The Ealing Club had proved to be too minuscular to accommodate the following we had built up by then. It was concert-type crowds trying to get into a biscuit box."

At the Marquee, however, Blues Incorporated could pack in excess of seven hundred dancing, jumping and wailing hipsters of all nationalities and age groups. They were also offered a much-sought-after guest shot on BBC Radio's *Jazz Club*, no small feat considering that they were not, strictly speaking, a jazz group at all.

"The budget for the [*Jazz Club*] programme," Baldry wrote, "precluded any vocal involvement by Mick and myself, so Alexis entrusted Mick and I to cover for the Blues Incorporated's absence at the Thursday night residency at the Marquee."

Jagger and Baldry hastily put together two bands and came up with band names for the Marquee bill, which advertised Long John Baldry and His Kansas City Blues Men ("Aaaarrghh, what a horrendous name," Baldry later moaned) and the debut of the Rolling Stones, although the band did not yet include Bill Wyman or Charlie Watts.

In a special 2006 issue of the U.K. rock magazine *Mojo*, original Stones bassist Dick Taylor described the audience's mixed reaction when the bluesy new band dared to play R&B for the Marquee's jazz-centric regulars. "Half the people liked it," Taylor recalled, "and the other half went 'Ahhhh, what is this crap at the holy Marquee?'"

In many downtown nightclubs, however, blues and R&B were the hip new alternative to the watered-down British rock 'n' roll of the late '50s. Speaking with Nick Orchard, Baldry commented on this changing of the guard. "I think people wanted to make it into pop music. In the early '60s there was an enormous amount of blues music making the charts. I remember 'Smokestack Lightning,' the Howlin' Wolf song, being in the top five. Sonny Boy Williamson's 'Help Me,' in fact, reached number one."

Top producer Jack Good had been a prime architect of the teenage pop scene of the '50s, bringing rock 'n' roll onto British TV through influential shows like *Oh Boy!*, *Boy Meets Girls*, *Wham!* and BBC television's popular *Six-Five Special*. Over the years, Good had worn many hats: music journalist, television presenter and record producer. He was to the U.K. music scene what Alan Freed and Dick Clark were in the U.S., and he would eventually be brought over to the States to produce the influential *Shindig!* series for ABC.

In 1962, Good was tapped by Decca Records to produce the first British electric blues album. On June 8, Good and recording engineer Jack Clegg entered Decca's West Hampstead studios with a slightly altered lineup of Blues Incorporated to record the misleadingly titled *R&B from the Marquee*. For the sessions, Korner had enlisted drummer Graham Burbidge, from Chris Barber's band, along with Spike Heatley, the bass player from Johnny Dankworth's big band, singer Big Jim Sullivan and bass guitarist Teddy Wadmore. The core of the band remained, with

Korner on guitar, Cyril Davies on harp, Keith Scott on piano and horn player Dick Heckstall-Smith, whom the album's liner notes described as "one of the most exciting and competent saxophonists on the scene today."

There was also mention in the liner notes of "the well-known British blues singer Long John Baldry," who appeared on the album doing lead vocals on Jimmy Witherspoon's "Rain Is Such a Lonesome Sound," Leroy Carr's "How Long, How Long, Blues" and a composition of Baldry's own entitled "I Thought I Heard That Train Whistle Blow." (A later reissue of the album on CD unearthed a previously unreleased Baldry vocal on Willie Dixon's "I'm Built for Comfort.")

R&B *from the Marquee* was released the following November on the Decca Records label. As was the custom of the day, Decca's detailed liner notes for the album were highly informative, if overwritten, and had an air of manifesto about them.

"The strength and vigour of R&B cannot be denied, and in the field of popular music they are qualities which have been lacking for too long. To an entire generation of young people musically weaned on diluted rock and roll, the sincerity and force of Rhythm and Blues have an irresistible attraction."

Particular attention is paid to two Korner originals, "Down Town" and "Finkel's Café," described as "soul-tinged blues... with a friendly nod in the direction of Mendelssohn." There is even an attempt to explain the origins of the word "mojo" as used in "I've Got My Mojo Working": "A mojo, en passant, is a sexual amulet which still enjoys great popularity among some urban Negroes. It is mentioned again in the lyrics of Hoochie Coochie together with its other variants, the black cat's bone and John the Conqueror."

In a 1971 *Rolling Stone* interview with journalist Andrew Bailey, Alexis Korner recalled his group's impact on the music scene.

"Technically, Blues Incorporated was the first professional British blues band," Korner told Bailey. "We were playing electric stuff by then, and Cyril and me were getting thrown out of perfectly respectable jazz clubs for doing so. It wasn't intended, but I suppose that sort of missionary thing about popularizing jazz was very strong 'cause we always had a very high proportion of jazzmen in the band. We all felt that jazz could be popular music if it were properly presented."

For Korner and Davies, however, a debate over jazz populism would eventually lead to a schism within Blues Incorporated. Korner favoured moving into a more jazz-based, progressive blues sound; Davies maintained that the Chicago sound was the only authentic blues. Baldry bypassed the conflict by fleeing to Germany, where he could always pick up work. Korner and Davies grew further apart while Baldry performed at German USAF bases with the Horace Silver Quintet hard-bop jazz band and did additional dates with vibe player Gunter Hampel's quartet.

By January 1963, when Baldry returned to a chilly London from what he jokingly referred to as his "Teutonic wanderings," the Rolling Stones had, in his words, "become a force to be reckoned with." Korner and Davies had dissolved the original Blues Incorporated, leaving two distinct entities—Alexis Korner's Blues Incorporated and Cyril Davies R&B All Stars—in its wake.

Both factions wanted Baldry. Rather than play favourites, he left his decision, like so many of his life's choices, to chance. He tossed a coin.

"It was a big silver coin," he told Holger Petersen years later, "what we called half a crown back in those days. I flipped it up, and I think it was tails for Cyril, so I started working with Cyril and the All Stars." He made his debut with the band on January 3 at the Marquee Club on Oxford Circus.

As Korner's Blues Incorporated soldiered on over at the Flamingo, with a rotating lineup that at times included future Animals singer Eric Burdon and an African-American ex-GI named Ronnie Jones, Davies scoured London to find players good enough to keep his side of the legacy alive.

One of the more exciting acts on the scene at the time was Screaming Lord Sutch and the Savages. Savages drummer Carlo Little, fed up with backing the mercurial Lord Sutch, jumped at the chance to join Davies. The disgruntled drummer suggested that Davies also rescue the other Savages, and the All Stars instantly acquired guitarist Bernie Watson, bass player Ricky Brown and piano genius Nicky Hopkins. Baldry was at the microphone, backed by the Velvettes, three "black chick" singers who had come to London direct from South Africa and were touring with a musical version of *King Kong*.

Rock historian Pete Frame had found it unfortunate that R&B *from the Marquee* was released by "the budget Decca label," rather than a more authentically bluesy label like Pye International. This time around, Davies accepted an offer to record for prestigious Pye International, the British distributor for Chicago's Chess Records. This meant that the All Stars were now labelmates with Muddy Waters, Howlin' Wolf and Sonny Boy Williamson.

On February 27, the band—Long John Baldry on vocals, Davies on harmonica and vocals, Bernie Watson on guitar, Carlo Little on drums and Rick Brown on bass guitar—entered London's Marble Arch Studio with producer Peter Knight Jr. to record four songs. "Country Line Special," a Davies-written and -sung composition on which Baldry did not appear, was chosen as a single, with another Davies tune, "Chicago Calling," selected as the B-side.

"Country Line Special" was a critical favourite, particularly with musicians. That didn't translate into the pop charts, however, which continued to be dominated by Cliff Richard's "Summer Holiday" and similarly safe rock 'n' roll.

The failure of the single was disappointing, but the All Stars were still a viable, hot new band with one of the best live shows in Britain. Radio be damned. The future looked promising indeed. Little did anyone know, however, that Cyril Davies was living on borrowed time. In just over a year, Baldry would bury his friend and mentor and assume control of Davies's All Stars.

hoochie coochie man

A<small>T THE OUTSET</small> of 1963, John Baldry's life was awash with contradictions. On the one hand, living at home with his parents, he was just John. His doting mother still did all his washing and ironing and laid out clean clothes for him each morning. On the other hand, in the Soho clubs, he was Long John, the highly visible man about town. A tall, handsome, twenty-two-year-old with innate social abilities and an apparently limitless tolerance for vodka, he would frequently return home in the wee hours of the morning after a long night on the tiles. A lot of his time and money were spent cultivating friendships and acquiring a sharp wardrobe. He relished the London scene and, by all accounts, the scene reciprocated. And in his new role as the front man for Cyril Davies R&B All Stars, he seemed poised for great things.

Giorgio Gomelsky, a tireless promoter of the blues movement, actively surveyed the London area for new venues where Davies and his band could play. His goal was to book blues shows every night of the week except Thursdays, the Marquee's own blues night. Gomelsky was keenly aware of the media's role in promoting any new movement. So, to give them "a scene" to write about, he took over a shoebox-sized club in Windmill Street and renamed it, literally, the Scene Club.

"I just wanted to add more venues so the nation's blues bands could get more gigs," Gomelsky explains today. "So I started renting places like the Jamaican Club, and I put some blues things there. I even had the gumption of starting a London Blues Festival—with Cyril and Alex, Long John, Blues By Six and a few others. We had about seventy to eighty people. It was winter, and I asked all my friends to stand outside in the street in a line so that when people walked by they would say, 'Oh, what's happening *there*, what are you guys lining up for?'"

Gomelsky conducted elaborate publicity stunts to give exposure to the emerging blues scene. "To promote the Scene Club," he says, "we found this old white piano and painted 'the Scene' on the side of it. Then we put it on a cart and dragged it around Piccadilly Circus in the middle of rush-hour traffic. That got us in the papers."

In June 1963, the All Stars appeared on television's *Thank Your Lucky Stars* and BBC Radio's *Saturday Club*. For a time, they enjoyed a residency on TV's *Hullabaloo*. Additionally, Baldry performed solo at the third annual National Jazz and Blues Festival in Richmond, which was organized by Chris Barber and Harold Pendleton.

In July, guitarist Bernie Watson left the All Stars to join Mancunian journeyman John Mayall in his Bluesbreakers. Carlo Little and Rick Brown also left, to return to Lord Sutch's Savages. Davies kept the momentum up by adding Geoff Bradford to replace Watson, with Cliff Barton on bass and drummers Micky Waller (and occasionally Bob Wackett) replacing Little.

"Cyril had kept me in mind," says Geoff Bradford today, "and when the occasion arose, he asked me to join the All Stars."

Bradford had been playing in Blues By Six, with former Blues Incorporated piano man Keith Scott. Davies would eventually enlist Scott to replace ailing keyboardist Nicky Hopkins, who was wrestling with Crohn's disease and had to be sidelined for over eighteen months.

A second single, "Preachin' the Blues," backed with "Sweet Mary," was released by the band with a minimum of fanfare in September. They weren't exactly huge, but the R&B All Stars singles, including a rendition of Buddy Holly's "Not Fade Away" featuring Jimmy Page, made a strong impression on a lot of musicians.

Despite their different approaches to the music, John Baldry told *The New Breed* magazine in 2001, Cyril Davies and Alexis Korner's core followings comprised the same people. "I think the audience was fairly interchangeable between the Marquee and the Flamingo at that time," Baldry said. "People went to both venues... Later on, people like Manfred Mann took over on Tuesday nights [at the Marquee], other odds and sods went on, and it was basically the same people coming to all of these shows."

Rock historian Pete Frame quotes Korner as remarking that he was always struck by Davies's intensity. "Cyril," Korner said, "was definitely aiming to be a working-class hero."

Certain venues, such as the Roaring Twenties on Carnaby Street, were frequented by sharp-dressed Mods who appreciated Baldry's fine taste in suits. In his book *Mods!*, author Richard Barnes says the neatly dressed young modern crowd was dismissive of the more slovenly Davies, whom he described as looking "near 40" and who committed the sin of wearing "lumpy jackets and baggy corduroys."

"The singer Long John Baldry," Barnes adds, "was tall, incredibly thin and young looking, and wore an immaculate silver-grey mod suit."

The old dance hall at the Eel Pie Island Hotel, sitting in the Thames at Twickenham, was by now one of the hot spots for blues and R&B. Mark De Novellis, curator of Twickenham's Orleans House Gallery, explains how club manager Arthur Chisnall's Eel Pie Island "experiment" had a far-reaching effect on British youth culture.

"People crossed the bridge," says De Novellis, "paid the toll and, to paraphrase Arthur Chisnall who made the music happen, 'entered another world.' Its heyday from roughly 1963 to 1967 revolutionized popular culture, and the musical repercussions are still reverberating around the world."

De Novellis's book *My Music*, published in 2005, includes a sampling of Eel Pie patrons recalling the island's significance. Their testimonials are evidence that the club was indeed the second front in the blues movement's war on musical boredom.

The book includes a review by Jules Acton of the *Richmond Informer*, who wrote in 1998, "The Eel Pie Island Jazz Club... was regarded either as a hangout for delinquents or the hippest thing this side of New Orleans. These days, it is widely recognized as a breeding ground for British Rhythm and Blues—along with the Richmond Crawdaddy Club—and was the launch pad for acts including The Rolling Stones, The Animals and The Yardbirds. What isn't as well known is that 'Eelpisland' as it came to be known, started out as a social experiment—a 'laboratory' for research into the changing values of British society."

Eel Pie's lynchpin, Arthur Chisnall, was a self-described "non-authoritarian observer, recording, experimenting, looking at the world" who was influenced by the writings of psychiatrist R.D. Laing and had been struck with the idea for the Eel Pie club while working at a local junk shop frequented by art students.

"From that all-important group of about 300 people," Chisnall says in *My Music*, "much of the later '60s cultural scene emerged including the later international R&B movement. How could their needs be provided for? The answer I came up with was a venue—a place where people could get together, make music, make a little noise and dance to it."

Sensing the potential in the faded island oasis, Chisnall began throwing noisy parties at the Eel Pie Island Hotel. These became so popular that the musicians, who had been playing for free, began to politely insist on payment. For that reason, and in an effort to comply with advice from the police, the Eel Pie Island Jazz Club became a proper nightclub. Chisnall even issued Eel Pie Island "Passports" as club membership cards.

Giorgio Gomelsky, similarly frustrated by the postwar drabness of London, had by now set up the Crawdaddy Club in nearby Richmond. "I wanted to stir things up," says Gomelsky. "London was a dead place when I got there. The pubs closed at 9:30 PM. I convinced a Greek coffee shop owner to buy an Italian espresso machine; there was no regulation about the coffee shops staying open all night. So he started the Olympic Coffee Bar, a tiny place in Chelsea with three tables and three chairs per table, but they had a hundred people in there getting stoned on coffee all night. This was right at the beginning of King's Road, which had been an artists' district. Mary Quant had a little atelier around the corner; she was one of the first ten people who came in. Her husband had a restaurant around the corner. When the restaurant shut, they kept drinking coffee all night. I lived just round the corner in Sloane Square, so for me it was very useful. We had jam sessions in artists' studios; we ran illegal gambling parties; rebellious stuff. My little town woke up!"

Marquee Club co-owner Harold Pendleton was not impressed with the over-caffeinated ambitions of his friend Giorgio.

"He got very upset," recalls Gomelsky. "He told me I was trying to steal his thunder. I said, 'Screw you! I am going to go as far away as I can from the West End, where you are, and I'll prove you wrong!' So I went to the end of the District Line and found a place in the back of a pub called the Station Hotel, in Richmond. I started a blues club there on Sunday nights, the worst night of the week. That's really how the Crawdaddy Club started. The Rolling Stones used to do their own version of a Bo Diddley tune called 'Let's Do the Crawdaddy.' When Long John asked, 'What do you call your place?' I replied that I didn't have a name for it. It just came out 'Crawdaddy,' and from then on we were the Crawdaddy Club."

Geoff Bradford recalls that although the Eel Pie Island Hotel was indeed a hotbed of musical activity, it was not a particularly *nice* venue.

"It was a decrepit place, really," Bradford says. "Being a damp sort of building in the middle of the Thames, it had gone into rack and ruin. You had to get over on a bridge, and you had to pay these two old women a toll. They held a bucket out, and you put money in as you went over. It was sweaty, but it had an atmosphere. It was a great gig. It used to get so crowded, and you could feel the floor moving, because of the weight of the people on it. It was an old-fashioned sprung dance floor."

Ian McLagan, keyboardist of the Faces, differs with Bradford on this last fact. "It wasn't sprung," he insists, laughing, "it was just rotted on the left side. It was an old hotel, and the joists that held the floorboards in front of the stage, to the right of it, were rotted. So if people started dancing, which they did, the right-hand side of the audience would be bouncing up and down."

Sprung stage or not, McLagan rarely missed a Sunday night at Eel Pie when Long John Baldry fronted the Cyril Davies All Stars.

"It was unbelievable," says McLagan. "They all knew the music and played it like they were forty-five-year-old Chicago residents. I fell in love with the band. Cyril was fantastic. He wasn't a great singer, but he was a great harp player."

McLagan was especially impressed when Long John Baldry stepped up to the microphone to belt out a lead vocal.

"When Cyril would take a break for a drink," McLagan remembers, "which he liked to do quite often, this extremely elegant, double-breast-suited Long John Baldry would hit the stage. He'd sing more 'city' blues than Cyril. Cyril was singing Chicago, but it was like from the Delta. John would sing the more sophisticated blues. I was amazed by this guy. He looked so smart. He towered over the audience. He'd sing maybe three or four songs and then Cyril would get back on."

McLagan says he often stood at the bar, near the short steps leading to the stage.

"A lot of people fell down those steps," he recalls. "When Baldry would come off, I'd usually be there. I was a familiar face to him, and he got to know me. It was a real high point in my life when, as he came off stage, he actually came over, reached down with his pointed finger, touched me on the head and said, 'McLagan, how are you tonight?' My whole week was made. I believe I bought him a drink, although I didn't have much money. I was in a band, but we were an opening band, the Muleskinners, and we'd play at the Marquee, opening for all kinds of people. Eventually, we opened for the Stones and other people at Eel Pie Island."

The Cheynes's drummer Mick Fleetwood, soon to form his own blues-based juggernaut in Fleetwood Mac, was among the many young musicians who were inspired by Korner, Davies and Baldry to play the blues themselves.

"I saw them play at Eel Pie Island," Fleetwood recalls today, "but they had a large following in the other clubs as well. Eel Pie was such a great place. I never played there, but I used to go see the Stones there and other groups. We were all beginning to listen to American Blues and all that stuff, and there was this host of newness for us."

Mark De Novellis's gallery book features first-person testimonials from punters and players alike.

"I first visited The Island sometime around 1963," writes Eel Pie regular John Adams, "and remember the affection and excitement of hearing The Rolling Stones, Long John Baldry, Cyril Davies, Buddy Guy, Memphis Slim... and many more fine artists. All for the princely sum of three shillings, plus of course the 3d toll collected by the two fur-clad ladies who guarded the footbridge."

Art Wood, Ron Wood's brother and the leader of the Artwoods, recalls in the book how Chisnall's club united disparate camps. "Arthur Chisnall... brought everyone together," writes Wood. "Pinstriped suits, early hippies, art students in duffel coats and sandals... everyone had a fantastic time on the island."

Andrew Loog Oldham, who later took over from Giorgio Gomelsky to manage the Rolling Stones, says today that there were never more than three hundred regulars at Eel Pie, the Crawdaddy or the 100 Club, although there are "a lot of people now who pretend they were there and they weren't."

Whatever the numbers, Gomelsky credits Chisnall's success at Eel Pie and his own at the Crawdaddy as key factors in getting the blues into the big leagues.

"Harold Pendleton kind of resigned himself to us," says Gomelsky. "He then asked me to run the Richmond Jazz Festival, which then became the Richmond National Jazz and Blues Festival. We put all these blues bands in there for the first year. Long John was a part of that. His sympathies were with us rather than with the trad jazz guys, which by this time was dying out."

Cyril Davies and the R&B All Stars were having the time of their lives. But for Baldry's good friend and mentor, time was running out.

Piano player Nicky Hopkins noticed that something was amiss with Davies, as he recalled in a 1974 interview with Britain's *New Musical Express*. Backstage at the Marquee, a loud crash had emanated from Davies's dressing room. When Hopkins ran back to check on it, he found that Cyril had smashed his fist through a mirror.

"His eyes were really tight-shut and everything tensed in his face," Hopkins told the *NME*. "You couldn't have moved him. He looked like a statue. You could see the pain in his face—not physical, but mental pain."

Geoff Bradford would later describe to Pete Frame, in the ledgers of Frame's Cyril Davies family tree, how even the bar staff had sensed Davies's imminent demise. "One night," Bradford recalled, "we had a gig at Eel Pie Island and this Irish barmaid said to me: 'Your man's got death sitting on his shoulders!' It sent chills through my whole body."

John Baldry had a similar experience. In 2002, he told the BBC's Spencer Leigh how Davies had made an eerily prescient comment to him one night as the All Stars were getting ready to play at the Eel Pie. "We were walking across the footbridge," Baldry told Leigh, "and he said, 'I think this will be the last time I will walk across this bridge.' It was kinda eerie. Within a month or two he did die."

Davies was walking with a cane by this point, and he generally appeared much older than his thirty-one years.

"It was very sad," recalls keyboard player Ian McLagan, "and a bit horrifying. He always looked like an old man compared to me."

According to most published reports, Cyril Davies succumbed to leukemia on January 7, 1964, a year and four days after Baldry had returned from Germany and flipped the fateful coin. Discrepancies have arisen over the years, however, about the exact cause of Davies's death. Some of his friends have perpetuated the myth that Davies died of alcohol poisoning. Others have speculated that he died from a combination of both. Pete Frame, for example, suggests in one of his books that Davies, after contracting pleurisy, began drinking vast quantities of alcohol to ease the pain. In another of his books, Frame lists the cause of death as endocarditis, an inflammation of the heart valves.

Giorgio Gomelsky pulled off one final coup for Cyril Davies, although Davies would not live to see it. Earlier that year, Gomelsky had convinced Irish businessman Ronan O'Rahilly to launch Britain's first "pirate" radio station.

"I had met Ronan," Gomelsky recalls, "and we became friends. Ronan's grandfather was 'The O'Rahilly,' famously associated with the Easter Rising in Dublin in 1919, and Ronan was a bit of a rebel, too. I wanted to get him involved in the new music business, because we needed more rebellious types; the old show-biz guys didn't have a clue what was happening. Pirate radio would be the ideal vehicle to promote this blues music that neither the BBC nor Radio Luxembourg would touch. I arranged a meeting with Ronan and an engineer who could explain what was required to go on the air. Ronan was skeptical at first, but I talked him into it. He drew on his family, who owned a fleet of trawlers in Ireland, and decided to go for it."

The official launch for the floating station, anchored in international waters three miles off the coast of Essex, would take place on March 28, 1964.

"It was Easter Sunday, fittingly," Gomelsky continues. "I remember getting the *Observer* and the *Sunday Times* and seeing a half-page picture of the boat floating in the North Sea. They said that the RAF would blast it out of the water come Monday."

It was a good thing for everyone that the RAF did not follow through with this notion. "Country Line Special," the single by Cyril Davies and his All Stars that had not charted with land-locked radio, fared considerably better on the uncharted waters of Radio Caroline after pioneering DJ Jerry Leighton adopted the track as his theme song.

The impact was immediate. In 1994, the Kinks' Ray Davies (no relation to Cyril) told the *Independent* that "Country Line Special" was an "unsung British R&B classic." The song showed British R&B enthusiasts like himself, said Davies, that it could be done: English people could play the blues.

rod the mod

O N JANUARY 7, 1964, the evening of the day Long John Baldry and his bandmates learned that Cyril Davies had crossed over into the afterlife, Baldry took the band over the bridge to Eel Pie Island for one last swing as the All Stars.

As a charismatic host and lead singer, Baldry was the obvious successor as bandleader. If there was to be a wake for Davies, it would be a loud one. Ian McLagan, who was in the audience that night, recalls that Baldry and his bandmates rocked especially hard in tribute to their fallen friend. "Well, it always rocked like hell," McLagan adds. "We knew how special Cyril was and how special that band was. It was pure Chicago blues. It was Muddy Waters personified."

It was tragic to think that Cyril Davies's harmonica would never again feel his boozy breath. There was no time for sad songs, though. "It was pretty down," remembers Geoff Bradford, who was on the bandstand with Baldry and the others that night. "But the show must go on and all that."

Ian McLagan, who was then keyboardist with Eel Pie regulars the Muleskinners, admits to closely studying the All Stars' musicianship.

"I played guitar as well," says McLagan, "so I used to look up at Geoff Bradford, trying to figure out exactly what key he was in, because he would do these crazy inversions. His hands would just move slowly up and down the neck and you could never tell. I was also transfixed watching Cliff Barton, who is just a fantastic bass player, and I talked to him every gig I could."

"Jeff Beck and the Tridents also played that night," Bradford recalls, "as the interval band." Baldry was impressed with the young Beck. "I'd tried to grab him [for my band]," Baldry later told *The New Breed*, "but his wife at the time, or a very intense girlfriend, would not let him give up his daytime job. She was happier for him to remain semi-pro and just do the odd gig over at Eel Pie Island with the Tridents."

Amid the mixed emotions of the evening, Ian McLagan noticed one particularly sharply dressed young man bouncing through the audience, transfixed by the band and swaying to the beat. His hairstyle, McLagan says, "was backcombed, big bouffant. He was very mod and seemed tall, although not compared with John, in a very smart suit, high collar and tie." The boy was named Rod Stewart.

As the sweat-drenched crowd filtered out at show's end, Stewart staggered through the doors and over the footbridge towards Twickenham station. Chicago blues still ringing in his ears, he took the harmonica from his back pocket and proceeded to blow a few riffs, if only to pass the time and keep his hands warm.

It had been a long night for Long John Baldry. Cyril was not yet buried, but the All Stars had shows booked, and Baldry would need to find a harp player, preferably one who could sing, to cover Davies's parts. When he heard Stewart's wailing harmonica from across the station, he thought, 'That's it!'

Baldry wrote about his auspicious first meeting with Stewart in a long letter to a friend in 1991. "I first met Roderick David Stewart," he began, "about ten minutes before midnight on January 7, 1964, on the London-bound platform of the Twickenham Southern Railway Station. It was a cold, damp and foggy night, and the station at that time still retained vestiges of its Victorian ancestry including gas lamp illumination. The platform was deserted, all sound quite deadened by the pea-soup fog, a perfect setting for a gothic thriller. Suddenly, through the mist I heard the eerie sound of a harmonica being played. It was the riff from Howlin' Wolf's 'Smokestack Lightning' and it was the real natchal blues!"

"Gingerly stepping along the platform," Baldry continues, "I went to investigate the source of this stirring sound, almost tripping over what I thought was a pile of old clothing spilling off a bench. Accustoming my eyes to the gloom, I realized there was a nose protruding from the swathing of a gigantic woolen scarf." ("It was the nose, you see," Baldry added, "that great glorious probiscus [*sic*] that still dominates [his] features.") "'Good evening' I said to the nose. 'You strike me as being a bit of a blues fan. Your harmonica playing seems very authentic.'"

As the two chatted about music, Stewart told Baldry that he lived in Highgate, not far from where Long John lived, and that he had very much enjoyed that evening's performance. Baldry said that the All Stars would be playing the following Friday in Manchester, and he extended an invitation to Stewart to come and sit in.

Stewart was slightly awed just to be shaking Baldry's hand. He was well aware that many of his blues heroes had shaken that hand before him. Today, however, he apologizes for forgetting the specific details of that momentous evening.

"I was usually blind drunk when I went to that Eel Pie Island place," he confesses. "But I do recall he was extremely tall, and

[that] I jumped at the idea. I think in the morning, when I had sobered up, I thought, 'God, what have I let myself in for here?'"

Stewart realized, however, that opportunity seldom knocks twice. "It was like a 1964 version of *American Idol* come true. Suddenly, I didn't have to go looking for a band. John had asked me to join his group, who were all wonderfully accomplished jazz musicians."

Stewart expresses an enduring debt of gratitude to the keen ear and good taste of Long John Baldry.

"The most important thing," he declares, "is just how much I personally owe to John. I think you can have all the talent in the world, but you do need a little bit of luck. My luck just happened to be that he was on that railway station and he heard me playing the harmonica and he heard me singing and he believed in me. It's a tremendous debt. I'm sitting here looking at my mansion, overlooking Palm Beach at the ocean. If it wouldn't have been for him, I may not have been here today. If there wasn't any John, there may not have been any Rod. If there wasn't any Twickenham railway station, there might not have been any Rod either."

Speaking years later with the BBC's Spencer Leigh, Baldry recalled that since Stewart was then just approaching his nineteenth birthday, his parents were more than a little concerned about him taking up with Baldry's band.

"His mum rang up," he told Leigh, "and asked, 'Are you paying him?' 'Yes.' 'Will you make sure he behaves himself?' 'Yes, Elsie.'"

Since Baldry lived quite near the Stewarts, Elsie Stewart also requested that he pick up her son and deliver him home again each night. Rod Stewart recalls that Baldry, with his posh voice and charming manner, made a lasting impression on the Stewart household.

"My family absolutely adored him," says Stewart today. "The first time he came around and picked me up, he brought a lovely bunch of flowers for my mum. I'll never forget that. That was the sort of guy he was. My mum used to love him."

Stewart says that his mother was also enthralled by Baldry's sophisticated-sounding speaking voice, which he describes as "a kind of Etonian, upper-class sort of accent."

"She used to say, 'Why can't you talk like that Long John? It's such a lovely accent,'" Stewart recalls. "Although I don't know where he got that from, because the rest of his family was working-class. His brother's a copper, his dad was a copper."

Onstage, as others have noted, Baldry's cultivated Etonian-isms took a back seat to a strikingly authentic rural American twang. "Well, we all do that," Stewart says. "Some do it better than others."

Baldry mourned the loss of Cyril Davies, his friend and mentor, but he was determined to soldier on. In light of their leader's passing, however, the band's name seemed rather "presumptuous."

"What was I going to do?" Baldry said in conversation with Holger Petersen decades later. "I didn't really want to call the band the Cyril Davies All Stars anymore. The name the Rolling Stones had been quite successful... so why not Long John Baldry and the Hoochie Coochie Men?"

Stewart became one of the newly christened Hoochie Coochie Men. In private, though, even Baldry would sometimes join others who took to calling the band "Ada Baldry and the Hoochie Coochie Ladies."

"In John's gay way he decided to call me 'Phyllis,'" Stewart explains today. "Later on, he called Elton 'Sharon.' Paul Jones [from Manfred Mann] was called 'Pimply Pearl,' because he had a horrible complexion. All John's idea. He was the ringleader."

Stewart says that while Baldry made no secret of his sexual orientation, it wasn't common knowledge beyond a small circle of friends.

"In those days it was looked upon as cardinal sin," says Stewart. "I never actually saw him with any young boys, but I know things occurred. We used to talk about it sometimes. But he was never one of those girlie sorts of queers. He was always masculine about it. You would never have guessed just looking at him. He didn't walk in any particular feminine style or wear anything that would have given the game away. But he was, I suppose, rather flamboyant and theatrical. Yes, that's a good word. Theatrical."

Stewart's first appearance with the band, as harmonica player and secondary vocalist, was an all-nighter at the Twisted Wheel in Manchester.

"I don't think John even called for a rehearsal," Stewart says. "We didn't have time."

In fact, Baldry only asked Stewart what he was going to sing as they bounded onto the stage. Stewart shouted back the title of the only song he knew well enough to perform: "Night Time Is the Right Time" by Ray Charles.

"He only wanted me to do two songs," Stewart remembers. "The other one was just going to be a twelve-bar blues. So I just shouted out anything that came to my mind."

Years later, Baldry recalled that the gig was also special because it was Stewart's birthday. "I think he celebrated it either there at the Twisted Wheel or the following night at the all-nighter in Hanley," he later told *The New Breed*. "The Wheel always booked us for the all-nighter, so you never got started till about one or two o'clock in the morning and you had to carry on until six o'clock. I don't know how we had the stamina to do it!"

Stewart attributes some of his own early stamina to chemicals. Worried about staying alert for the long night's show, he turned to bass player Cliff Barton, who readily prescribed a cure. "I said, 'I'm really nervous, Cliff, I don't think I'm going to be able to stay awake if it's an all-night affair,' so he said, 'Just take one of these and have a beer'."

Barton had given Stewart an amphetamine tablet, affectionately known to jazz players as a "black bomber." The effect was dramatic.

"They had to get a hook and drag me off the stage," Stewart laughs. "I just kept on singing, singing and singing until I was hoarse. That was my initiation."

As many of Baldry's later bands would do, the Hoochie Coochie Men structured their sets in the manner of an R&B revue. Stewart's assigned job was to open with two or three solo numbers, warming up the crowd before Baldry, the star, took centre stage to do three or four tunes by himself.

"It was mostly Muddy Waters and Jimmy Reed," says Stewart. "I used to sing 'Bright Lights, Big City,' and songs by Ben E. King and Howlin' Wolf, all real blues stuff. Then we'd do a couple together, and that was the end of the show. We only played for an hour in those days."

Baldry was making good money as leader, and Stewart was paid the princely sum of £35 a week, which he felt was a pretty good wage for four nights' work. He recalls Baldry as an open-handed and encouraging boss.

"I think, as a bandleader," says Stewart, "he was more than generous with the financials of it. In those days, thirty-five pounds a week was a heck of a lot of money. I know most of the band were earning more than I was. He was generous to a fault with his money."

To Stewart's good fortune, the sartorially elegant Baldry was a sympathetic ally with an equally keen sense of style.

"John always stood up for me," says Stewart. "I found him a great bandleader, because a lot of the guys in the band didn't really like me. They were a lot older and considered themselves serious musicians. They didn't like my haircut or my clothes. John would put the band down, and say, 'Give the kid a chance.' So they did. In the end I won over their respect. It took me a couple of gigs to find my feet and then a few stage movements, and it was wonderful. John told me to never stand at the micro-phone with my legs together: 'It makes you look unconfident.'"

Timid at first, hiding behind the amplifiers between his numbers, Stewart was groomed and egged on by Baldry. As he gained confidence, he became a star attraction in the group.

"I hadn't heard him sing until he sang a couple of songs," Baldry recalled in *The New Breed*. "Although he was intensely shy back then... the crowd loved him. That was it. I said that we should capitalize on this."

He elaborated on the rapid rise of his protégé in Tim Ewbank and Stafford Hildred's *Rod Stewart: The New Biography*.

"He was an impressive singer from the word go," said Baldry. "His voice was even higher pitched then, but there was a bit of Sam Cooke in there even in the early days."

Baldry also noted that, as Stewart acquired both self-confi-dence and notoriety, some club owners began to promote per-formances by "Long John Baldry and the Hoochie Coochie Men with Rod 'The Mod' Stewart." Baldry insisted in the *New Breed* interview, however, that there was never any rivalry between him and Stewart. "People used to say to me: 'How can you let him take the spotlight? It's your show.' But I've never been greedy for the spotlight."

To the Mods on Carnaby Street, the two singers were as influ-ential for what they wore as for what they sang. Looking back today, Faces keyboardist Ian McLagan recalls the visual splen-dour of the Hoochie Coochie Men onstage at the Eel Pie Hotel.

"Long John was slim," he says, "wore double-breasted suits, and at six feet seven inches tall was an imposing presence on the bandstand, wailing Big Bill Broonzy's blues. When he felt the need to take a break, he'd bring up Rod, this big-nosed, skinny Mod with a bouffant hairdo, all three-buttoned suits and high-heeled boots."

Mick Fleetwood also appreciated Baldry's style.

"London in those days," says Fleetwood, "was about fashion, the vibe, and everybody doing something interesting. Not just within that little framework of music, but the whole cultural thing. John knew all about English tailoring. I was just a little kid, but I fancied myself as a bit of a clotheshorse because my sister used to hang out with some of the early fashion designers and artists in London. But when I first saw Baldry, I thought, 'Shit, this guy's just stunning!' I marvelled at his sense of style, which of course Rod took after. Rod was his little fledgling, star pupil. He and Rod used to wear these beautiful, immaculately tailored, silver sharkskin suits."

At six foot six, Fleetwood was only an inch shorter than Baldry, but he says that the singer seemed "larger than life" on the scene. "He was always immaculate and very good looking, with this incredible gangling body. He did this funny scoop up of his hand to his ear, when he sang. We just loved to watch him. His size lent him an incredible presence."

Fleetwood thinks of Baldry as a maverick, totally in command of how he wanted to look and sound. "Long John was very much one of the pioneers, and he knew the whole deal. He'd gone from this sort of a bluesy thing into soul, and he always had great players."

Still, Fleetwood often wondered how Baldry and Stewart could afford such nice clothes. The answer, according to Giorgio Gomelsky, was that Baldry, along with the other thrift-conscious clotheshorses of London, had simply wandered off Carnaby and over to the more affordable Greek tailor shops, where, as Baldry said, you could pick up a whole suit for just over ten pounds. Besides, with what he called his "abnormally long arms and legs," he could rarely wear the Carnaby "clobber" off the rack, anyway.

"Ten guineas," adds Gomelsky, "was quite a lot of money, but it was still not as much as you would pay on Carnaby Street. So we showed pictures of all this mod stuff to this Greek tailor, and he started making knock-offs for all of them."

Baldry also relied on his connections with hip, young designers like John Stephens, who would frequently lend him freebies to wear in promotional pictures. This was a time, Baldry later told the mod-centric *The New Breed* magazine, when the entire Mod movement was taking off. "The 'winklepicker' shoes, Italian suits, Lambretta scooters and parkas, all that stuff," Baldry said. "I always kept ahead with the fashions."

As Mick Fleetwood notes, Baldry's sharp dress sense was perfectly in keeping with the traditions of all the best blues and jazz musicians.

"There were no better dressers than the big band singers and blues players," says Fleetwood. "Some of those older guys couldn't have had two bucks to rub together, but there they were, turned out in crocodile shoes, silk socks and big suits. I never saw one second, onstage or off, where Long John Baldry wasn't turned out immaculately. He came from the generation before us, when it was all about the turnout."

Baldry would often say in later years that although nobody was making a fortune back then, they were all just happy to make a living by making music.

"It was a treat to be doing what we loved and getting paid for it," he told *The New Breed*. "And enough ale to get a little headstrong with!"

In between gigs with his band, Long John Baldry accepted an offer from United Artists, an American film and music company who had recently established a British record label, and managed to turn out his first full-length solo album. Released that year, *Long John's Blues* was credited to Long John Baldry and the Hoochie Coochie Men, but for contractual reasons Rod Stewart appeared only once, relegated to backing vocals with P.J. Proby on "I Got My Mojo Working." Other highlights included blistering recordings of "Goin' Down Slow," "Hoochie Coochie Man," "Times Are Getting Tougher Than Tough," "Rock the Joint" and "Everyday I Have the Blues."

Baldry was understandably happy to have a long-player out under his own name, even if the rush job in the studio left him little time to worry about whether it was any good. The live-sounding approach was entirely suitable for a blistering album of blues tunes, and Geoff Bradford, for one, is adamant that the album remains a milestone in British blues history. "*Long John's Blues* is still valid now," he says today. "When you hear any of the other '60s blues bands, it sounds so creaky and unauthentic. I think John made a wise choice. He got jazzmen in to give the rhythm section a bit of flexibility. That set it apart from the other bands, because it swung more."

The Hoochie Coochie Men enjoyed some profitable and high-profile shows up and down the U.K., although Baldry would admit later that the breakneck schedule, which included multiple bookings and all-nighters, wore him out.

"You'd double-up, even triple-up, gigs," Baldry explained to *The New Breed*. "I remember even quadrupling—that was like a real killer. It usually culminated in the Twisted Wheel, because they didn't care what time you started so long as you had the stamina to keep going until six in the morning."

The band also supported a great many touring American players, such as Sonny Boy Williamson, Little Walter, Chuck Berry, Buddy Guy, James Cotton, Charlie and Inez Foxx, Howlin' Wolf and Hubert Sumlin. Baldry's English players were shocked by some of the more violent antics of their visiting American counterparts. Rod Stewart recalls the time he was threatened by a razor-wielding Little Walter.

"He was very drunk," says Stewart. "He'd done his set, and he knew I was scoring big time with some of the girls. He just said, 'Can you go and get me a girl?' I took no notice of him, and then he suddenly drew out a knife. He didn't point it at me, just showed it to me. I said 'Yeah, yeah, I'll be right back with a couple!'"

In his interview with *The New Breed*, Baldry spoke about yet another incident, this time involving Sonny Boy Williamson and keyboardist Johnny Parker. Sonny Boy had exploded after a disagreement with Parker and run after him with a large knife. Baldry more or less agreed with Williamson.

"We had to hastily drop Johnny Parker," Baldry recalled, "who was getting on my nerves a bit anyway with a bit of 'backstage lawyer' shit. Then Ian Armitt came in to the band and that pacified Sonny Boy. He and Ian got on very well."

On April 7, 1964, Baldry, the Hoochie Coochie Men and Sonny Boy Williams joined a stellar lineup that included the Yardbirds, Memphis Slim and Jimmy Witherspoon for the grand reopening of the Marquee Club at its new home on Wardour Street. Journalist Graham Wood, then a writer for *Melody Maker* and the *New Musical Express*, recalls the music and atmosphere of opening night.

"It was stifling and packed with people," says Wood today. "It was the first time I'd ever seen the Yardbirds with Clapton, and I was very impressed, but I really went down to support John. Sonny Boy was this legend as well, and I wanted to see him live. John did a sterling job backing him up."

Baldry returned to the cobblestone streets of Soho in 2001 with Nick Orchard, recalling the event as the cameras rolled.

"I had flown in from Amsterdam," Baldry told Orchard, "and somehow the night before I ended up with an enormous black eye. I remember going on stage with a big black eye and swollen cheek. It was a great night, and there were many great nights at the Marquee."

Much to the chagrin of musicians and patrons, the new Marquee did not, at first, have a liquor licence.

"It was always coffee and Coca-Cola," said Baldry. "Of course, a lot of the musicians didn't want that. So we actually opened up a little nightclub called La Chas. The only way we could get licensing for that was to have it run by a board of directors, us, who would take turns on the bar. So I used to have to put in one night a week's time, serving drinks. They got rid of me pretty quickly, because I was giving people far too hefty a shot in the drinks."

Baldry also revealed to Orchard that Jon Anderson, later a founding member and lead singer in the progressive rock group Yes, held a job as the Marquee Club's busboy and live-in janitor.

"We let him sleep on the banquettes," Baldry laughed, "in exchange for picking up empty glasses, emptying the ashtrays and that sort of thing. I don't think too many people knew about that."

According to various unscientific reports, Long John Baldry would play the Marquee more than two hundred times over the next ten years, which is considered a record. Baldry's sister, Margaret, would frequently attend. Having sworn off the damp, sweaty Eel Pie Island, she found the Marquee more to her liking, and she marvelled at her brother's ability to sing and tell funny stories. Baldry's humour was informed by British comedians of the day.

"John had a wicked sense of humour," Margaret says, "and he was a great fan of *The Goon Show*. He often socialized with Spike Milligan. He was also a big fan of Tommy Cooper, this comedian who used wear a fez hat. He was so silly. The only time I ever saw John do a real belly laugh was if he was watching someone like him.'"

John had become a great mimic, according to Margaret, and he would often imitate people's accents and physical mannerisms.

"Sometimes it was embarrassing," she admits. "He'd mimic someone, and you'd think, 'Please, please stop.' I do think, however, he'd be mortified if he thought he'd really hurt some-one's feelings."

Margaret also puts forth the notion that her brother's larger-than-life social tendencies were in fact the product of Baldry coping with chronic low self-esteem. "It's almost as if he came alive in front of an audience. Yet there was that bit of him that felt that people didn't care about him at all."

When not holding down weekly residencies at the Marquee, the Hoochie Coochie Men toured incessantly, appearing at descriptively named venues like the Dancing Slipper in Notting-ham and the Ricky Tick in Windsor. After a few of their long drives, Rod Stewart became keenly aware for himself of Bald-ry's legendary aversion to vehicular travel. Baldry's feelings were only compounded by the band's jerry-built van and the rather odd man they had hired to drive it.

Baldry had paid £40 for a decrepit delivery van, which he'd had customized, adding windows on the sides, a few old aircraft seats for the band to sit on and an outdated paraffin stove tied to the floor with ropes for heating.

Stewart still shudders to think about the vehicle. "All the band were inside sitting on seats that were tied down with bits of string and in the middle," recalls Stewart. "It was bloody dan-gerous. If we'd had an accident we'd have all gone up in flames." Baldry himself would later call the old van "a death trap."

Stewart describes their driver as an eccentric ex-RAF pilot, whom they all knew as "Mad Harry."

"He'd done out the dashboard like a Lancaster bomber from the Second World War," Stewart recalls. "He used to wear a fly-ing helmet and ear muffs and gloves, the whole flying thing. He thought he was in a Spitfire or something."

Harry's duties also included introducing the Hoochie Coochie Men each night, dressed to the nines in a full tuxedo embellished with his wartime decorations.

"John used to sit up the front," says Stewart, "and if Harry was taking a corner too quickly, he'd smack his hands on the dashboard and scream, 'Slow *down!*' We had a few near misses where the old oil stove went over a few times."

Holger Petersen recounts a tale Baldry shared with him about another close call.

"He told me about a couple of car accidents he'd been in," Petersen recalls, "particularly this one time, when Rod was a little more well known, and they'd gone out together in London for Indian food. After the meal, they had a couple of bags of left-overs and got into Rod's limo. They get to an intersection when suddenly the limo gets T-boned and everything gets thrown around all over the car. There was a lot of damage, and it was quite a serious accident. The way John tells the story, Rod was calling, 'John, I'm dying, I'm dying. Look, I'm covered in blood!' So John puts his finger in it, licks it and tells him, 'It's not blood, Rod, you're okay. It's only the leftover chicken vindaloo.' It shook John up, though."

One night on tour in Scotland with the Hoochie Coochie Men, Stewart remembers, Baldry made an uncharacteristically ill-advised fashion choice. "It was pretty hairy, you know, to go and play up in Scotland in those days, because they didn't particularly like the English people. In fact, they still don't. We went up and played Dundee University. Beforehand, John had said, 'Tomorrow morning we're going to go out and buy some tartan trews, you know, to placate the audience and please them and they'll be knocked out.'"

Baldry would recall the incident years later in a separate interview. "We'd got some Royal Stewart tartan trews," Baldry told *The New Breed*, "and of course that was right for Rod, but I had no right to be wearing Scottish tartan!'"

"So we walked on the stage," Stewart continues, "and they didn't even wait for us to start playing. They fucking booed us, threw beer cans at us, told us to get off the stage; they took umbrage. We only played about three numbers, went back to the dressing room and from there on to the hotel. What with me and my haircut, which looked, at the time, like Dusty Spring-field, they must have thought, 'What have we got here with these two?'"

In fact, more than a few people in the London scene had speculated, behind their backs, about the nature of Baldry and Stewart's relationship. Stories began to circulate about the two them sharing a bed on the road. This did happen once, but both parties were adamant that nothing sexual had transpired between them.

"I know Rod fairly well and [knew] John extremely well," says keyboard player and producer Jimmy Horowitz today, "and I can tell you there was never anything between John and Rod. Rod is pretty hetero and always had leggy blondes around. He's so confident in his own heterosexuality that he finds [the rumours] kind of funny. People always talked about it, but it was nonsense."

Certain members of the audience openly heckled the bouffanted Stewart and the flamboyant Baldry, but the two of them had developed an unbreakable bond that was beyond sex. Although Stewart would come, over time, to view John Baldry as equal parts Svengali, mentor and older brother, Baldry would forever look upon his beloved protégé as "Roddy," his closest and most reliable friend.

meet the beatles—again

As the Hoochie Coochie Men continued their breakneck touring schedule through the spring of '64, Long John Baldry received an unexpected courtesy call from his old mates, the Beatles. He had become friendly with the Fab Four in Hamburg and met up with them again when he played the Merseyside clubs with Ken Sims. Baldry spoke of their connection in an interview in 2002 with the BBC's Spencer Leigh.

"I'd been coming to Liverpool a lot," he told Leigh, "and there were a number of occasions... when the Beatles were my intermission group, but things turned around in 1962. The first time I heard Paul McCartney, I was sold for life. To this day he is one of the best Little Richard impersonators."

The Beatles performed with Little Richard in Hamburg that year, as Baldry explained in the liner notes to a late-career live album. "In November of 1962," he said, "I had a residency on the 'Jazz Boat' in Lübeck and I would drive into Hamburg on my free Sunday nights. At that time, Little Richard (with a twelve-year-old organist in short pants, Billy Preston, in his band) was head-lining at the notorious Star Club with my old friends the Beatles and Gerry and the Pacemakers as support acts, for the month."

Roy Young, an English keyboard player who had turned down an early offer to join the Beatles—and who would later play piano with Baldry, during his Canadian years—was at the time the Star Club's talent booker.

"I booked everyone," says Young, and he saw firsthand the effect Long John Baldry had on the young Liverpool band. "The Beatles looked up to John Baldry, and he had a lot of influence on what style of music John, Paul, George and [then drummer] Pete Best were going to play."

Paul McCartney recalls today that he and the other Beatles admired Baldry, whom he describes as "tall, dark and bluesy" at the time.

"He was one of the first great white hopes in Britain," says McCartney. "He had a unique style and great presence. He was an important part of the '60s scene. I saw him quite a bit, on and off. He came round to my house for tea. He was a bit of a mate. A lovely man."

Back in Liverpool, Paul's younger brother, Mike, an accomplished musician and photographer in his own right, would often tag along with the Beatles when they swapped records and stories with Baldry. Long John's enthusiasm for the blues inspired them to explore records by Little Walter, Howlin' Wolf and Muddy Waters. Mike McCartney immortalized the connection in a well-known photograph he snapped of Paul standing with Baldry at Liverpool's Lime Street railway station.

While the Liverpool kids picked up Chuck Berry and Little Richard discs from the dockers in their seaport town, Baldry brought them the more obscure blues albums from London.

"I presumed that Baldry got his records from the dockers in London, as well," says Mike McCartney. "We'd say, 'I'll swap you a Bo Diddley for a Chuck Berry.' Baldry had all the oblique ones. We didn't know it was black music or blue or green or whatever, because they didn't have any photographs in those days. All you had were these bits of vinyl. You'd put it on and it was, 'Oh, I like that one,' and so on. So he influenced us all in a way that not many people know. He knew what he loved, and so it was marvellous for him to come up here and find all these people with strange accents before the [Merseybeat] explosion."

According to popular legend, John Lennon was so inspired after Baldry had played him the harmonica blues of Little Walter that he picked up the instrument himself to create the distinctive opening riff on the Beatles' "Love Me Do."

"The climate was very underground," says Mike McCartney. "It was all tom-toms and smoke signals. It was all just word of mouth with musos. We'd all share our knowledge."

By 1964, of course, the beat boom had found its way onto the nation's radar, and its television sets. It was a highly televised year for Baldry, who appeared on *Hullabaloo,* with Sonny Boy Williamson, Peter, Paul and Mary, the Clancy Brothers and Sister Rosetta Tharpe; *Road Show,* reuniting him with folk troubadours Robin Hall and Jimmie MacGregor; and a televised *Tribute to Cole Porter.*

With the world now overwhelmed by Beatlemania, the Fab Four proved that they hadn't forgotten their old mate. They invited Baldry to appear, without the Hoochie Coochie Men, on their own TV special, *Around the Beatles.* Also at the Beatles' request, Baldry's old friend and producer Jack Good was flown back from America to produce the program, taped on April 28 at Wembley Studios. The finished sixty-minute production was broadcast in Britain on May 6 by London-area ITV franchise Rediffusion (a.k.a. Associated-Rediffusion).

The Beatles performed ten of their current hits and appeared in a *Goon Show*–esque parody of Shakespeare's *A Midsummer*

Night's Dream. Because of the band's hectic schedule—they were filming *A Hard Day's Night* at the time—the program was padded out with performances from artists hand-picked by the Beatles themselves.

"We liked [Baldry], so we suggested him for it," says Paul McCartney. "It was great."

Millions of Britons tuned in to witness Baldry belting out an incendiary version of "I Got My Mojo Working" while the camera cut away to shots of the Beatles cheering him on from the side of the stage. Additionally, Baldry performed two other numbers: "Lover Please," and "Movin' On." The show also featured Fab friends P.J. Proby, Cilla Black, Millie Small, the Vernon Girls, the Jets, Sounds Incorporated and American disc jockey Murray the K.

Back at home, Baldry's mother nervously watched her oldest boy on the telly. In a rare interview for the pop magazine *Rave* in 1968, the doting mother would discuss the anxiety she felt whenever her son was on television.

"I remember the first time," Mrs. Baldry told *Rave*. "I just sat there and shook like a leaf. Even now I almost put my fingers up to my face, almost frightened to look because I think he might mess it up. He never does, but I always think he might!"

Baldry did not "mess up" on the Beatles special, and his appearance announced to the whole country what people in the clubs and at festivals had known for some time: Long John Baldry's mojo was indeed working, and he was a force to be reckoned with.

Although the special was a coup for Baldry, it did nothing for his relationship with his bandmates, particularly Stewart. In the month leading up to the broadcast, Baldry was tied up with various rehearsals, and the schedule became so demanding that, on the afternoon before a gig in Portsmouth, he was forced to stay behind while the rest of his bandmates slogged it out in the panel van. Baldry shuttled up by train. By the time he arrived, the show was already in progress; Stewart and the band struggled as they tried to stall for him. A tense vibe was in evidence as Baldry approached the bandstand, and Stewart fired off a verbal onslaught from the stage, asking facetiously why Baldry had bothered to show up at all. Baldry was furious.

After an almighty row backstage, Baldry kicked his protégé out of the band. He would reinstate Stewart a week later, though, when the band entered the studio with Jack Good. Good had stayed over after the Beatles special, at Baldry's request, and on June 19, Baldry and the Hoochie Coochie Men recorded a single, "You'll Be Mine," for United Artists. Perhaps as a peace offering, Stewart was given a solo, and he made his recording debut on the B-side, singing the Sister Rosetta Tharpe song "Up above My Head."

At only twenty-three years old, Baldry was already something of an elder statesman. Although he remained a blues purist, he was now having his first taste of both pop stardom and the Fleet street music press.

"I'm a blues singer," Baldry declared in one interview. "I don't really *have* to make records, but this chance turned up after goodness knows how many people asked me when I was going to make a record."

Speaking to Sidney Nelson in his "Round the Turntable" column, Baldry said: "I've been listening to the blues for a decade or so now, and I think I've absorbed a little of what it is about. To sing the blues you have to be 'aware' they have a greater relevance to life than any other form of music."

"I don't like this phrase 'R&B'," he insisted. "It seems to have been coined by the Americans to describe anything that wasn't pop or jazz."

"Half the kids who are playing rhythm and blues today," he told Anne Nightingale in the *Hastings Evening News*, "don't even know what it means. But I don't believe that you have to be a Negro to be able to sing the blues. After all, the present-day Americans can hardly have worked on chain gangs, and, anyway, I don't believe that there's any difference between black and white emotions. I can have exactly the same feelings as someone from the Deep South, and I can sing the blues just as sincerely."

In several articles, possibly culled from the same press release, Baldry expressed his desire to sing with the Count Basie Orchestra and dismissed his own recordings as fun folly.

"It doesn't mean anything much," he was quoted as saying to Bob Farmer in the *Lincolnshire Echo*. "I'm not bothered about having hits, although it would be nice if my records were bought, because I like money as much as the next man. To have people interested in your music is great, and popularity is fine so long as you don't get lumbered to the extent that you can't move around without being leapt upon and seized. Just think of the Beatles—they must have the patience of Job."

Record Mirror's David Griffiths staged a meeting between Baldry and a visiting American hero, John Lee Hooker, who expressed his gratitude that "guys like Long John are helping people to get to know the blues. You can't like what you don't know, and I don't think the blues had been heard much until the last few years."

Although the pop life was a welcome distraction, with Baldry becoming a well-known habitué of London nightspots like the Bag O' Nails, the Scotch of St. James and the Cromwellian, things weren't easy for the Hoochie Coochie Men. By the end of 1964, the entire enterprise had become a nuisance not only for Baldry, who claimed to be losing £400 a week, but for Stewart, who by now had signed as a solo artist with Decca, releasing a cover version of Sonny Boy Williamson's "Good Morning Little Schoolgirl." Bass player extraordinaire Cliff Barton left the band amid speculation of a nasty drug habit.

Baldry's management was in financial disarray, with Martin Davis crying bankruptcy and informing Baldry that he was in debt, despite having solid bookings. Guitarist Geoff Bradford walked out, temporarily, in a dispute over fees.

"I had trouble getting wages, so I left," remembers Bradford. "I went back doing odds and ends. Then Baldry asked me to rejoin him a month later, on the condition he paid me what he owed me."

When Stewart left the group to take up with Southampton combo the Soul Agents, the writing was on the wall. Although the Hoochie Coochie Men were all but over, Baldry soldiered on from Christmas 1964 until the following July, when the band opened for Chuck Berry and the Moody Blues. In addition to newly reinstated guitarist Bradford and amicable pianist Ian Armitt, Baldry was now backed by sax player Rudy Jones, trumpeter Pete Peterson and former Humphrey Lyttleton players Pete Blannin on bass and Eddie Taylor on drums. The new jazzier sound, however, didn't suit Berry's rock 'n' roll audience.

The band split up for good in the fall. It had been a good run, but Baldry appeared to have played all his cards and folded. It also seemed that he would never again perform with Stewart. As it turned out, he was wrong on both counts. In a year's time, his career would be steaming hot.

launching the steampacket

EVEN THOUGH it was a long time coming, the dissolution of the Hoochie Coochie Men came as a surprise to many on the scene, including some band members. Piano player Ian Armitt later told Stewart biographers Tim Ewbank and Stafford Hildred that he only found out when Baldry's manager, Martin Davis, told him one day that the band was "finished." "There was an idea for another band," said Armitt. "That, of course, was Steampacket."

Launched in July of 1965, Steampacket is commonly believed to be England's first supergroup. And indeed, the promise held by the group's component parts convinced Baldry and Stewart to put aside petty squabbles, temporarily abandon their respective solo careers and unite for the greater good.

Steampacket's talent-rich lineup found Baldry sharing lead vocals with both Stewart—after his less-than-impressive stint in the Soul Agents—and a relatively unknown female vocalist named Julie Driscoll. The instrumental soul of the group was organist Brian Auger who, along with guitarist Vic Briggs, drummer Micky Waller and bass player Rick Brown, had been performing for some time as the Trinity.

Steampacket was the brainchild, if not the love child, of three distinct managerial factions, a fact that would later prove to be its undoing. Martin Davis and George Webb represented Baldry. The young team of Geoff Wright and John Rowlands handled Stewart, and Giorgio Gomelsky brought Auger's Trinity and Gomelsky's singing secretary, Julie Driscoll, to the group.

The "supergroup" concept was cooked up by Gomelsky, who had recently handed over the management of the Rolling Stones to Andrew Loog Oldham and was now presiding over a stable of artists that included the Yardbirds and Auger's jazz group. According to Gomelsky, trad jazz was finished. Modern jazz hadn't yet established a following, but in his mind the younger jazz musicians were the true hope for the future.

"These younger jazz players had no problem with Ray Charles or R&B," says Gomelsky today. "So that's how I got involved with jazzers like Brian Auger, Graham Bond and Dick Heckstall-Smith."

Auger, a rising star, had been voted Best New Jazz Pianist in the prestigious *Melody Maker* jazz poll. Although the piano had been his forte, everything changed when he heard the Hammond B3 electric organ.

"I had heard some Jimmy Smith records," Auger explains today, "and I was fascinated by the Hammond. So I went out and bought my first B3 with a loan from the Shepherds Bush Branch of the National Provincial Bank in London."

Julie Driscoll, at that point, was just another pretty young woman with singing ambitions. She worked in Gomelsky's office, where one of her tasks was answering fan mail addressed to the Yardbirds.

"It was a pretty considerable job, too," recalls Auger, "because the Yardbirds had Eric Clapton in the band, just before Jeff Beck came in. I was doing some sessions at the time as well, and I played on the Yardbirds' single "For Your Love"... Julie was in the office, just waiting to get out on the road with a band."

Gomelsky says he discovered Driscoll's singing abilities one evening after she had been out at his Crawdaddy Club in Richmond. "I drove her and her sisters back home to Lambeth," he remembers. "The radio was on, and Julie started singing along with it. I said, 'Wait a minute, Julie—you can sing.' So I asked her, 'Do you want to be a singer?' She said yes, so I started taking care of her and helping her along."

The idea for Steampacket was more than just a marriage of convenience. Gomelsky says he had an ideological belief that the next wave in music would stem from the cross-fertilization of blues and modern jazz. "I always thought we were going to have a universal, global, popular music sooner or later," he says. "It was all just lying there, and I was connecting the dots. But England was very insular, and nobody knew about that stuff."

Auger, with his new Hammond in tow, was touring with his mainly instrumental jazz trio. He was open to new directions, however.

"About March or February 1965," he says, "we were playing as the Hammond Trinity, me, Micky and Rick. I was one of the only people that had ever won a jazz poll for piano at that point, so I was able to play at Ronnie Scott's, for jazz snobs. But because I'm also an organ player I could play in the R&B clubs, too, so I got to meet up with all the rock 'n' rollers on that scene. I knew that rock was still in its infancy and felt poised to drive it forward with the Trinity. They were very exciting times for me. We were breaking down these barriers, you know?"

Gomelsky, for his part, sought one unified endeavour that would consolidate his many different artists and interests. "There are only so many hours in a day," he says. "So I thought, 'Who is doing nothing out there?' Long John was going round in circles doing one-off appearances here and there. Brian was playing piano at Peter Cook's Establishment Club, filling in for Dudley Moore. Julie was an aspiring singer, and Rod wasn't really big yet. That's really how the Steampacket came about."

Baldry was intrigued enough by the proposition to make the trip up to Manchester's Twisted Wheel, to give Brian Auger's trio a listen. Auger recalls seeing Long John from the stage, a tall figure at the back of the Wheel nodding his blond head to the beat.

"He didn't actually introduce himself or anything," says Auger, "but we recognized him in the crowd. John, in those days, was a household name. The Beatles TV special had been seen by so many people; it was the kind of thing that could really launch a career. So we all knew who he was."

Baldry liked what he heard, and, besides, he had an implicit trust in Gomelsky's instincts. "Giorgio always seemed to have access to something," he later told *The New Breed*. "He was always in there at the beginning of a lot of things like the Scene Club... the Stones."

The following Monday morning, Auger received a call from Baldry's managers. The Hoochie Coochie men were in chaos, they said, and they were wondering whether Auger would be interested in discussing a proposition with them.

"They told me that John was no longer able to deal with it," says Auger today. "They said they were looking for someone straight up who could put together and run a band, keep John in line, and make sure we turned up on time and collected the money. Basically, I was being asked to be responsible for the whole damn thing."

Auger recalls discussing the triple lead singer concept with Baldry.

"I had been doing some vocals in the Trinity," says Auger, "although I wasn't a great singer or anything. John said he'd like to have this other guy in the band called Rod Stewart. Of course, I knew Rod; he had occasionally sat in with my band. So I said, 'John, no problem, but what are we looking at here, some sort of Sam and Dave kind of revue-type thing? How's this going to work with two singers? Why not add a girl singer, like Julie Driscoll?' So that was it."

The instant success of Steampacket added another musical flavour to Baldry's repertoire. He and the band incorporated some of the best new American sounds, such as Stax-Volt soul from Memphis and Tamla Motown from Detroit.

"We just beat everyone to the punch with hearing all the new Tamla records that people didn't know about," Baldry would tell *The New Breed*. "Then we basically appeared on the scene and people went nuts... they were hearing all this... and they thought 'Where is this bloody music coming from?' Then it filtered out to become more of the Northern Soul thing and everything else."

"It was one hell of a band," says Stewart today. "Once again it was basically jazz musicians that had a great pedigree playing in an R&B style. We had Julie Driscoll, a touch of extreme beauty, and then we had John and me. It was just a great package."

The show was structured like a soul revue with the main singers staggering their entrances, coming on stage one at a time.

"I proposed that I could go on first," says Auger, "and play a couple of Jimmy Smith tunes, then one of my own, plus all these little kind of jazzy teasers. Julie was into Nina Simone and all those Tamla Motown people. And then Rod could come on, and Julie and I would sing backup for him. Then John could come on, basically doing straight Chicago blues and Delta blues things and some gospel stuff which we could all sing backup on."

"In those days," remembers Stewart, "we only had to play for three quarters of an hour. I'd sing three Sam Cooke or Otis Redding songs, Julie would sing three songs, and John would sing about four."

"Then all three would come on for the finale," recalls Giorgio Gomelsky, "a gospel song like 'Oh Lord, You Sure Have Been Good to Me.' It was a real rebel rouser and people were up and clapping."

"Then," Stewart says, "when it was all finished, we'd go round to the pub. I remember John saying to me that we were earning five hundred pounds a night, and we didn't even have a hit record. But it was all because we had just a great show, with these three figures backed by a fabulous band."

Auger tells the story of how he came up with the group's nautical-sounding name. "Back then," he says, "when a musician really gave you 150 per cent on stage, you'd say, 'Boy, he's a steamer' or 'She's a steamer.' They'd get on and they'd just be steaming. So I thought, it's a package, what about 'Steampacket'? It evoked New Orleans riverboats and a kind of bluesy Mississippi Delta thing. John liked it, and so did everybody else. Steampacket got off to a flying start and was incredibly successful."

The newly christened revue was among the most happening acts of 1965. The band was asked to open for Baldry's old mates the Rolling Stones, who had by now become, to quote the subtitle of their most recent album, "England's Newest Hitmakers." A press release from the time heralded the news that Steampacket "could well give a completely new look to British pop music! The idea is to take big names out of the various groups and band them together as one group... three or four good vocalists for the price of one! The audience at the Odeon, Exeter, saw the first 'rehearsed ad-lib' performance from the group on the first three-night bill with the Rolling Stones last Friday."

After their London debut at the Marquee in July, Steampacket set their sights on a showstopping appearance at the fifth annual National Jazz and Blues Festival in Richmond, Surrey. Auger recalls that although they played a lot of festivals, the Richmond Festival was by far the best of the lot: "It was such a great spread and a great show. We had a great time."

The lineup for the three-day festival that year included, among others, the Yardbirds, the Who, the Moody Blues, Ronnie Scott, Manfred Mann, Georgie Fame, Graham Bond Organization, Chris Barber, Kenny Ball, the Animals and Spencer Davis. Steampacket were listed in the program as "Brian Auger's Trinity with Rod Stewart, Julie Driscoll, Long John Baldry."

"Steampacket, the name, meant nothing to the public at that time," says Auger today, "so the festival promoters went with our individual names, which *did* mean something to the festival ticket buyers."

Nineteen sixty-five was the Richmond Festival's most successful year to date, with an estimated 33,000 fans—among them, John Lennon and George Harrison—packing the Richmond Athletic Grounds. Steampacket's set was filmed for posterity, although Baldry later complained to *The New Breed* that the filmmakers had "ruined it by putting that silly scream track on it from beginning to end, which they used to do with pop things back in those days. People never went to the Richmond Jazz Festival and screamed."

Steampacket's dates with the Rolling Stones went down so well with the Stones' core constituency that the band was asked to join them on a summer tour of the U.K. While on the road, Auger got to know Baldry, or "Balders," as Auger called him, very well. He remembers discovering Long John's talent for drawing, which he demonstrated backstage at Eel Pie Island. "Baldry drew these hilarious caricatures, right onto the walls, of everybody in the band. But I noticed that every time I returned to Eel Pie Island, we all began to resemble the wall drawings more and more. It was a bit scary. John had grabbed everybody's personality and just exaggerated some of the features. I thought we'd better be careful. We were starting to look more and more like John's caricatures!"

Steampacket was drawing huge crowds, playing at colleges and universities with bands like the Who and with crooning pop balladeers the Walker Brothers. Scott Walker's deep-voiced, vanilla-soul sound would inspire Baldry to explore his own string-inflected crooning. "At that particular time," Baldry later told *The New Breed*, "I had seen the possibilities of working with big orchestrations, and of course that formula did prove successful later in the Pye years."

Rod Stewart recalls fondly the frequent college bookings, where girls were always in abundance. "I remember I always used to get laid, just shagged rotten, up at Sheffield University. I always used to like playing in Sheffield."

Auger, however, had less time for carousing. Serving as the band's musical director, resident keyboard ace, tour manager, roadie and driver meant countless hours behind the wheel and no shortage of heavy lifting.

"It was like *everything*," says Auger. "They had one roadie, Eric Brooks, so all the rest of it was basically down to me. We were working sometimes six nights a week, and no one else in the band had a licence, except for Eric. And when we were doing one-nighters, out of town, I'd have to leave at least two hours earlier than anybody else to go drive all the way around London to pick everyone up. I lived in Twickenham, so I'd drive to Vauxhall to pick up Julie, then cross the river and pick up John in Colindale [his parents' house] and then over to Mill Hill to pick up Rod."

"We used to travel around in Brian's old Audi," Stewart confirms today, "although when I got my licence, he didn't have to pick me up anymore. Still, I didn't drive myself to Birmingham or to Manchester or all those places."

Auger recalls a troubling incident on the road one rainy night, which likely exacerbated passenger Baldry's already heightened auto-phobia. "We were driving up to Manchester on the M1," Auger says. "John's in the back of the car for leg room, along with Julie, and Rod was in front. We came to a bit of two-lane highway that was extremely dangerous, particularly when it was dark and it rained, which it was on this night. I was driving blind in the rainy night, when all of a sudden I hit the lip of a foot-high median and launched the car, for a few seconds, into the air. As we got back onto the road, the suspension on the car went down to the ground, scraping the road, sending a huge curtain of sparks on our right-hand side. Balders nearly climbed through the headliner [ceiling] of the car. I managed to pull it over, down the road, then stop and get out to take a look at it. John was pretty upset about that. But Rod actually complimented me on a great bit of driving. Still, I think that may have contributed to John's fear of car travel."

Whereas Auger had to report to the management offices at 9:00 AM every Monday morning, to review the tour details and settle accounts, Baldry, Stewart and Driscoll's only homework was to go out and meet the press.

Pop journalists had grown tired of the "Gosh, he's tall" caption for Baldry and were always fishing for a new angle. *Disc* magazine featured a photograph of him, with up-and-coming pop singer Kiki Dee, at a trendy Carnaby Street restaurant under the subheading, "Clothes aren't the only things swinging in Carnaby Street. Vegetarianism is trendy too!" Elsewhere in the story, readers learned that "Julie Driscoll was once labelled an eccentric for living on raw carrots and fruit juices," but that now "she's just one of an increasing number of pop stars who have caught the Health Food Bug."

The *South East London Mercury* wrote that "Rod Stewart... looks more like a college boy than a blues singer." A wide-eyed, eighteen-year-old Driscoll confessed that she was "working very hard, but... having a wonderful time."

Driscoll wasn't kidding. With their fortunes rising, the band members, Auger included, were having the time of their lives playing to packed houses every night, earning a good wage doing it and becoming celebrities. Naturally, Long John Baldry made sure they were all dressed for success.

"I remember wearing these very bold striped suits that Rod and I had made up," Baldry told *The New Breed*. "White with a dark blue stripe... more like pyjamas than suits!"

Living in such close quarters with him, Auger finally caught on that Baldry was gay and realized why Balders routinely brushed off the advances of his many female fans.

"I just must have assumed he had a fiancée stashed away somewhere," Auger laughs today, "because there were always these mini-skirted mod birds—the dolly-birds of London—coming around. Which, of course, was wonderful for the rest of us. It was like we had died and gone to heaven. But John wasn't interested. So I figured that one out. But you know, it didn't matter to me anyway."

The band did have their tense moments. Auger resented the workload. Driscoll and Stewart fought sometimes over who got to sing which song, and Baldry had the odd tantrum or pulled rank as the most established star. But by and large, Baldry called upon his own humility and diplomacy to smooth out their differences.

Unfortunately, however, money and management would ultimately sink the Steampacket.

"It's sad," Baldry confessed in a later interview. "A lot of infighting broke out, and that usually centered on Brian's need to have more share of the dough."

"The big problem," says Giorgio Gomelsky, looking back, "was that they all had different managers. When it came time to record the band, we went to the studio and did a kind of a demo recording, which has [since] been bootlegged as an album over the years. But it was only meant as a demo."

"I was with United Artists," Baldry explained in a 2001 interview. "Rod was with Decca, Brian and Julie were with Parlophone and none of the labels would agree. So we never ever recorded, apart from those awful lousy recordings... for which we never received a dime. Both Rod and I would prefer they would just go away and die, rather than ever want any money for it, because it was totally embarrassing. Awful, awful!"

Gomelsky feels that the band had become too successful, too soon, and their fragmented management situation only complicated matters.

"Success spoils things," says Gomelsky, "and Long John was not that clever with regard to the business. Artists on the whole are not terribly good at seeing the big picture."

"There were too many managers," confirms Auger today, "and too many cooks spoiling the broth. Rod's manager, though, only turned up when there was money for him. We were doing all the work, and this [manager] was kind of blithely turning up at certain points and asking to get paid for doing basically absolutely nothing. Everywhere we went, we got stronger and stronger in the marketplace, but there was this managerial problem. So that was it on the recording level. Still, we worked solidly, live, for two years, did a lot of festivals in Europe, and we played all over the place."

By the summer of '66, band members were becoming frustrated and tired of the road. Their managers had arranged a residency in the south of France. It was supposed to be a tonic for the troops, but it ended up creating more trouble than it was worth.

"We were booked to go to St. Tropez in August," Auger explains. "The band had probably been on the road for about eighteen months at that time, and I desperately wanted a holiday. We were booked in the best club there, the Papagayo, which was popular with French film stars and the hoi-polloi of the south of France holiday crowd. Brigitte Bardot actually came in on two or three occasions and gyrated in front of the band in a very short little mini-dress. We tried our best to keep playing and disguise the fact that we were drooling."

The Papagayo residency proved to be a tipping point for the band, fracturing the final shreds of goodwill and solidarity that existed among the various factions.

"Before we left London," Auger recalls, "we found out that the money they offered was terrible. John didn't think the money was suitable, and so we ended up going up to the office. Rod and Julie weren't there. Giorgio came up with me—Rod's manager never showed, of course—it was just John, Giorgio, George Webb, Martin Davis and myself. They told us that there wasn't enough money to pay everyone; somebody would have to stay behind. John was drinking a bit at the time, and I remember thinking the amount of money left over wouldn't even cover his drink tab. Still, John said that he'd like to do the gig anyway, because he'd already told Lionel Bart and Leslie Bricusse [musical-theatre friends of Baldry's from London], and they had all decided they were going to be there. George Webb said, 'Look. The way to do this is, John, you're gonna have to go. Brian, you're gonna have to go.' And we only had a four-piece band; we couldn't leave the guitar player behind, 'cause we needed him. It's a blues band. So the band members are going to have to go, you know. You and the band, that's four people. They told John, 'You can either take Julie or Rod.' There was a vote, and everyone voted for Julie, including John who was the real power in the band. He could have said, 'If you don't take Rod, then I'm not going, and so we can all have the month off.' But I think because his mates were gonna be there, he wanted to go, and since all the votes up

until his casting vote had gone for Julie, he voted against Rod.
It probably would have helped if Rod's manager had been at the
meeting."

Steampacket, without Stewart, proceeded to head south—in
more ways than they knew. Auger explains how it all went terribly wrong.

"The first week went by, and everything was good," he says.
"We were bringing a lot of business to the club, and it was packed
every night."

Unfortunately, in the holiday atmosphere of the French seaside, Baldry's once restrained drinking habits had become, in
Auger's judgment, out of control. "John's drinking started to get
the better of him, and he began not to show up for the second,
third or fourth set. In the last two weeks, he just didn't turn up
at all. I thought that was really unprofessional. But we just went
on and did the gigs without him, Julie, myself and the band."

Rod Stewart was not there to judge for himself. Looking
back today, though, he swears he can't recall Baldry's drinking
ever interfering with his work.

"I never saw John fall down or throw up," says Stewart. "He
was always wonderfully in control. But he *could* drink the hard
stuff, which I think was left over from his influence by all the old
blues guys who could really drink. John thought, 'Well, if *they* do
it, *I'm* going to do it. It'll make me more authentic.' And he really
could drink. He used to laugh at me because I'd have a couple of
pints of beer and be as pissed as a fart, but he could go through
a bottle of whiskey, stand up and sing perfectly in tune and
converse with people. Not that that's anything to be proud of."

Steampacket was sinking into an abyss of bad vibes and
strained business dealings. The Papagayo residency caused
another minor rift between Baldry and Stewart. Auger went
back to the National Provincial Bank in Shepherd's Bush and
took out a loan to bankroll his new, funkier, jazzier version of
the Trinity, with Driscoll on lead vocals.

"The Steampacket had started to implode," says Auger today, "and I already had this thing in the back of my mind that I had wanted to try musically. As it turned out, John dropped out, so there was Julie and the rest of the band, and what I wanted to do at that point was start a band that could play some straight-ahead jazz stuff over a kind of funky rhythm section. So that's what I went off to do."

Baldry, saddened by the dissolution of Steampacket, poured himself into his solo career once again. At least on his own, he would have some recorded output to show for his efforts. Still signed to United Artists, he wasted no time in releasing two solo singles. "I'm On to You Baby," backed with "Goodbye Baby," was followed up by "House Next Door," backed with "How Long Will It Last." Although both drew mixed reviews, the critics were kinder about the release of Baldry's second full-length album, *Looking at Long John.* The new disc reflected a stylistic shift away from the ensemble R&B of *Long John's Blues* towards deep-voiced soul ballads with lavish orchestral accompaniment not unlike that of the Walker Brothers, on whose version Baldry's cover of "Make It Easy on Yourself" was clearly modelled. Baldry's interpretation of the Righteous Brothers' operatic opus "You've Lost That Lovin' Feelin'" set him against a Bob Leaper–orchestrated wall of sound almost worthy of Phil Spector's original.

Martin Davis's sleeve notes for *Looking at Long John* promised "a little taste of everything for his many fans." "Throughout the British Isles and Europe," Davis wrote, "his singing has brought him a respect and acclaim almost unique in his field. However, in this, his second album, we have set out to show the years of training have given John far wider vocal accomplishments."

Baldry discussed the record with the *Melody Maker*'s Richard Green shortly after its release. "I wanted to record with a big backing and strings and do new or little-known numbers," he told Green, "but the label thought the LP should contain well-known numbers. They're probably right."

The cover photo for the United Artists album was a bit of a stretch: it featured Baldry, dressed in John Stephens "freebies," being torn apart by adoring females. "I remember the photographer flew me out to San Tropez to take that picture," Baldry later told *The New Breed*. "Stephens would be saying 'Ooh try and get more in the photo.' As you can see [on the album cover], I've just got the sleeves rolled up because the sleeves on John Stephens's shirts were never quite long enough."

Rod Stewart, meanwhile, had grown a beard and accepted an offer from the Flamingo Club's managers, Rik and John Gunnell, to front an outfit called Shotgun Express. The Gunnells saw money-making potential in a Stewart-fronted revue band emulating the Steampacket template. Only this time, Stewart would be the leader, with Beryl Marsden as his female foil and a kind of Trinity-ish trio comprising organist Peter Bardens and two future Fleetwood Mac members, guitarist Peter Green and drummer Mick Fleetwood.

"Shotgun Express," Fleetwood admits today, "were the poor man's Steampacket. Rod basically fronted our three-piece band, with Pete playing all that Booker T–type stuff, early Billy Preston-ish, organ music. We were covering the Auger Trinity role, and Rod was now the Long John Baldry, basically."

Shotgun Express released one single, "I Could Feel the Whole World Turn Around." They stayed together for a while, until Stewart went off to more solo work and a successful stint fronting the Faces, with Ronnie Lane, Ian McLagan, Kenny Jones and Ronnie Wood.

Despite the Steampacket's inelegant demise, Auger maintains that the band was a great experience, at least on a musical level, for all involved.

"As far as I was concerned," says Auger, "Long John had given us the chance to be seen and to develop in front of larger audiences and gain a foothold in the market, which, personally, allowed me to step off into the deep end and try to put my own project together. He was really a gentleman, and very intelligent. You could talk to him about just about anything. He was also one of the kindest human beings I've ever met in the music business."

Over the next two years, the music business would come to know a softer, gentler side of Long John Baldry. His career, which had begun in the cellar clubs of London, Liverpool and Hamburg, was about to skyrocket straight to the top of the pops.

the heartaches begin

WHILE LONDON was named "the style capital of Europe" by the editors of *Time* magazine in 1966, Londoner Long John Baldry regularly flitted from Carnaby Street to the Cote D'Azur, Hamburg and Amsterdam, seeking distraction after the Steampacket's painful breakup.

Nineteen sixty-six was also a turning point for two important bands with whom Baldry was friendly. The Beatles' new album, *Revolver*, with its string quartets and tape loops, had solidified the group's reputation as artistic innovators. The Rolling Stones, meanwhile, had returned to Britain as conquering heroes after capturing the hearts and minds of America. Manager Andrew Loog Oldham invited Baldry to join the Stones' homecoming tour, *Rolling Stones '66*. It was their way, he says today, of saying thanks to their fans, and to Baldry for being an early influence on their music.

"It's not even a question of what John did for them," says Oldham, "but what John *was*. The tour itself was our way of saying we'd been away a long time, here's a thank-you tour for our English fans. But it was really so they wouldn't fucking resent us too much while we're running around in Rolls-Royces trying to pretend we've made as much money as the Beatles."

The tour also included the Yardbirds and the seventeen-piece Ike and Tina Turner Revue, whom the Stones had brought with them from the States. Oldham says that having so many people on stage left little room for Baldry to sing; that's why the Stones hired him to be their eccentric compère on the tour.

"That way," says Oldham, "he's got a regular gig, and they could all hang out on the road together. Plus, he gets to keep all the money, because he ain't gotta share it with a band, you know?"

Baldry relished his role, cracking wise and telling jokes as he introduced the band and their guests. "The Stones always insisted on having a good black supporting act with them when they were on tour," he would tell Nick Orchard years later, "Muddy Waters, Ike and Tina Turner and all of those. Mick Jagger and the Stones went out of their way to promote these artists."

Fun though it may have been, touring with the hard-partying Rolling Stones might not have been the best choice, healthwise, for Baldry. His personal habits were posing an increasing danger to his well-being. Drinking loosened his tongue and his inhibitions, and there was always the possibility that he might say or do something that could end up in the Fleet Street gossip pages. There were layers to what people could know; people could be blackmailed, careers ruined, if certain secrets got out.

Baldry's theatre friends could be just as bad an influence on him. Among his best friends in the theatre was Lionel Bart, an important figure from the 1950s British rock 'n' roll scene who had gone on to write and produce stage musicals, including the runaway 1960 hit *Oliver!* In addition to sharing a sexual preference, Bart and Baldry were each burdened by careers that hit peaks of success followed by valleys of failure and depression. Both were fond of self-medication via the socially acceptable British depression cure, alcohol.

In a liner note written in 1968 for an unreleased Baldry album, Bart wrote the following account of their initial meeting: "I first met Baldry in my early days around pop music in Soho, when a skiffle board made you a musician; and when, for a no-account bum like myself, a loan amounting to the price of a cup of coffee made you a millionaire. That about sets the scene around ten years ago when my own attention was first drawn to my incredibly tall friend; who not only carried a brand-new guitar case that wasn't empty, but who was also sporting a very flashy fawn mohair suit, not to mention a white spear-point collared shirt and hand-painted tie. A working musician! Man! Not only was this a definite touch for a cup of coffee, but with any luck, a guy with a pad and a bed and a place to kip down for the rest of the night, or the week, or the month. Had I known at the time that Baldry's pad was a semi-detached in the suburbs living with the rest of his family; who, on account of their mutual hereditary great height, all just happened to be cops; I would have taken the steps that my natural inclinations would have, at that period in my life, most certainly have dictated. As it was, I stifled the now-familiar exclamation of awe; and, squinting up at the halo around the blond head eclipsing the rising sun, I ventured these famous and endearing words, 'Hullo, hullo, hullo, what have we here?'"

Andrew Loog Oldham had met Baldry through his own association with Bart, when the three of them were regular patrons of the 2i's coffee bar in Soho.

"Lionel and Long John were just outrageous together," says Oldham today. "This was at a time when being gay was still scandalous. But the truth was, most gay people were talented, so there were a lot of 'em in show business!"

Baldry's sister, Margaret, took a job for a time as Bart's secretary.

"Not a very good one," she says today. "I think I was probably about twenty, and I did it for about a year." Reluctant to go into sordid details, Margaret will allow only that her brother was, by her account, "extremely promiscuous" at the time.

"I say it doesn't really matter to me," she confesses now, "but it really did. I found a lot of the gay scene very seedy. I just thought it was a tragedy that all these young boys were... male prostitutes. Some of them were very young. I felt like the mother hen. I used to think, 'What if this was my kid?' John was blackmailed on a couple of occasions. The solicitor who was involved at that time, Brian Epstein's lawyer David Jacobs, and I used to meet a lot of these young guys who were way beyond their years, and they were clearly out to get his money. I find that abhorrent as well. The tabloid journalists are just so seedy and such horrible, horrible people."

Bart was fond of throwing elaborate parties at his house in Fulham, to which Baldry would bring Rod Stewart and their various friends. "Lionel Bart's house was a den of iniquity," Stewart recalls. "All sorts of things used to go on around there, with two-way mirrors and sausage sandwiches."

Oldham would encounter Baldry at Bart's parties. It wasn't until much later that he discovered he was a singer. "I knew this part of Baldry in London," Oldham recalls, "but until I met the Rolling Stones, I didn't really experience him as a musician. I'd only seen him try to pull something in a pub. Sadly, John and Lionel had a common interest in straight kids, which was an awful dilemma, if you think about it, because it's doomed from the start."

Baldry was infamous for flirting with straight musicians, too, including Zoot Money's guitarist Andy Summers, who would later join the Police. Summers, who wrote about one such incident in his memoir *One Train Later*, swears that Baldry was ultimately a gentleman, backing off when it became obvious that the guitarist wasn't interested.

Kinks guitarist Dave Davies was remarkably candid in his 1996 memoir *Kink* about an intimate evening he spent with Baldry, which began in the Cromwellian pub and ended in the nearby Ashburn Hotel.

"Long John Baldry," Davies wrote, "was a famous habitué of the Cromwellian, and I enjoyed talking with him about Lead Belly, Muddy Waters and music in general until the weé hours of the morning. One night, when I noticed that Long John had been drinking too much, I suggested he stay with me at the Ashburn. I didn't know he was gay. To save the hotel manager embarrassment, I asked for a room with two single beds. Nevertheless, once we got in the room we sat on one of the beds and kissed. It felt like a kiss of friendship rather than a kiss of lust or sexual intention. Long John and I sat talking, kissing, and holding hands. It was very beautiful. I always remembered that feeling of being close to another man, of being intimate in a respectful way."

Music biographer Philip Norman has written extensively on British musical acts from the 1960s. In his biography of Elton John, *Sir Elton,* Norman described quite eloquently Long John Baldry's on- and off-stage personas.

"Among British blues singers of this era," Norman wrote, "none was so distinctive as Long John Baldry. A London policeman's son, six foot seven and a half inches tall, blond of hair and pink of face, he combined a voice oozing Southern molasses and hominy grits with a manner which, in either sense, could accurately be termed high camp."

Norman points out that, in the macho bluesy circles in which he travelled, Baldry's camp act was atypical.

"As well as being immensely tall," Norman continued, "he was a notable dandy, fond of flipping open his jacket to display the

LJB monogram patterned over its silk lining. The Deep Southern voice that growled macho blues ballads each night was by day exercised in all the parodied gambits of a screaming old queen. Whereas other musicians called each other 'man' or 'cat,' Long John preferred the appellation 'dear' or 'she,' as in 'She's bold today!' Onstage, he was equally unlikely, his immaculate figure towering through the cigarette smoke, a Savile Row suit straight out of some Mississippi bayou."

Extracurricular activities aside, Baldry still had his new album to promote and, with Rik and John Gunnell now on board as managers, a career to maintain.

"I've been off the scene for about three months, except when I did the Stones tour as compère," Baldry told *Melody Maker* in the fall of 1966, "but when I start in December I'll be changing my act quite a bit. It's the thirteen- and fourteen-year-old girls you've got to appeal to on the circuit, and I must do material to suit them."

Now all Baldry needed was to assemble a superb backing group who could not only play a wide selection of his music—including the orchestrated material from *Looking at Long John*—but also withstand the inevitable comparisons to the Steampacket. Making the rounds in South Kensington one night, Baldry dropped down to the Cromwellian, where he was delighted to hear the house band, Bluesology, belting out renditions of the songs of Jimmy Witherspoon, Lightnin' Hopkins and Muddy Waters.

Bluesology had been touring in many of the same places as Steampacket—including Hamburg and a residency at the Papagayo—and had backed a great many visiting American artists, like Major Lance, Patti LaBelle, Doris Troy and the Ink Spots. Even their frontline vocal approach was similar, with singer Stuart A. Brown trading off lead vocals with a female singer named Marsha Hunt, recently of the London cast of the musical *Hair*. Instrumentally, they were supported by bass player

Rex Bishop, drummer Mick Inkpen and, on the Vox Continental organ, a chubby keyboard player by the name of Reggie Dwight, the future Elton John.

"Bluesology," Elton recalls today, "was the kind of band that played clubs like the Cromwellian, the Speakeasy and also the Scotch of St. James and Sibylla's; basically, all the kind of hip clubs of the day. Everybody used to go to those clubs. I mean, we're talking about the mid '60s, so you'd get the Beatles and the Animals coming in."

Reg Dwight immediately recognized Baldry in the Cromwellian that night, having seen him perform at the Kenton Conservative Club in Middlesex and other venues. "I'd seen him with Rod," Elton John recalls, "who freaked me out because I'd never seen anything like it. Then I saw him quite a few times after that playing gigs."

Elton recalls being impressed with Baldry's acoustic twelve-string guitar prowess. Like his fellow Bluesologians, Elton had been influenced by Long John's groundbreaking efforts in popularizing the blues in England.

"He really was a fantastic blues guitarist," Elton remembers, "just him on his own, singing Lead Belly stuff. It was just amazing. He was definitely a pioneer and at the forefront of British blues music; he was right up there. Without John there wouldn't have been a blues scene as such. He was up there with Alexis Korner and Cyril Davies. And he always wore very smart suits and ties. He was this incredibly tall, imposing man who had this fabulous fashion sense."

After a perfunctory audition in Soho, at the Ken Colyer Jazz Club, Baldry asked Bluesology to effectively become the new Steampacket. Bluesology, however, was under contract to manager Arnold Tendler. After the Gunnell brothers made Tendler an offer he couldn't refuse, their contract was hastily broken, and Bluesology became the core of what was promoted as "The Long John Baldry Road Show."

Baldry, though excited about the new venture, played up his deference towards his old Steampacket-mates in a *Melody Maker* article. "I sometimes wish Julie could join us," he told Richard Green, "but I suppose she's happy with Brian. Rod's doing well with the Shotgun Express, have you heard their record? I must pop round the corner and buy it."

Long John Baldry's sense of style did not fail him with his new band.

"I remember 'flower power' happened overnight," Elton John recalls. "Suddenly we were all in kaftans and bells and things, and John loved all that. I remember one time in Newquay, John had this brand-new kaftan, which he thought had been exclusively made for him by somebody in Carnaby Street. There was some guy in the front row with exactly the same one, on and John went absolutely nuts, saying, 'Where did you get that jacket? Take it off immediately.'"

Baldry made some musical alterations to Bluesology, replacing Bishop and Inkpen with new bassist Freddy Gandy and drummer Peter Gavin and adding lead guitarist Neil Hubbard. A third male vocalist, Alan Walker, was enlisted to back Stuart Brown. Baldry also added Marc Charig on trumpet and Elton Dean on tenor saxophone. Dean's arrival would acquire historical significance years later, when Reg Dwight left Bluesology to launch a successful career as a singer-songwriter and adopted the names "Elton" and "John," based on Elton Dean and John Baldry, for his stage name.

"I thought, 'Elton John sounds pretty good,'" says Elton today. "I wanted to have a name that was unusual, so I chose those two names, and they've worked out pretty well for me. I remember choosing the name on the way back from the airport, on a bus into London. I said 'That's it! *Elton John!*' It was done very quickly."

Although Baldry could sometimes be quite demanding of his band, Elton says that his time in Bluesology was more or less enjoyable. "I have the fondest memories of everything about John. I can't think of one negative thing to say about him. He was one of the biggest, and certainly one of the kindest and most lovable, people ever in the business."

He recalls, however, that Baldry could be eccentric to a fault. "I remember sometimes John would stop the number halfway through to tell people off or tell a joke. Of course, the audience lost interest, and you'd have to get them back all over again. He was a complete and utter eccentric. That and the fact that he liked a nice drink of brandy now and again."

Rod Stewart had also witnessed some strange stage behaviour during his time with Baldry.

"One night we were doing this concert in Britain," Stewart recalls today, "and we'd all had a couple of drinks. There was this huge audience, and we were going down extremely well. The people in the audience were waving at John, putting one hand in the air. Suddenly he stopped, right in the middle of a number, and said, '*How dare you* give the "Heil Hitler" to me!' I think he actually said, '*How dare you* turn this into a Nuremburg rally?' Then he ranted on about the Nazis. They weren't really doing Heil Hitler, but it did look a little like it. The evening fell apart from that point and never recovered."

While Elton acknowledges Baldry was "a boozer," he doesn't recall any hard drugs around.

"John was never a drug addict at all," he says. "He was a brandy man, without question, and a really heavy smoker. He *was* a bit of a self-destructive person in the fact that he drank too much. But he was fantastic to work for, and I haven't got a bad word to say about John; there was absolutely never a dull moment. He would always call me 'Reggie'; in fact, he never, ever *stopped* calling me Reggie! I used to live in Northwood Hill, and John lived in Colindale. I used to go park my car round at John's house and then travel in the van with him up to the shows. He had a 45-RPM record player installed in the van, and he would play all these great blues records on the way up. Then he would sometimes drop me off at home, if it was on his way."

Like so many who worked with him, Elton John claims to have had no clue about Baldry's sexual orientation then. "I cannot believe I never realized that he was gay. I mean, I didn't realize *I* was gay at that time, but, looking back on it now, John couldn't have been any more gay if he tried. It wasn't on my radar at that time. Of course, when I came out of the closet John was very, very happy about it."

Throughout 1966, Baldry and Bluesology slogged it out on the road without the benefit of a hit single. Long John was eager to change that, however. "There's so much you can do when you have a hit," he told Richard Green in *Melody Maker*. "Take Georgie Fame. He could have worked for two years solid without having 'Yeh, Yeh' and 'Sunny' but it opened up new things for him."

In 1967, Baldry made a move towards pop stardom by leaving United Artists to sign with Pye Records. "It seemed to me," he later explained to *The New Breed*, "that they had... complete faith in what I was going to do and they paid United Artists for me... bought me out. It was like being shuffled around like a football player."

Pye's star in-house producer and songwriter, Tony Macaulay, had come to the label after being a "song-plugger" for EMI. Once at Pye, he immediately scored a massive hit for the Foundations with "Baby, Now That I've Found You," and he was soon outshining Pye's former production ace, Tony Hatch, as the new go-to guy for hits.

Macaulay had grown up near Epson, and he spent a lot of his teenage years over on Eel Pie Island, watching artists like the Rolling Stones, David Bowie (then David Jones) and Long John Baldry. Today, Macaulay admits he was surprised when he heard the news that Louis Benjamin, Pye's managing director, had signed Baldry and that the blues pioneer was now interested in recording chart-friendly material.

"Louis called me into his office one day," remembers Macaulay. "I'd had this big hit, and I was, you know, the blue-eyed boy. Louis asked me, 'Are you aware of Long John Baldry?' I said, 'Yes, but he doesn't do that kind of thing.' Louis said, 'Well, he wants to.'"

A few years earlier, Macaulay had written a song called "Let the Heartaches Begin," an uptempo number for which he had failed to find a suitable recording artist. For Baldry, though, Macaulay was thinking at first "of something like Chris Farlowe's 'Out of Time.' Farlowe had this very ragged, very blues-orientated voice, and somebody said, well, you know, maybe Baldry could do a record like that. We actually tried various songs. Baldry's piano player, Reg, was even drafted in, and the three of us wrote a song called 'Lord You Made the Night Too Long,' which wasn't all that good. Suddenly I remembered 'Let the Heartaches Begin.' Then my songwriting partner, John MacLeod, came in and wrote the lyrics for the second verse and added a chord or two."

As he played the song for Baldry, unaccompanied on the piano, Macaulay still wasn't sure if it was hit material.

"I wasn't getting any thrills from it," Macaulay says. "Usually, if I play a song alone on the piano or guitar, I know instinctively whether it's gonna make it or not. If I'm not certain, it's usually a flop. So while I was not convinced it was a hit by any means, I had nothing else."

He credits John MacLeod for greatly improving the song by the time Baldry went in to sing it. "I was just a guitar-playing twat who knew about six chords and had this combination of energy, vitality and a grasp of what was happening in the music. But MacLeod's expertise as a musician was very strong, and he was a great arranger."

Still uncertain, Macaulay took Baldry into the studio with a live orchestra to record the song. There he faced another obstacle: he had never produced an orchestra session. Luckily, he could again lean on John MacLeod.

"At that point," Macaulay says, "I didn't have the capacity to do it all alone. So we discussed the orchestrations, then John [MacLeod] went away and wrote it all up. The minute I heard the orchestrations on the track, I thought, wow. It just sounded so emotional, and then Baldry came to sing it. He wasn't used to singing absolutely on the bar line as written, so he really was struggling with it."

Music critics have often described Baldry's vocal on "Heartaches" as sounding "brandy-soaked." According to Macaulay, that's precisely what it was. "He must have dropped about half a bottle of Courvoisier by the time we got the vocal down. The voice he has on the record, that really sort of lived-in, emotional sound, an Orson Welles–on-record kind of thing, came from alcohol and his nervousness as much as anything. Once the vocal track went on, I thought, 'My God, this is something and a half!'"

Macaulay says that mixing the epic production was "a helluva job. We mixed it about five times, in one Sunday. I think it took about four hours of teaching myself where to suddenly push that fader up just to get that guitar lick through. And I was so enamoured with John MacLeod's orchestration. I don't think it would have been a hit without that."

Anya Wilson, now a successful music publicist in Toronto, recalls her days as an eighteen-year-old secretary at Pye Records, where she met Macaulay and Baldry.

"Tony," says Wilson, "was actually my boyfriend at the time. He was one of those writer-producers who was given these bands and told, 'Okay, it's up to you to record an album, record singles, make some hits.' When he was given John Baldry, it was a very diverse change of pace. John had done blues and really wasn't particularly what you would call 'hit material.' Tony thought a ballad would turn John's whole thing around, because of his warm, gravelly voice. I was actually there, in the studio, when they were recording 'Let the Heartaches Begin,' and I met John, who just seemed like a wonderful guy."

Before the single was released, Macaulay played the final mix for an associate of his from a music publishing company. "She said, 'God, it's a great song; if you'd done it with anyone but Baldry, it would be a hit. But he's been around so long, you know, no one's going to play it.'"

Yet, in the wake of his earlier success, Macaulay found that anything he touched turned to chart gold.

"Because of my sudden notoriety," says Macaulay, "and the fact no one had heard Baldry sing like that before, it went straight into the charts, somewhere in the top ten."

Wilson left Pye Records shortly after the sessions, and she was working as a temp at the BBC Television Centre when the Baldry single began to gain momentum. "Tony was still my boyfriend, so I was very up to date on what was going on with John Baldry. 'Heartaches Begin' was climbing up the charts, and now they wanted to get John on *Top of the Pops*. There was a lot of competition from everybody, and, of course, they liked younger, hipper bands on there. Once you got to top ten, though, you were a contender."

"Anya," Macaulay says, "was this little northern girl with this absolutely amazing personality. She worked at the BBC, so I said to her, 'Look, if you can get Baldry on *Top of the Pops*, I'll buy you a fur coat.'"

Wilson's boss, Paul Shields, held a high-ranking position at BBC's Television Enterprises department. "He and I had a drink one evening," Wilson remembers, "and I said, 'You know, we can't seem to get John on *Top of the Pops*, but I wish we could.'

He said, 'Well, wait a minute, I know Johnnie Stewart,' the producer of that show. 'He owes me a few favours.'"

The favours were called in, and Long John Baldry made his
debut appearance on *Top of the Pops*, ten years into his career.
Within a week, on November 22, 1967, "Let the Heartaches
Begin" shot straight to number one.

"It was a very exciting time," Anya Wilson recalls. "In the end
I didn't get the fur coat, but I got a suede coat, so that was good!
Of course, later I became a professional record promoter, lobby-
ing to get records on radio and television."

Macaulay was gratified by Baldry's number-one hit.

"I don't think anybody thought it would go as fast as it did,"
he says, "and I knocked my own number-one off the top of the
chart, which had never been done before. So that went to my
head a bit."

Unlikely as it would have seemed to him a decade earlier, in
the blues clubs of Ealing, Richmond and Soho, former busker
Long John Baldry was now a bona fide pop star. Success, however, would prove to be a mixed blessing.

9

it was a very good year

Having a number-one hit single did wonders for Long John Baldry's morale, not to mention his social standing. If the Fleet Street pop press had been vaguely interested before, they were positively clamouring for him now. A cartoon in the *Daily Mirror* depicted a young fan balanced precariously on stilts, with the caption: "See you later. I'm off to get Long John Baldry's autograph."

Critics shook their heads in disbelief, though, as the printing presses busily churned out tabloid stories for Baldry's new audience, middle-class mums and dads and teenage girls who had never heard his earlier, bluesier work.

Pop writer Simon Lewis produced an incredulous column about it. "Long John Baldry didn't seem the type... to set the ladies swooning in the aisles," Lewis wrote. "Respectable housewives go wobbly at the knees and funny in the head at the sight of Tom Jones's rugged manliness, Frank Sinatra's sophisticated charm, or the Latin looks of Engelbert Humperdinck. But Long John Baldry? It doesn't add up... [Yet] Long John sings his songs directly into the hearts of the women who... shed their inhibitions and sit quivering as he winds a spell around them with his sometimes deep, sometimes high and always husky voice."

Maureen O'Grady, of *Rave* magazine, wrote a puff-piece entitled "A Bird's Eye View of Long John Baldry" in which the singer marvelled at his own accomplishments.

"It's amazing what one hit record can do," he told O'Grady. "I played in Manchester the other day... I earned a small fortune that night! It would have taken a couple of weeks to earn that before. And the audience... just went mental! In fact the place got so crowded that people were actually turned away! After about ten years in the pop business it's very hard to grasp this overnight success. A No. 1 record really has power... so many doors are now open for me... I get asked for my autograph in the street, which I don't mind, but I just can't stand screaming girls!"

Baldry also expressed an interest in leaving music, eventually, for a career in the movies. "A film agent from America saw me on *Top of the Pops* and cabled that he was interested in me," he told O'Grady. "I've got a television series lined up this spring where I play a singing tycoon. I'm really looking forward to that. And my new LP should do well, too."

The television project never materialized, but it was typical for Baldry to both believe it would happen and announce it prematurely. Over the years, he had been promised many things and had followed a lot of bad advice in the process. Now, staring down his thirties, Baldry was looking for something, anything, that might make him a *real* singing tycoon.

"I'm in my mid-20s," Baldry told George Tremlett in another article. "That's too old for a pop singer. I want to go on to acting."

Baldry was unusually candid with Tremlett about the financial situation of his former managers. "In 1964, one of my managers went bankrupt, and I was advised to do so as well because I owed various people about £3,000. But I refused. Going bankrupt is a terrible thing. Nobody trusts you again, and you have to pay for things in advance. I'm completely clear now... but I've been conned so many times that I get suspicious of people who haven't got money."

Baldry compared the fees he was commanding now with those he received playing compère to the Rolling Stones. "I can get £150.00 for one evening's singing," he told Tremlett, "but when I compèred the Stones tour I received £250.00 for 12 nights."

In other interviews, however, he began to complain that having a number-one record, and the notoriety it brought, was exhausting.

"I think I must have aged ten years," he claimed in one. "I've never worked so hard in my whole life. I'd like to have a week in a health farm and then a week somewhere in the sun, like Tangier or Morocco."

Much of Baldry's pain was self-inflicted, since he generally followed up a hard day's work with a long night of cocktails and other amusements. At one point, his manager Rik Gunnell assigned a "minder" named Ruby Bard to keep Baldry out of trouble.

Baldry was spending increasing amounts of time immersed in the swinging London scene. At twenty-six, he was already a nightclub veteran, and he knew the after-hours culture like the back of his long-fingered hand. One popular haunt was the Ship Pub, which had been, in the days before the Marquee got its liquor licence, the pub of choice for musicians.

"In fact," Baldry would tell Nick Orchard years later, "the very first night that Jimi Hendrix arrived in England, back in 1966, Chas Chandler [Hendrix's manager and Animals bassist] brought him into the Ship, because he wanted to have a drink before he went down the road to the Marquee to see Eric Clapton that night. [That's how I ended up being] one of the very first people to meet Jimi Hendrix on British shores."

Amazingly, considering his burgeoning pop status, Baldry continued to live with his parents in Colindale.

"Baldry has found that living at home has its decided advantages," wrote journalist Peter Oakes in a 1967 column. "Few of his fans know where he lives—and even fewer find their way to the house. Because of his size he has the largest bedroom in the house and it just manages to accommodate a portable TV set, a record player, his clothes and a big bed for his giant frame. With another record being released next month, Baldry could well become richer still. He has a tour of America lined up and whether he likes it or not things will have changed at home when he gets back. For his mum, Mrs. Margaret Louisa Baldry, told me that she and her husband are having the loft converted into another room for their pop star son."

Rave magazine was granted an interview with Baldry's mum, who candidly expressed a preference for her son's earlier, folkier work over his recent "commercial" pop music.

"I've always preferred him as he was in those days, doing folk," she told the magazine. "Somehow, there's more heart, depth and soul in that music. Today John is more commercial, and I don't like the sound quite so much. He's always coming to me saying, 'What do you think of this song, mum?' I just say no, I don't think so, or yes, that song's for you. I tell you, one song I would have loved John to record was Dusty [Springfield's] 'I Count To Ten.' Every time I hear that song I can just hear John doing it, you know. It's him. If only you got a hold of that one, I say to him. Why the hell didn't you get a hold of it first?"

Mrs. Baldry was also forthcoming about the domestic duties she performed for her pop star son. "I like to see him looking good," she said. "He always takes care in looking nice whether casual or formally dressed. I love to see him looking immaculate. I take personal interest in his clothes—you ought to see my hands, love! I'm so proud of my boy, and I know and hope, please

God, that one day he'll be in the class of someone like Sinatra.
He was just born talented, a born actor and clown!"

Mrs. Baldry admitted that she and Jim Baldry rarely went
out to see their son sing in person, "because it seems to upset
him to know we're out there watching him. If we do go, however,
we never tell him, because we've learnt that he gets nervous if he
knows."

In an interview with Bob Farmer published in *Disc* and
Music Echo, Baldry was candid about his desire to conquer the
American market.

"It's great of course to get a No. 1," he told Farmer, "but after a
week of it you're screaming for the chance to get away from it all
for a while and relax. My next single will be in the same vein as
'Heartaches,' in the same sort of nostalgic mood. The main thing
now is to get my act sorted out, because I will probably be going
more into cabaret... I want to get a very polished... American
act. America, of course, is the next step in my career. It's the biggest market there is."

Anya Wilson had become great friends with Baldry after her
Top of the Pops coup. The two would often do the town together.

"I remember one time," says Wilson, "it was my birthday,
and Tony was away somewhere, so I took a chance and called
John. I said, 'Are you doing anything tonight? It's my birthday.
I'm miserable and Tony's out of town. You want to go out to dinner or something? I'll pay.' John was great. He said, 'Oh God!'
and came right over to pick me up. He'd even brought a gift for
me and then he took me to Mr. Chow's, which was a big, fancy,
trendy, Chinese restaurant near Kensington."

One time, while Tony Macaulay was recording with Baldry,
he and Wilson were invited to the Baldrys' family home for high
tea.

"His mother used to fuss over him beyond belief," recalls
Macaulay. "She would come out and polish his shoes. I mean, he
was six foot seven or whatever, and in his mid- to late twenties,

and she would *still* polish his shoes for him before he went out. She'd say, 'Can't go out with those shoes, John!' And his father, who was a policeman, was this really perfectly down-to-earth fellow. God knows what he thought of John, who always had these boyfriends around there."

"His mother may not have actually known that John was gay," says Wilson, "although I know Margaret knew. He and his sister were very, very close."

Roger Baldry disputes the notion that anyone in his family was in the dark about John's sexual orientation. "Both my parents knew, as indeed we all did," he says. "Although he did not hide his homosexuality, he never flaunted it and would have been very upset that he would be remembered for his sexuality rather than his ability to entertain."

Margaret Baldry admits that there were times, after "Heartaches" had made him famous, when she bristled at her brother John getting the "pop star" treatment.

"We were staying at my parents' house when it all happened," says Margaret, "and I really found it so hard to deal with. I remember when John would come on the radio—which happened sometimes ten, twenty times a day—our mother would run round the house and open all the windows and turn the radio up so that all the neighbours could hear. And I know, you know, as a more mature person now, I understand what that was about, but oh God, did I hate it. My mother used to say, 'Oh, come on, you've got to help me with John's shirts.' I used to think, 'There he is, jammy swine!' It wasn't so much sibling rivalry as, you know, he was like the ultimate in golden boy, at that time."

As 1968 began, manager Rik Gunnell began to parlay the success of "Heartaches" into steady work for Baldry and Bluesology on the lucrative northern cabaret circuit. Playing amidst the constant whirring of gambling machines in smoky casinos and working men's clubs, the band was now pulling in as much as £20,000 a night, a far cry from the small change Baldry had gotten in his earlier coffee-house days. While lucrative, though, the northern clubs could be harsh and challenging to play.

"I remember one club in Southport," Baldry told *Sir Elton* author Philip Norman. "The owner told us to play for twenty minutes, no more. When I overran a couple of minutes, the curtains closed in front of us. Just as if someone had got a nasty shock and snatched their front-room curtains together."

Other changes were afoot within Bluesology. Baldry had let Marsha Hunt go and added a new guitarist, Caleb Quaye, but Reg Dwight, still only the piano player, was itching to become a legitimate music star in his own right. He resented having to play what he felt was a dreary cabaret circuit. Then there was the abject humiliation of having to play—or not play, as it turned out—the hit single the crowds had come to hear in the first place.

"It was very embarrassing," Elton recalls, "because we would still be playing a very bluesy set and then suddenly, halfway through the set, we'd have to stop and John would have the backing track to 'Let the Heartaches Begin' on a tape recorder. We just stood there while he sang it to the tape. He had all these girls screaming at him. Then, all of a sudden, these girls are trying to grab the microphone, and he'd say, 'You break my microphone and you'll pay me fifty pounds' and promptly hit the girl over the head with it. It was very, very funny."

Although he was happy his friend John was having his first taste of huge chart success, the future Elton John loathed the song itself.

"John loved it," Elton recalls, "because he had got a success, a number-one single. He had a lot going for him at that time, but it was not the music of Long John Baldry, really. It was this hideous Tony Macaulay stuff. I mean, John was one of the great blues pioneers of British music. In fact, he was recognized as one of the best twelve-string blues guitarists that Britain ever really had. Unfortunately, he kind of laid that to waste when 'Heartaches' became a hit. It's a shame."

Anya Wilson recalls attending some Bluesology shows with Macaulay around this time. She was struck, like many, at the seeming disconnect between "Heartaches" and the rest of their set. On one occasion, she and Macaulay were on hand to witness Reggie and the band openly mocking the song and its string-laden backing tape.

"They were playing in London," says Wilson, "and they just tacked the hit on at the end. Reg started doing a parody of it, which made Tony furious. John was trying to keep it together, because he knew Tony was there, but he couldn't help but laugh."

Shortly after this, Wilson was hired to do PR for the band. While on the road, she discovered that Baldry's core audience had changed dramatically.

"I went to a gig in Manchester with him," Wilson recalls. "Before, his crowd used to be like-minded kids who loved the blues and stuff like that. Now it was all middle-aged housewives who aligned him with Engelbert Humperdinck because 'Heartaches' was that type of a song. It was very strange to see John afterwards signing autographs for all these ladies of all shapes and sizes."

Speaking with the BBC's Spencer Leigh in 2002, Baldry remarked that although he found "Heartaches" to be an albatross around his neck, it wasn't the worst thing he'd ever recorded.

"It is not a bad song," he told Leigh. "If it had been treated in a different manner, I feel it could have been an R&B standard. I liked anything at the time; I was happy that people were even employing me. It was a thrill that people were investing money to put me in a recording studio. I was hugely flattered that they would consider recording me at all."

After the surprise success of "Heartaches," Tony Macaulay was less than thrilled with the follow-up that he and John MacLeod wrote for Baldry.

"When it came time to write another hit for John," says Macaulay, "I didn't have another ballad, so I got out a bottle of whiskey and tried to write one. What I came up with was 'Hold Back the Daybreak,' a very poor song that followed along the same lines as 'Let the Heartaches Begin,' but with none of the magic. It was a completely crappy song, in all truth."

Macaulay and MacLeod tried to replicate the chart magic of "Heartaches" with a succession of less successful singles, such as "Long and Lonely Night," but nothing else managed to come close. Pye assigned Baldry to songwriter Mike D'Abo, but he failed to generate much excitement with D'Abo's song "When the Sun Comes Shinin' Through." "Mike D'Abo," Baldry told Spencer Leigh, "wanted to do the song more like the Four Tops. It turned out very differently. I think Mike's original conception was better, but he was overruled by Tony Macaulay, [whose production] came out more poppy than we would have liked."

The *Let the Heartaches Begin* album, released by Pye in early 1968, did not enjoy the same sales as the single, and the critics were divided.

One review gave the album "four stars" and gushed, "The once pulsating blues raver Long John Baldry is now a singer of sad, dramatic songs. His first venture brought him a fast-selling 'Let The Heartaches Begin' hit, and the authors of that, John MacLeod and Tony Macaulay, have added four more songs to the big hit—'The Long and Lonely Nights,' 'Better by Far,' 'Wise to the Ways of the World,' 'Since I Lost You Baby'—all on the low-key, sad yet dramatic style of 'Heartaches.' In contrast Nicky Welsh has produced another six tracks in which Baldry sounds a bit like Nat King Cole, clipping his words and putting on an American accent. Tony Hatch arranged his (and Jackie Trent's) 'We're Together,' which John dramatizes effectively. There's good instrumental and vocal backing for him throughout. An impressive LP debut."

At the other extreme, reviewer James Johnson declared the LP to be "a ghastly memento of Baldry's foray into cabaret after the success of 'Let the Heartaches Begin.' Pye have obviously put together a collection of tracks recorded at the time—a real club-land selection including 'MacArthur Park,' 'Spanish Harlem,' and 'Spinning Wheel,' all of which Baldry croons with unaccustomed blandness. One might have imagined 'River Deep Mountain High' or 'How Sweet It Is' to be a little looser, but with a crashing orchestra and girl chorus, [they] remain suffocatingly ponderous. The sleeve proudly proclaims the album contains sixty minutes playing time. I wish it had been less."

In an ironic fluke, Baldry would return to the charts briefly in 1968 with a non-album single that neither he nor Macaulay liked very much.

"The only song that we had any success with after that," says Macaulay today of the hit single, "came when Sir Lew Grade, head of ATV [Music], approached us and said 'Tony, we want a theme for the Mexico Olympics.'"

It was almost as an afterthought that he asked Baldry to sing "Mexico," a sunny throwaway tune Macaulay and MacLeod had written in haste for a televised fundraiser. The event, filmed at the London Palladium and attended by Queen Elizabeth II, was held in honour of the English Olympic team as they headed off to the XIX Olympiad in Mexico City.

"It was odd," Baldry told *The New Breed* in 2001, "because Tony only wrote it to perform at the Royal Command Performance that year. I was like a cheerleader with all these athletes around me 'just take my hand, dah dee, dah dee.' And then people said, 'Oh what a wonderful song, it's fabulous,' and Tony said, 'I only wrote it for this show,' and they said, 'No you've got to record it.' And then someone at Pye had the idea of submitting it to the BBC for them to use as their [Olympic] theme music. The BBC turned it down but ITV said 'Ooh, we want it, we want it.'"

"I don't think we spent more than an hour on the whole song," says Macaulay today, "in my lunchtime between two other projects. John MacLeod did the arrangement the next day, then we went straight to the studio and recorded it."

Hoping to capitalize on Olympic fever, Pye rush-released the quirky novelty song as a single. "It was way too late," says Macaulay, "given that the Olympics only lasted about three weeks. Still, it went to number ten, and I think if we'd come out with it earlier it would have gone to number one. I think I mixed it and then never listened to it again. Of course I heard it a couple times coming out of shop windows and things."

Baldry made it clear to Spencer Leigh that he never wanted to sing, or hear, "Mexico" ever again. "It was constantly on the radio," he recalled. "I wanted to scream every time I heard the damn thing. Talk about overkill. There are no international functions that would give me a reason to sing 'Mexico' again. Maybe they can play it at my funeral."

The truth was, by 1969, after a dizzy year at the top, Baldry's career as a pop star was dead in the water. He would chart again in January of that year, peaking at number twenty-one with the prophetically titled Macaulay number "It's Too Late Now," but Pye had run out of ways to promote a tall, gravel-voiced ex-blues singer. To add insult to injury, a planned U.S. tour had been scrapped at the last minute, in response to the "Mexico" single's unexpected success.

"I was going to go to America... and do a load of TV appearances," Baldry told the *Record Mirror*'s Ian Middleton in November of 1968. "But as 'Mexico' is happening it's better that I delay the trip and concentrate on my new single."

The postponed U.S. tour was never rescheduled, and Baldry's pride was dealt a further blow when he learned that the blues sound he had cultivated was gaining acceptance through the music of John Mayall and other late arrivals. Baldry had abandoned his roots to go pop, and he was now stuck in limbo between the two worlds.

Pye gave Baldry one last shot, this time with Tony Hatch presiding over lavishly orchestrated and echo-drenched singles such as "Wait for Me," "Well I Did" and "When the War Is Over," but none of these troubled the charts in any real way.

As far as Macaulay was concerned, Long John Baldry's year at the top of the pops was a fluke in the first place. Today, he has several theories about what killed Baldry's pop career. "He had credibility issues on a whole number of levels," says Macaulay. "I had started to hear all sorts of rumours about his dalliances with men. He had all these young, pretty, vacuous boys running around in his wake, and he associated with lots of well-known gays like Lionel Bart, who was always turning up to the studio in the middle of sessions with cases of champagne. To be a pop singer in the industry in the '60s, you definitely had to be heterosexual, and he never made any secret of the fact that he wasn't. Unless a male artist was overtly heterosexual, and could generate a strong female fan base in the sort of twelve- to eighteen-year-old age bracket, it was impossible to consistently have hits in those days. When the second single flopped utterly, I remember thinking, 'God, we've created no fan base here at all.' Usually, after a number one, with most artists you can at least get in the top ten even if the song is only half-decent. So it was then I realized Baldry was really a one-off, and we were never going to build up the kind of fan base we needed. He'd had this instant hit, but he was a man who didn't fit in any of the moulds. Plus he wouldn't do the song in his act, which was what the audience he was drawing live at the famous working men's clubs like the Fiesta, Stockton and Batley Variety wanted to hear. Those venues drew a lot of pretty hard-nosed people, who probably would have thought that he was a big 'poof' standing up there."

Years after the fact, Baldry told one interviewer that he considered his pop chart experience a double-edged sword. He had enjoyed all the adulation and attention, but he was saddened by the rejection coming from his original fans. "A lot of the people who'd followed me right through the sixties and the blues thing suddenly threw up their hands in disgust saying 'Baldry! How dare he? Sold out.' Hell, if I'd stayed with the whole blues thing like Mayall and the rest of them, I probably would have achieved a greater degree of success. But you know, sometimes we all make silly mistakes."

In the same interview, he could not resist pointing the finger at some of his peers, whom, he noted, had engaged in similar flirtations with mainstream pop. "There are people more established than me that have made more foolish mistakes. I'm not alone in this. I'm not the only one who's done sucky things, you know."

Today, his lifelong friend Elton John finds it "totally tragic" that some people in Britain remember Long John Baldry only for his brief tenure as a melancholy cabaret singer.

"John is a very important historical figure in the face of British music," Elton says. "But the songs that were written for him were such a million miles away from where he really was at. Even though he enjoyed his success in the charts, it did him more harm than good in the long run. If people go over and study his earlier records, they'll find someone who was fantastic. John didn't really like pop music very much. He was into jazz singers, blues singers and folk singers and, obviously, soul music. He didn't really like white music very much, except for folk music like Woody Guthrie and people like that. That was why it was so astounding when he did something like 'Heartaches,' because it was totally foreign to everything that he loved. Tony Macaulay was riding high, and John had signed to Pye Records, so they just put them together. It was very successful, but it was totally alien to what John was all about. It's a shame that people remember him for that. It's horrible."

Rod Stewart remembers he was upset with Baldry at the time for changing horses in midstream. "We really had a big falling-out when he had that horrible hit single," says Stewart. "He'd gone and recorded this terrible Engelbert Humperdinck kind of stuff, and it was dead against the grain. It was not blues, and I think that was a turning point in his career."

Paul McCartney, however, whose own songs with the Beatles kept Baldry from a protracted run at number one in the late '6os, totally empathized with Baldry's predicament.

"Perhaps the records were a bit too pop," McCartney allows today, before coming to Baldry's defence with the assertion that "most R&B or blues singers were trying for hits around then, so it was not unusual that he would."

Andrew Loog Oldham, for his part, faults his friend Baldry not for going pop, but for not "taking it all the way." "He was a total schmuck, man," says Oldham today, "in terms of when he had that number-one record, of not going for it. I mean, what's so fucking difficult, you know? Tony Macaulay was *it*. You know, 'Build Me Up, Buttercup' and the like, they're great songs. I don't get it; a song is a song. And besides, I would have thought an old queen would have *wanted* to be in cabaret."

Baldry's old mentor Chris Barber, who stopped in at a Bluesology show in Redcar one night in 1968, remembers being struck by what he too felt was Baldry's unnecessary embarrassment at singing the hit.

"I had the impression he might be singing it with his tongue in cheek," Barber recalls. "I don't see why. If Tony Macaulay cares to write a nice song for you, and that way you get a new lease on life, and you get paid for it, how can you complain? Tony simply wanted John to have a hit record, because he needed money and support, and it got John known to a bit wider public. There are plus sides to things and minus sides. It works both ways."

Eric Clapton, though, admits he joined the ranks of the shocked when the man who had shown him that white English guys could play the natch'l blues suddenly went pop.

"John," says Clapton today, "was probably one of the only guys who, to begin with, anyway, was solely a blues musician. He really was very interested in Muddy Waters, but he grasped the whole genre. So I was a little shocked and a bit disappointed that he would go that Engelbert Humperdinck kind of way. But I also probably thought, if you've got the kind of background John's got, it doesn't really matter. I'm not sure if it alienated his fans or not, but I thought his credibility was always pretty solid. I mean, if you can then pick up a guitar and go and play it with an entirely different repertoire, in a little club, who gives a shit?"

Mick Fleetwood echoes Clapton's assertion that though Baldry may have stooped temporarily to conquer the charts, he knew in his heart he was above it all.

"John had the *real* shit," says Fleetwood, "and I think as time went on he might have thought, 'My God, what was I doing!' But he probably said, 'Well, fuck it, I'm gonna go and just do it,' you know? You need to make a living. His *essence* is what I always admired, and in truth he never lost that."

Guitarist Geoff Bradford was another friend who didn't fault Baldry for being drawn towards solvency after so many years on the road. "You can't blame the guy," says Bradford today. "He was earning money; it must have put a few pounds in his pocket."

In looking back, Ian McLagan compares Baldry's so-called sellout with that of another of his heroes, organ whiz Georgie Fame.

"Georgie had done the same thing," says McLagan. "I used to go and see him play at Eel Pie Island. I couldn't believe it when he had a hit with something awful like 'Yeh, Yeh.' Same with John; he ended up being a terrible pop singer. I never understood why he needed to do it, but you can't blame the management. He made the decision. Managers can't tell you what to do. You need to want to not be commercial."

In 1971, Baldry defended his late '60s output in an interview with the *Record Mirror*'s Keith Altham. "I did that for one or two reasons," he told Altham, "some of which were economic. I earned quite a lot of money out of that situation, although not as much as I might have done had I stuck to rock 'n' roll. By far the best thing to come out of the situation was the experience of working tough working-class audiences in the Northern clubs. After them, you never have to fear another audience. I don't regret the decision—it's all experience."

He was still explaining his decision, in 1973, to journalist Chris Salewicz.

"I fitted into the whole 'Mexico' and 'Let the Heartaches Begin' thing very easily but it didn't suit me," he told Salewicz. "I jump into things feet first and then I think, 'No this isn't for me,' so I'm a difficult person to take care of, because my mind runs around all over the place, plus the fact that my head has never really been governed by financial things. I never really think what this is going to earn me which must be very frustrating for the people on the business side."

Ultimately, says Elton John, Baldry's greatest achievements happened on stage. In his opinion, no one record ever captured his power.

"He never really made the quintessential John Baldry record," laments Elton today. "I can remember him live, on stage, singing stuff like 'It Was a Very Good Year' or blues stuff, like Muddy Waters, and it was just sensational. But he never made the great record that he should have done."

At the dawn of the 1970s, however, Baldry's star pupils "Reggie" and "Roddy" would unite with a simple goal: to try to give their friend and mentor the recorded legacy each felt he so richly deserved.

it ain't easy

As BALDRY'S initial run at chart success wound down, Bluesology was barely holding together. Their inevitable demise had been foretold by the departure of their ambitious keyboard player, Reg Dwight, who had left "the circuit" and was now building a songwriting and recording career with Bernie Taupin under the name Elton John. The band hobbled on for a few months more with a replacement keyboardist named Jimmy Horowitz.

"Long John was holding auditions," says Horowitz today, "and I went down to meet him. He said, 'Oh, I remember you. Elton says you're very good.' I wasn't aware that Elton knew about my playing. I played one song, and he said, 'Yes, can you join the band?' It was very prestigious to play in Bluesology. It was kind of a musician's band. The gigs were very well organized, and we got paid, which was a rarity in those days. We played a lot of jazz at all these working men's clubs and the Batley Variety Club and the like, where John would do all of his 'sugary' hits, interspersed with Oscar Brown Jr., Nina Simone, some Ray Charles and some Jimmy Smith–type organ stuff, which I loved because I was a Hammond player."

Horowitz recalls getting a taste of just how recognizable—or not—John Baldry had become when, lost in the Midlands, they stopped the car to ask a farmer for directions to a gig.

"John," Horowitz explains, "puts his head out the window and stops this guy walking along the street and says, 'Excuse me, sir, can you tell me how do we get to the Batley Variety Club?' and the guy looks at John and he looks down and says, in a heavy regional accent, 'Eeh, by gum, I know thee. No, don't tell me, you're that *Manfred Mann!*' Then he suddenly realizes, and shouts, 'No! Tell you what, you're that *Big Jack Bradley!*'"

Bluesology's extended life was short. After the band folded, Baldry scrambled to fulfill his obligations in the U.K. and Europe, and then returned home to an uncertain future.

He was still friendly with Elton, even as his former piano player's star began to eclipse his own. Although it would be another year before Elton became a worldwide overnight sensation, he felt he already owed a lot to Baldry. In 1969, something occurred that would leave Elton feeling he owed his very *life* to Long John.

As he and Taupin struggled to write the songs that would become their legacy, there was an underlying problem: Elton had not yet come out, even to himself, as a gay man. To further complicate things, he had convinced himself that he was in love with Sheffield secretary Linda Woodrow, with whom he and Taupin were sharing a basement flat on Furlong Road, Islington. Woodrow had convinced Elton to propose marriage.

"I was going to get married to her because she said she was pregnant," Elton recalls. "I didn't even think about it. I said, 'Okay, we'll get married.'"

What happened next would become the basis of Taupin's lyrics for "Someone Saved My Life Tonight," the epic song from their semi-autobiographical 1975 album, *Captain Fantastic and the Brown Dirt Cowboy.*

"One night around this time," Elton remembers today, "Bernie, John and I went to the Bag O' Nails on Carnaby Street—P.J. Proby was there, too—and we all got incredibly drunk. At the club, John had said to me, 'Why are you getting married to this woman? You are more in love with Bernie than you are this woman.' Of course I knew he was right. I wasn't in love with Bernie in a *carnal* way, but he was like the brother I had always wanted. So I was coming home to the flat with Bernie, and we staggered up Furlong Road, falling and setting off car alarms as we went. I went home completely drunk and called off the wedding that night, so, yeah, John was the catalyst for 'Someone Saved My Life Tonight.' That song is about John Baldry at the Bag O' Nails saying, 'You've got to call the wedding off; otherwise your songwriting career, which you want, will be over and you're going to ruin everything.' Without that it could have been an entirely different story. He really did change the course of my life, bless his heart."

Elton says today that the entire *Captain Fantastic* album was a testament to the hard times he and Taupin endured. "It was the first first-person album I had ever done, because I don't write lyrics, and every song was about how we were struggling to make it. The follow-up, *The Captain and the Kid,* covers from 1970 to 2006, how we struggled *after* we made it. But the times when we were struggling to make it were some of the best times we have ever, ever had, and John was a big part of that."

He may have saved someone else's life, but Baldry's own life was unravelling. After a few whirlwind years of pop celebrity, he found himself adrift, severed from his blues roots. As the new decade beckoned, a change was sorely needed to get him back on track.

One change was to move out of his parents' home, with sister Margaret, to a flat in Muswell Hill, which he rented from Rod

Baby John gets some rare quality time with his dad, Jim Baldry, late summer of 1942. COURTESY PERSONAL COLLECTION OF JOHN BALDRY

above: Margaret Louisa Baldry holds John's new baby brother, Roger, on January 18, 1945, days after John's fourth birthday. COURTESY PERSONAL COLLECTION OF JOHN BALDRY

facing page: Baldry at school, already mugging for the camera by the age of six. COURTESY PERSONAL COLLECTION OF JOHN BALDRY

above: Some of Baldry's peers from Zoot Money's band, featuring future Police guitarist Andy Summers (*second from right*), hang out in front of the Flamingo in 1961. © JEREMY FLETCHER / REDFERNS

facing page, top: Brighton, 1957 (*Baldry back row with guitar raised*). "Once we'd got to Brighton," Baldry later recalled, "all the guitar players would get their guitars out." COURTESY PERSONAL COLLECTION OF JOHN BALDRY

facing page, bottom: Baldry (*left*) consults with Willie Dixon (*centre*) and Chris Barber at the Marquee Club, 1959. © JEREMY FLETCHER / REDFERNS

above: Baldry takes the mike while Cyril Davies wails on harmonica
at the old Marquee Club, Oxford Street, 1963. © PETER DYER / PETER DYER
PHOTOGRAPHY

facing page: A pre-Beatlemania Paul McCartney discusses the blues
with John Baldry outside Lime Street railway station, Liverpool, 1962.
© MIKE MCCARTNEY

R&B from the MARQUEE

ALEXIS KORNER'S BLUES INCORPORATED

mono

LONG JOHN'S BLUES

LONG JOHN BALDRY
and The Hoochie Coochie Men

top: R&B *from the Marquee*, the first electric blues album in Britain, released November 1962. DECCA RECORDS / COURTESY JEFF EDMUNDS COLLECTION

bottom: Released in 1964, *Long John's Blues* "is still valid now," says guitarist Geoff Bradford. UNITED ARTISTS / COURTESY EMI ARCHIVES

left: Eschewing his usual twelve-string acoustic guitar, Baldry poses with an unplugged Telecaster at the Marquee, Wardour Street, 1964. COURTESY EMI ARCHIVES

top: Long John Baldry, barely fitting onto a London park bench, Manchester Square, 1964. COURTESY EMI ARCHIVES

bottom: Steampacket, the world's first supergroup. *Left to right:* Baldry, Rod Stewart, Brian Auger, Julie Driscoll. PROMOTIONAL SHOT, CIRCA 1965 / THANKS TO BRIAN AUGER

facing page: Wistful promotional pose, 1967. COURTESY PERSONAL COLLECTION OF JOHN BALDRY

above: November 22, 1967, Baldry performs "Let the Heartaches Begin" on BBC's *Top of the Pops*. Within a week, the single shot to number one.
BBC PHOTO LIBRARY / REDFERNS

facing page: Pye Records promotional photograph for "Let the Heartaches Begin" single, 1967. MICHAEL OCHS ARCHIVE / GETTY IMAGES

below: Baldry, *John* Baldry. Looking very 007 in '67.
COURTESY PERSONAL COLLECTION OF JOHN BALDRY

facing page: Baldry backstage at one of the many television appearances from his pop star years, circa 1968, with the band Grapefruit (*back row*) and the Three Bells (*front*). COURTESY PERSONAL COLLECTION OF JOHN BALDRY

Most of Baldry's adoring female fans were likely unaware of his well-guarded sexual orientation. Circa 1970. COURTESY PERSONAL COLLECTION OF JOHN BALDRY

Stewart. He had rescued a pet goat and brought it home as his pet. He called her Mayley, and most afternoons Baldry could be found stumbling out of bed in his red-and-blue dressing gown into the garden to feed "May" her chopped cabbage and other table scraps.

As he retreated into domesticity, his protégés were enjoying their first international successes, on what seemed to be a parallel journey to the top. Elton's ballad-laden second album, *Elton John,* was dominating the U.S. airwaves, largely on the strength of its breakthrough single, "Your Song." A year earlier, Rod Stewart had garnered solid interest for his debut, *An Old Raincoat Won't Ever Let You Down* (released in America as *The Rod Stewart Album*). His 1970 follow-up, *Gasoline Alley,* established him as a solo star.

Back in Muswell Hill, Margaret Baldry remembers that her brother, now long-haired and bearded, was living it up at night while trying to live it down each morning. He was suffering a serious crisis of confidence about both his life and his career.

"It was a hard thing for John to cope with," Margaret says today, "although it must have been very exciting to have gotten to the pinnacle of whatever was expected of him. He had suddenly become this celebrity, earning a lot of money, with a lot of new clothes. He had always spent a lot of money on clothes, even when he had none."

Baldry also spent a great deal of money on the self-medications—drinking, gambling and carousing—of a man deeply troubled in mind.

"It wasn't a very grounded life," says Margaret, "but then, I don't think John was a very grounded person anyway. He did like going to casinos, but I don't think it was a big problem."

Margaret did have a problem with her brother's increasing sense of entitlement. Without their doting mother to do the domestic chores, John assigned the ironing and washing to her.

"I'd tell him, 'John, I don't know what you would ever do if you actually had to look after your own basic daily needs,'" says

Margaret. "He would always find a way to have people waiting on him. I don't know how he did it. It was like he thought it was a *privilege* for people to do it. But, you see, then, it doesn't go with the other bit of him that was so lacking in self-esteem, just in what he did to himself or what he let people to do to him. He didn't take care of his body."

Nor did he take care of his body of work. Speaking to the *Record Mirror*'s Keith Altham in 1971, Baldry seemed almost indifferent to his British legacy.

"I think, for better or worse, I can regard myself as a household name in England," Baldry told Altham. "It's not as though I ever completely disappeared like poor Alexis... On the other hand I feel very proud that people like Reggie and Roddie have achieved what they have because it shows, if nothing else, that I have good taste in the people I work with."

Baldry drew warmth from the heat of his friends' careers at a time his own flame appeared to be rapidly burning out. His star pupils had not forgotten him, and both felt nothing but gratitude and concern for their troubled mentor. In 1971, they joined forces to co-produce—for no fee—an album that would introduce to the world a refreshed, re-energized and reinvented John Baldry.

By now, Billy Gaff was managing the careers of Rod Stewart and his raucous associates, the Faces. Gaff had known Baldry previously, and he provided some key career guidance.

"I first met John at Cooks Ferry Inn, in North London," recalls Gaff, "with Rod singing backup, when I was at university. I fell in love with the music, and then I kept running into him at gigs after that. There were a few great bands on the scene back then: the Graham Bond Organization, Zoot Money, the Yardbirds, Georgie Fame, and Long John Baldry and the Hoochie Coochie Men. But the three best were Long John, Georgie and Graham. I must have seen John at Eel Pie Island about a hundred times. It was always sweaty and packed, but it was always brilliant. Then, when I went into the music business myself, we ran into each other for a few years after that."

After the dissolution of Bluesology, Jimmy Horowitz had started working as a house producer for Gaff's GM Records. "Jimmy had signed a singer to the label named Lesley Duncan," recalls Gaff, "who later became his wife. Now he wanted to bring over John Baldry, who was leaving Pye Records."

"John had been unhappy in his deal with Pye," Horowitz says today. "He no longer wanted to do what they wanted him to do. So I brought him to Billy, as I did with most of the artists we signed. Billy suggested that we really needed to kick-start John in America, so we needed to get a couple of big names on it."

"This was 1971," remembers Gaff, "and Rod was just becoming successful. So I said to John, 'Look, let's do an album, and I'll ask Elton and Rod to see if they'll produce it.' Rod always felt an awful lot for John and felt he owed him everything. So Rod and I were talking one day, and I said, 'I'd love to do an album with John; would you produce it?' He said, 'Yes, I will.'"

Horowitz himself had become friendly with Elton through Duncan, whose composition "Love Song" had appeared on Elton's *Tumbleweed Connection*. "She had sung that as a duet with Elton," he says. "And then he had played on Lesley's album, which I produced. We had all become friends over that. I talked to Elton and told him that Rod had agreed to do half the album and said, 'Why don't you do the other half? I'll put it all together and help you get the musicians and come in and help mix it, take some of the production burden off you.' Elton agreed."

The next step, Gaff says, was to go about finding a label to get Baldry's album released in America. "I called Joe Smith at Warner Bros. and said, 'Look, I've got Long John Baldry, and I'm making an album. One side is being produced by Elton, the other by Rod; will you take it?' And he said, 'Oh Christ, yes. Just do it.'"

"I think Warner Bros. wanted Gaff's other acts, like the Faces," Horowitz recalls. "Rod was signed to Mercury Records as a solo. The Faces had a contract with Andrew Loog Oldham and Tony Calder's Immediate Records, which they wanted to get out of."

Baldry's version of the story was a bit different. In the liner notes for the 2005 CD re-release of *It Ain't Easy*, he tells Sid Griffin that he first introduced Rod and Elton at a 1970 Christmas party at Billy Gaff's cellar apartment in Pimlico, shortly after Stewart and the Faces had signed with Warner Bros. "Rod and Billy," Baldry recalled, "mentioned me to Joe Smith, president of Warner Bros. at the time, and Joe said he would love to record me but in a rootsy setting."

Speaking with the *Record Mirror*'s Keith Altham in September of 1971, however, Baldry had given the impression that the project was more casually conceived. "When Reggie—who is very much a friend and joins me in some projects we do together—heard that Roddie was going to help out, he asked to join. I said the more the merrier—bring me the whole world!"

Elton John says, though, that he and Stewart made it their mission to get Baldry back on track to repay him for the early encouragement he'd given them.

"When we both became successful," recalls Elton, "we were able to help John get signed to Warner Bros. Rod and I had parallel careers, although Rod was slightly ahead of me in America. One of the things Rod and I could do was to produce a side each for John. Here we were, his two protégés who had become big stars, and now we could turn round and do something for someone who treated us so kindly and was such a great man to work for. It was something we could give back to him. Rod has always looked after John, and he's been so kind to him."

Stewart apologizes today for recalling little about the actual sessions.

"It was such a long time ago," he says, "and there was a lot of drinking going on, without a doubt, so the memory is gone for that period of my life. The point was that Elton and I both said, 'we need to pay our dues back to John.'"

The sessions for *It Ain't Easy* were divided equally, with each of the two star producers working with different teams at separate locations on opposing schedules. The Stewart-helmed side was recorded between January 15 and February 4, 1971, and Elton's sessions ran from February 1 to 11.

"Rod's sessions were done at Morgan Studios in North London," Jimmy Horowitz recalls, "while Elton did his sessions at IBC Studios. I did a lot of sessions at IBC—I had a good studio rate there—and Elton liked it there as well. The Who had recorded *Tommy* at IBC, and their client list also included the Beatles, the Kinks, the Stones and many others."

The twin-producer approach provided *It Ain't Easy* with two slightly different visions of what would constitute an ideal Baldry album.

"Each of them used their own different musicians," says Horowitz. "Rod used the musicians that he'd been friendly with, like [drummer] Micky Waller and Rick Brown, who played bass on that. Lesley sang background vocals along with Madeline Bell, who was a solo session singer, and Rod also brought along Maggie Bell, from Stone the Crows, to sing on 'Black Girl.'"

In addition, Stewart enlisted a mutual friend of his and Baldry's, pianist Ian Armitt, and hired Baldry's newest discovery, slide guitarist Sam Mitchell.

"I turned Rod on to genius players like Sam Mitchell," Baldry told Sid Griffin in 2005, "whom I found at a folk club on Greek Street where he was emcee and swapping licks with innovative players like Bert Jansch and John Renbourne."

Mitchell himself recalled their meeting in Griffin's liner notes.

"One night in 1970," Mitchell explained, "... he came in with Rod Stewart. I was playing host... and introducing people and of course John knew everyone! To my surprise and pleasure

Long John invited me onstage, and we did 'Amazing Grace' and the old Blind Willie Johnson tune, 'Dark Was the Night,' and something else. Hardly anyone else but me and Fleetwood Mac were playing bottleneck at the time."

"I just loved working with Sam," remembers Jimmy Horowitz. "He was the most inventive bottleneck slide player I ever worked with."

Mitchell shared with Griffin a particularly telling image from the sessions. "The main thing which sticks in my mind," he said, "is that I turned up at Morgan Studios with my guitar in a plastic bag and Rod showed up driving his Jaguar!"

For his side of the album, Elton drew largely from his backing band at the time—bass player Dave Glover, drummer Roger Pope and ex-Bluesology guitarist Caleb Quaye—collectively known as Hookfoot. Quaye later told Griffin that it had been "an honour" to work with Baldry.

Baldry let his star producers run the sessions, but did take an active role in song selection.

"It was mainly John who found the songs," Jimmy Horowitz remembers. "I would send things over to him, too, like Lesley's song 'Mr. Rubin,' from Elton's side."

In his 1971 conversation with the *Record Mirror*'s Keith Altham, Baldry described the Stewart sessions as drunken mayhem. "Roddie is, of course, one of those people who likes to work in the early hours of the morning or very late at night when everyone is drunk out of their minds and falling off stools."

He continued this line, years later, with Sid Griffin.

"Rod loved to record well after midnight and very loosely," Baldry said. "I think that is evident on some of the tracks, especially those recorded on my thirtieth birthday when he showed up with cases of Rémy Martin cognac and several measures of good quality champagne! Therefore I had to record 'Don't Try to Lay No Boogie Woogie on the King of Rock 'n' Roll' whilst laying on the floor."

Horowitz readily acknowledges the alcoholic frivolity, but disputes somewhat Baldry's account of Stewart's timetable.

"Rod was always pretty disciplined," he says, "when it came to recording. He liked to start his sessions late afternoon, like five or six [o'clock], and he liked to finish by eleven and go home and watch football. He was not an overnight player. In fact, one of the reasons he later left the Faces was that they just got out of control in terms of turning up for sessions."

Elton's side, by all accounts, was a decidedly more regimented affair. In his 1971 interview with Keith Altham, Baldry playfully mocked Elton's day-based schedule. "Reggie is a bit of a sadist," he said, "and likes to work at nine in the morning. When we did the album, I got about thirty minutes sleep a day!"

He expanded the story years later for Sid Griffin.

"Elton's work ethic was to start at eight o'clock in the morning," Baldry said. "I was doing two weeks residency up in Manchester so I would do my show till 2 AM and then sleep a few hours, grabbing the early plane to London to do the Elton sessions and then I would fly back in the late afternoon. I was actually quite worn out from all this."

Baldry also admitted to Griffin, "Rod was just feeling his way, Elton was just feeling his way and I doubt I was feeling anything."

It Ain't Easy could not have been released in the U.S. at a better time. It was harder to convince U.K. audiences that Baldry was back in the blues-rock game, but untainted American rock critics, FM radio programmers and, most importantly, audiences took to the album immediately.

"The album sold relatively well," remembers Elton, "and got him back on track with the people and with his core audience, which was a blues audience, a music-friendly audience rather than the 'Let the Heartaches Begin' shit. I don't think 'Heartaches' was a hit in America, anyway, so they were saved from it, thank God. We just wanted to get John back to the bluesy,

rootsy stuff, and he did a great job with 'Burn Down the Cornfield' and stuff like that."

A clear highlight of the *It Ain't Easy* album—credited to the
artist "John Baldry" without the prefix "Long"—was its opening
track, "Conditional Discharge." The spoken-word introduction
was the product of Stewart's desire to capture something that
had been missing on Baldry's albums up to then: the charming
Mr. Baldry himself.

"Conditional Discharge" was Baldry's autobiographical solil-
oquy, over Ian Armitt's good-natured barrelhouse piano riff,
recounting the details of his arrest for busking on Wardour
Street in the late '50s. It was punctuated by Baldry's amusing
voice characterizations of the judge and the arresting officer, the
latter modelled on his policeman father, Constable Jim Baldry.

Once he had eloquently introduced himself, Baldry and the
band wasted no time in issuing the album's rocking manifesto,
"Don't Try to Lay No Boogie Woogie on the King of Rock 'n' Roll."
The juxtaposition is one of the great one-two punches in the
recorded history of rock. Says Sid Griffin, "It was as if Oscar
Wilde had successfully submitted material to the MC5."

Many assume that Baldry penned the declarative anthem,
which was in fact written by Jeff Thomas. "You think, 'John
must have written it,'" says Jimmy Horowitz, "but that's what
makes a singer great. 'Burn Down the Cornfield' doesn't sound
like a Randy Newman song when John does that one, either."

Horowitz says that Baldry's undisciplined manner often
betrayed a very "disciplined voice," which made him something
of "an anomaly in the blues scene."

"His big love was blues," says Horowitz. "You can hear that in
his take on Willie Dixon's 'I'm Ready,' but he really had so many
influences. We think of the blues as John Lee Hooker, Muddy
Waters and all those guys. That was their shtick, and that's all
they played. John could sing anything, but he happened to love

the blues. Just like Tom Jones, who has a great command of his voice and has therefore also done all of this legit kind of stuff: cabaret, standard-type things and big bands."

On the second side of *It Ain't Easy*, Elton John conjures up some gospel-tinged boogie reminiscent of Baldry's Steampacket days, from "Burn Down the Cornfield" to the Baptist fire of Elton's own "Rock Me When He's Gone" and the rousing, celebratory finale on the Faces' raver "Flying."

Rock historians have correctly noted that Stewart's side of *It Ain't Easy* was a virtual blueprint for his own breakthrough, *Every Picture Tells a Story*, released later that year. Stewart's single from *Picture*, "Maggie May," did for his worldwide stature what "Your Song" had done for Elton the year before. By the end of 1971, their combined career prominence dwarfed that of their six-foot-seven mentor by leaps and bounds.

"At that time when we did the album," says Elton, "*our* albums were selling quite well, and because of his association, his history, with us, the album did really well. It established him in America. He toured [there], and he became more known in America because of those albums than he did through the English hits, thankfully!"

Filmmaker and music journalist Cameron Crowe was a young rock writer in the early 1970s, and he recalls first hearing about a man named Long John Baldry when interviewing Baldry's two protégés in Los Angeles.

"When Elton came over for the Troubadour shows and all that stuff," Crowe remembers, "he was talking up Long John Baldry. So was Rod Stewart. Both of them would identify him as their roots mentor. Then, when Baldry put out *It Ain't Easy*, I noticed that he had got them to play on it and produce it. So that became like a flashpoint. It sounded so good on the radio. In many ways it was a definite template for Rod's *Every Picture Tells a Story* album."

Baldry was understandably excited at the prospect of finally getting to tour in America, the land of his beloved Lead Belly. He was upbeat about his tour plans in an interview with *Melody Maker*. "I'm doing about four off the album, live," he told Roy Hollingworth. "I can't do things like 'Flying' because they were so lavishly arranged in the studio. I get into all sorts of things, you know, old crawly things like old Baldry's gonna put a spell on you."

His career flying high once again, Baldry and his band boarded a plane to bring their English blues home to America. If England couldn't appreciate him, he felt, then it bloody well wouldn't have Long John Baldry to kick around any more.

everything starts, everything stops

THE *It Ain't Easy* tour wound its way through the U.S.A. and Canada, with Ian Armitt on piano, Sam Mitchell on guitar, Pete Sears (later of Jefferson Starship) on bass and old friend Micky Waller on the drums. Baldry and the band spent a lot of time in North America during 1971 and well into 1972, doing club dates, festivals and tours with Tower of Power and Delaney & Bonnie and an arena-ready package tour with British blues disciples Fleetwood Mac and Savoy Brown.

Mick Fleetwood and John Baldry had been nodding acquaintances since the swinging London club scene of the early '60s, when both men were among the tallest in the room at the Flamingo or the Marquee. While Baldry had steered away from blues and rock to more mainstream pop and the cabaret circuit, Fleetwood had gone from backing Rod Stewart in Shotgun Express to taking guitarist Peter Green and joining with bassist John McVie and singer Jeremy Spencer to form the blues-based, original Fleetwood Mac.

"We all used to look up to John," says Fleetwood today. "I always have this happy memory of his very English music-hall sense of humour. He had a dry wit and he loved telling little stories and then, you know, he would make a sort of quip, then say, 'Well, that's enough of that.' Then off he'd go into a song. He had a great rapport with his audience. We were all youngish, the generation after Cyril Davies and stuff, you know, in these little tin-pot bands trying to make a go of playing Bo Diddley, but John and Cyril and those guys seemed like the *real* blues to me. As a young musician looking at that, I thought, 'How cool is that?' Then it sort of filtered down, vicariously, to guys like myself, Peter and Jeremy, and John McVie, who was such a great bass player. We just had a connection."

Baldry and McVie, as it turned out, shared a unique family connection in that their fathers had once gone into business together.

"Reg McVie and my father had a carpeting and furnishing store in Acton High Street, when Dad retired from the police force," Baldry told Nick Orchard years later. "They had called it Celebrity Carpets and Furnishings. In fact, Christine McVie, who was then Christine Perfect, actually married John McVie right there in this damn shop. At that particular time, they couldn't afford to have any kind of a function other than this wedding breakfast in the shop. So they had stuff brought in, drinks and minor catering, and got married right in the store."

By 1971, however, Fleetwood Mac's fortunes had improved. Now it was John Baldry who was on the bottom of the bill, along with second-billed Savoy Brown, as they brought the blues home to the arenas of America.

"We enjoyed his music," says Mick Fleetwood, "and he was always surrounded by high-calibre players like Micky Waller, a great, swinging drummer, who had also played that classic loose drumming on Rod's 'Maggie May.'"

Cameron Crowe caught up with the tour when it reached the San Diego Community Center.

"It was fantastic," recalls Crowe. "There was a packed crowd and [Long John] just sauntered out, stoop-shouldered, with a tambourine, wearing satin pants—I believe he had a top hat on, too—and kind of joined the band, already in progress. He only had a primitive light show, but he totally had the crowd on his side. If I remember correctly, he closed with 'Don't Try to Lay No Boogie Woogie on the King of Rock 'n' Roll,' and it was just great."

Baldry told another journalist on the tour how much he loved to connect with rock audiences. "I like to see them have a damned fine ball," he said. "Let it be marvelous, let's let our hair down. There's too much boredom around."

Although Billy Gaff had successfully delivered Baldry to America, he says he was never, contractually at least, Baldry's actual manager. "Well, maybe I was, but for free, as a favour. I was very much involved for a couple of years, though, with things like setting up the American tours. I had a couple of other acts going there, and I knew the system in America better than in England. The album was taking off at the time, and there was a lot of airplay for the single. He was being treated very well by Warner Bros., which was a spectacular company in those days."

Capitalizing on Baldry's increased U.S. exposure, United Artists released the Hoochie Coochie Men album, *Long John's Blues,* in the States along with a single, "Up above My Head," marketed as a "duet" with red-hot Rod Stewart.

Melody Maker's Roy Hollingworth asked Baldry if he minded his old stuff coming out in the States. "Christ no," Baldry shot back, "I have no qualms. *Long John's Blues* is nothing to be ashamed of, and you can play it now, and it doesn't sound in the slightest bit dated. It's an historical documentary."

Besides, Baldry said, it was better that the U.S. fans of *It Ain't Easy* were exposed to his 1964 output than, say, his 1967 pop material. "What I am now," he told Hollingworth, "is surprisingly close to what I was in the Hoochie Coochie, Steampacket days. I've not really had to bring anything up to date. The things we were doing in '64 were the blues for a minority audience, and now it's a big deal. Well, that's great. I look back on those old days with great nostalgia."

He did confess to one regret: that he hadn't gone to America sooner. "I was very lucky," he told Hollingworth. "My name had been mentioned for a long time in the States as a daddy of the English blues... [so] they knew me when I went over."

In the circus-like atmosphere of a '70s road show, with seemingly endless parties and a near-constant flow of liquor at his disposal, Billy Gaff recalls that Baldry sometimes got a little carried away.

"John Baldry was a total gentleman," says Gaff, "*most* of the time. But he was complete bollocks when he'd been drinking. During the touring and the promotion of the album, his drinking just got too much, and it kind of ruined things a bit. I'm not sure if John was an alcoholic, but I think he probably just drank too much. A lot of people did. Unfortunately, when he was drinking, he went off the rails and he got very aggressive. He brought me to tears on a number of occasions when we were doing gigs. He would be late. In his mind he was already a star, and of course everyone treated him like one. He didn't exactly behave like a superstar, but he started making silly demands and power tripping."

Gaff cites one unfortunate incident in which Baldry became unruly at the Bottom Line club in New York. "We just wanted John to play it alone with his guitar," he remembers, "which was when he was actually at his very best, and maybe a bass player and a drummer. We didn't want to put the whole band in there, because it was just too big. I remember John went on stage, very drunk, and basically insulted the audience. He just looked at them and said, 'I suppose you have all come here expecting an evening of *hard rock*. By the looks of you lot all I'm getting is an evening of *soft cock*.' It was actually sort of funny, but the audience did not like it."

"[John] liked to drink," Cameron Crowe concurs, "so he was very English in that way, too. I got the feeling that he was kind of a roaming royalty figure, moving through all the circles because he was anointed, but who still knew how to flip out there and kick ass himself. He was a great character who wasn't so lofty that everyone didn't dig him."

Gaff elected to hire an American road manager, John Peters, to ensure Baldry got to his gigs on time, in one piece. Peters had been promoting artists such as Stevie Wonder and Don McLean. Long John Baldry, on tour with Savoy Brown and Fleetwood Mac, was the first English act he'd handled.

"It was my job to take care of John," says Peters today, "plus thirteen people and two tons of equipment, and take him on a two-month tour throughout America, a different city almost every day. I was about twenty-two at the time, so it was a big deal to me, to take care of somebody like him."

Peters was immediately impressed by Baldry's ability to connect with any audience. "John would open the show," he remembers, "for these hard-rocking blues groups in these incredible, packed places like Cobo Hall in Detroit. The only difficulty was, being on the bottom of the bill, we were always fighting with the soundboard for good sound. John didn't act like he was the third guy on the bill, though. He jumped right into it and totally rocked those crowds. They were just insane gigs. He was already thirty-two at that time, but all the younger people in the audience loved him. They didn't care that he was an older guy."

"Frankly," Cameron Crowe acknowledges, "Baldry *did* seem a little older than the other people that were on the show, but he got down and funky and won over the crowd on a real 'slug back the beer, have a good time, rock 'n' roll' level."

According to Peters, the other musicians on the tour expressed a genuine respect for Baldry. "All the Fleetwood Mac guys sat with John, on the plane, many times," he recalls, "and you could see they all loved him and would help him in any way possible. We also did a lot of Rod Stewart dates, with the Faces, which were obviously big, fifteen thousand– to twenty thousand– seat stadiums. Ronnie Wood was an extremely kind gentleman who also loved John."

Peters swears that, at least on his watch, Baldry was a true professional and a consummate artist when it came to perfor- mance and staging. "John Baldry had the power to walk out in front of five thousand people, clamouring for great blues and rock 'n' roll, and he'd deliver. He'd open his mouth up, start sing- ing, and floor everybody. He always gave 110 per cent and com- manded the same of his musicians. No matter how hungover he might be, no matter what condition. I don't think I can ever remember John missing a gig, except maybe a plane got can- celled because of a snowstorm. He had a lot of professional pride and felt that he had an image he had to keep up."

The hours in between shows made Peters's job as road man- ager challenging, though. He wonders today if the pressure Baldry felt to live up to his own legend was at the root of his tendency to tamp down his anxieties with alcohol and pills. "The intensity of life sometimes overwhelmed him," says Peters. "There was a gruelling aspect to taking two or three flights a day, commercial flights. He wasn't travelling by private jet or anything."

And Peters acknowledges that getting Long John Baldry onto a plane was like getting a cat into a bathtub. "I would literally hold his hand," he recalls. "He would shake, he would sweat, and he would break out in rashes. So he was flying like this, every day to a different city, for three weeks. The drinking was possibly a way of trying to heal that extremely sensitive part of him. He was really tall, and sitting in those planes could be really difficult. A few vodkas or a few Valiums would help. I would calm him down and just talk to him. I can remember one time we were 37,000 feet in the air. The pilot came down the aisle and ripped up the carpet and started reaching down into a hold, to try and get the wheels down. There's John sitting right next to this guy, freaking out. That type of thing would totally throw John into another dimension."

Back in the office, Billy Gaff had noticed that Baldry's room service bills were outpacing his income.

"John was generous to a fault," recalls Gaff. "He always looked after his band very well. I think they will tell you that he always paid the best wages. He always had the biggest car, the best van. He was always the first to buy a drink. The reason that he was terrible with money is because he was always 'a star,' even though he never really earned an awful lot. And when he did, he would spend it. He never managed to save anything. The only time he'd ever had massive success was with 'Heartaches,' but he didn't own the publishing on that, and personal appearances didn't pay anything like they do now. We had to subsidize the tours [we did] in America because nobody had heard of him there."

Peters recalls one particularly dramatic incident from the Fleetwood Mac tour where he had to show his boss some tough love.

"We were in West Palm Beach, Florida," says Peters, "and we had to get up at seven or eight o'clock the next morning to fly to Pittsburgh. I gave everybody wake-up calls in the morning, but John wouldn't answer his phone. So I bang on his door, and he starts yelling, 'What do you want? Get out of here!' He had somebody in there, some guy he'd picked up the night before, and he'd been partying all night, so he was in one of his *moods.* I said, 'John, got to get up, man. We've got a plane to catch at nine o'clock.' He just yelled back, 'Get the fuck out of here!' Then somebody opened the door up, the chain was on, and he threw something, maybe a shoe, at the door. He had never done anything like that to me. I was shocked and hurt. I had put my heart into getting this guy to every gig, and here he was throwing a shoe at me through the door. We were like a month and a half into the tour, we were all losing it at different points, so I walked away, feeling a little sad. But I still had to get the band up and get them to Pittsburgh. I had to figure out how to get the band to the next gig without him. I had a stack of tickets, for thirteen people, so I went to the hotel clerk, pulled out John's ticket and $100, and I told them to tell Mr. John Baldry to get the next flight to Pittsburgh when he decides to get up. Then I took the rest of the group and flew to Pittsburgh."

A few hours later, Peters recalls, Long John Baldry sauntered into the Pittsburgh gig accompanied by Fleetwood Mac. "They had helped to get him get to Pittsburgh, but this is the interesting part: each member of Fleetwood Mac came up to me, one by one, at some point and said that I had done the best thing for John. He was out of control. That night, John gave me the silent treatment, but the next evening we were somewhere alone and he eyed me up and down and he said, 'John Peters, you have an unusual genius. I want you to know that.' I never forgot him for saying that. He appreciated that I was putting my heart into it, trying the best I can to get him to each city, get everything on stage, setting up the radio interviews, publicity, magazine business, everything. He had a way of being the kingpin, yet at the same time making everyone around him feel special."

While staying at Hollywood's notorious Continental Hyatt House (affectionately nicknamed the Riot House by the rockers and groupies who did everything but sleep there), Peters witnessed firsthand Baldry's connection to the rock royalty of the day.

"Within hours of checking in," says Peters, "Mick Jagger or Rod Stewart would be calling him on the phone. These highly respected people were all his friends, and they all kept in touch. It was great to hang in a hotel room with John, playing his acoustic guitar, and just singing. I met Elton in his room one afternoon, and I remember Led Zeppelin would also come around. They all knew him and loved him. These guys had grown up, back in England, watching him."

Cameron Crowe remembers that, for years, whenever he spoke with Stewart or Elton, Baldry's name would continue to crop up in the conversation.

"They still gossiped and talked and told stories about him," says Crowe, adding that Stewart, Elton and Baldry "were all in this kind of a club. Elton had been so public about exploring his sexuality, so I never knew if they were together, but they all spoke in those little codes, calling some men 'she' or 'her.' This further made Baldry this great character, this mentor figure who was exciting to talk about, beyond just the music."

In Los Angeles, Peters discovered that there was an elite, underground team of male groupies who catered exclusively, and discreetly, to the needs of discerning gay rock gentleman.

"In those days," Peters reveals, "when guys like John Baldry would arrive in L.A., there would be this group of twenty-year-old gay guys who would come and take care of them. They'd phone and say, 'John, we're here to do whatever you need,' and then they would do whatever he needed. It was kind of a groupie scene, but they took it very seriously, and they did a good job. I mean, they catered to more than just his sexual needs; they'd take John out to get new clothes because they also knew all the good stores and the best places in L.A. to get your hair done or to get a manicure. John was tapped into this gay party scene, and he'd hang out with Billy Gaff and their friends. Since I wasn't gay, they would only occasionally take me around the clubs with them."

Canadian alternative radio legend David Marsden got to know Baldry when the tour reached Montreal, where Marsden was working at CKGM-FM, the first free-form progressive radio station in Canada. One evening, before his on-air shift, Marsden was hosting a party at his apartment when a mysterious, tall Englishman in a wide-brimmed fedora arrived with an entourage in tow. "I went to answer my door," says Marsden today, "and who should I see but this tall guy we'd seen in town earlier, who wore this big, Leon Russell [type of] hat. He was here at my party, suddenly, with a group of his friends. We didn't really know who he was at that point. So I called a friend of ours over, and he said, 'Oh John, John, come on in.' So then I was officially introduced to John and some of his band. I think Ian Armitt was there, and Micky Waller, too."

Marsden had to leave his own party, to go to work. "I was due on the air at eight o'clock," he says. "So around seven thirty, I invited this John Baldry guy to come on the air with me. I knew nothing about him at the time, but I knew that he knew a lot of players. So John and I walked over to the station. We went on and, for about an hour, he played some of his music and talked about what he liked. In those days it was quite accepted on progressive FM radio that when you were on the air, you'd be stoned. It was what you did. After the first hour, John left to go back to my apartment, pick up his pals and be on his way. I didn't get off the air till about 1:00 AM, when I ambled home, stoned. When I got back to my apartment, Baldry and his friends were all still there, and everybody was either completely pissed drunk, or stoned on something, sitting in what remained of my living room. The party went on until sun-up, and it was my first introduction to someone who later became my friend, Long John

Baldry. You know, when you party with someone for more than twelve hours, you get to know a lot about them."

After the strong critical and commercial response for *It Ain't Easy*, Warner Bros. ordered a second album. In August of 1971, Baldry had told *Melody Maker*'s Roy Hollingworth that although he was "fairly pleased" with the first album, he and his superstar twin producers were hoping to improve upon it with the follow-up. "Rod and Elton did a good job," he said, "but it will be better next time. I hope Rod and Elton work closer next time, instead of doing one side each."

Everything Stops for Tea, released in 1972, featured an album cover adorned with a Lewis Carroll–inspired drawing, by Ronnie Wood, depicting Baldry as the Mad Hatter from *Alice in Wonderland*.

As with *It Ain't Easy*, the January and February sessions were split into two teams, with Stewart's crew back at Morgan Studios and Elton at IBC Studios.

"I do remember a little more about *Everything Stops for Tea*," says Stewart today, "although I think I only did two or three tracks for him on that one. And John wasn't actually there for a lot of the sessions. We'd get the keys from him and lay down all the tracks. I think I used the same guys I used on *Every Picture Tells a Story*. I didn't know many musicians in those days, so I was bound to use just the players I knew, like Madeline Bell—she sang on my album—and Maggie Bell, who was a good Scots girl. She used to like a drink, but nothing else. She was wonderful. I don't know what happened to her. And of course Woody couldn't make it, but he did do that lovely cover drawing. The title song, 'Everything Stops for Tea,' was a Noel Coward number. I loved it when John sang all that stuff, so I said, 'Why don't you try it on the album?' And he did a marvellous job with it."

Stewart joins Baldry on the album for a guitar and banjo duet on an old favourite of theirs, the traditional song "Mother Ain't Dead." "It was a song we always used to sing in the dressing room at rehearsals," Stewart recalls, "because I'm an old folkie at heart, really, so I knew all these songs as well. I'm pretty sure we didn't track it together, though, because I was on the other side of the board. I think John just went and played it on guitar first, and then I went in and did my banjo part later."

Just as Stewart drew upon his *Every Picture Tells a Story* crew for his side of the second Baldry album, Elton John's side tapped into the musical style of his own 1971 album, *Tumbleweed Connection*. This time Elton adorned the tracks with players like guitarist Davey Johnstone, drummer Nigel Olssen and percussionist Ray Cooper, with whom he would end up working for the rest of his career. Bass player Klaus Voormann was also enlisted, on John Lennon's recommendation. A native of Hamburg, Voormann was a friend of both Baldry and the Beatles. He had played bass on various Beatles' solo albums and also created the distinctive cover art for the Beatles' *Revolver*.

In the studio, Elton ran Baldry through a set that included the Dixie Cups chestnut "Iko Iko" (Baldry's version would actually chart in Thailand), a stirringly bluesy version of Willie Dixon's "Seventh Son" and a John Kongos tune called "Jubilee Cloud."

"I think the element of fun is there," Baldry told Sid Griffin years later, "even in the music on the serious songs, and between that and the talent and respect of the players, the combination allowed these two albums of mine to touch a great many people."

Elton says today he loved every minute of working on the albums. "I had the best time. There was no better person to work for. He was always very kind. He was a dandy, a gentleman, a heavy drinker and heavy partier who liked a good time and loved his music. For me, when I was young, that was all I needed to be influenced by him."

When he toured for the second album, Baldry once again brought along his right- (and left-)hand man, pianist Ian Armitt. In the liner notes for *Everything*'s 2005 CD reissue, Baldry raved about Armitt to Sid Griffin. "Ian Armitt was just the most amazing piano player," he said. "He had that Otis Spann style down so well, and yet it was impossible to typecast him, he could do so much."

Baldry also drew upon an otherwise brand-new lineup, which included guitarist Bob Kulick, bassist Dennis Ball and drummer Joey Forgione, plus female backup singers Ellen Clark and Myra Cooper. Piano man Ian McLagan sat in with Baldry when the Faces shared a bill with the Baldry band at a major rock festival in Puerto Rico.

"We played with John," McLagan recalls, "and lots of other bands at the Mar Y Sol—which means Sea and Sun—Festival in Vega Baja, Puerto Rico, on April 3, 1972. Ian Armitt had actually fallen off the back of the stage, so I had to sit in for him."

Baldry's live version of "Bring My Baby Back to Me," recorded at the festival, was added in 2005 to the CD release of *Everything Stops for Tea* as a bonus track.

John Peters once again kept the show on the road throughout North America, as Baldry and his band did shows with Alice Cooper and Fleetwood Mac. Peters recalls that, around this time, Baldry had increasingly begun to express a profound interest in Canada.

"He always had a deep love for Canada," says Peters today, "even back then. He loved to play in Toronto and in all the cities in Canada, especially Vancouver. The city seemed so clean. I mean, the first thing you noticed in Vancouver was how clear the air was, how sharp the edges of the mountains were because the air was so clean. He'd say, 'John Peters, can we please stay extra days in Vancouver?'"

The Fleetwood Mac tour also took Baldry to Edmonton, Alberta, a city that would later be significant to his career. "We played some big cow-hall palace thing there," Peters recalls, "with seven thousand or ten thousand people or something. It was wild. He could get the audience going nuts."

Looking back at that time, Mick Fleetwood says he always felt there was something of an Édith Piaf quality to Baldry.

"She was just this little creature standing there," says Fleetwood, "but they all loved her. That, for me, was partly the essence of John. Much later on, we [would do] another funny tour in the States, again with Savoy Brown, but this time Long John was only the compère. He didn't really do a full show, but he did a standup thing with his guitar, doing this sort of Lead Belly thing. Then he would introduce the bands, and he was the sort of master of ceremonies, 'Well, 'ello, 'ello, how're we all doing tonight? Okay then, now we're gonna do... ' Then suddenly he goes from that to something from the back wall of a fuckin' [Mississippi] Delta drinks bar, you know?"

Cameron Crowe noticed the same dichotomy, both on stage and off. "Sometimes guys who have important affiliations talk down to the audience, but Baldry was not that guy. He carried himself well. On the one hand he was all 'dear boy' this and 'my dear' that, but then he'd go out there and shake it on down with the people."

In July of '72, Baldry drunkenly spilled his guts to his old friend Roy Hollingworth, getting in some knowing jabs at the pigeonholing U.K. music industry for a piece that he knew would run back home in the pages of *Melody Maker.*

"I just don't care about England anymore," Baldry declared. "They still think I'm playing the bloody Batley Variety... there's nothing there for me, is there? I mean it's getting to the point of having to make it [in the U.S.] before you can make it in England. And there the English animosity creeps in—if you're making it [in the States] then they seem to be ready to put you down when you get home. Sorry I'm on such a downer. For God's sake let's cheer up!"

Baldry seemed to have returned to his senses, but it was too late. He was now officially on a rant.

"Let's be truthful," he continued. "Selling me in England is like taking an old horse up to the starting gate, keeping him there for a while, and then taking him to the knacker's yard to have him shot in the head. Whereas if one comes to the U.S.A.... there are all kinds of stray people going around, like the Cockettes and Alice Cooper. On stage [in America] you can act out your every fantasy. If you're a fool, then you can be a fool. If you're a monster, then they love a monster, and you can be a monster. I'm doing lots of things that I would never have dared to do back home... At long last I'm finding myself. I'm beginning to see that I should be an outrageous person—and all that time in England I was stifled. Out here you can do just what you like."

It was true that Baldry had become more outrageous. However, the U.S. wasn't embracing him with quite the open arms he had hoped for. Despite an extensive tour, roaming from Puerto Rico to Hawaii and points in between—including his Carnegie Hall debut—he felt increasingly let down by the lacklustre response to his second Warner Bros. album, which had only troubled the lower reaches of the American album charts.

"When the second album didn't do that well," remembers Billy Gaff today, "he became impossible on tour. It was a nightmare. But we never really fell out. When I couldn't get any more money to do any more albums, then one thing led to another, and we just sort of drifted apart. I would still see him sometimes, in Los Angeles, and Horowitz, who was my partner in the early days in business, went off to work with him in Canada as his musical director. So we stayed in touch through him."

Looking back on his Warner Bros. albums during his conversations with Sid Griffin in 2005, Baldry said that he never had a clear favourite between the two. "There were many magical moments," he told Griffin, "... and they've gone down in rock history as fond memories for a lot of people. I think this is partly because, unlike today, there was no big guiding hand standing over the proceedings back then telling us to do this now, hurry up, chop, chop."

No one was telling Baldry what to do in 1972, but now, with Warner Bros. out of the picture, no one was asking him, either. Diminishing sales had forced the label to politely decline to order a third album. It was becoming a familiar pattern: just as everything was starting, everything had stopped. The buzz of American arenas still ringing in his ears, Baldry retreated to the domestic tedium of his North London home and waited, as he always did, for another shot at the top.

good to be alive?

A<small>T THE AGE</small> of thirty-two, John Baldry had already lived more lives than most.

After his years at the top in the late 1960s, he had been brought down to earth by the realization that the blues movement, a movement he had started, had moved on without him. Roddy and Reggie had bailed him out, but even after two well-received "rock" albums in America, he could never seem to get past third billing. Now, without a new U.S. album on the horizon, he wondered what would happen next. Every time he found success, it seemed, heartbreak was sure to follow. The emotional roller coaster was beginning to take a toll on his mental health.

Although his beloved Roddy regularly checked in on him, Baldry couldn't fault his old friend for being distracted; as 1973 began, Stewart was, after all, one of the biggest names in rock 'n' roll. Elton, for his part, was soaring above the pop stratosphere in his customized private jet, the Starship.

Jimmy Horowitz recalls the frustration felt by everyone in the Baldry camp at the time.

"With the second album," he says, "we were trying to follow on with the success we'd had with the first one. But in the end, I guess the energy wasn't there. The second album had been very disappointing saleswise, so Warner Bros. didn't pick up the option for a third. I remember it was also frustrating for Joe Smith, who actually loved John, who'd say, 'John always seems to snatch defeat out of the jaws of victory.' Joe was a great guy, but we still had to find somebody else to pick up the option. As a result, it would be a while before we made the third."

British singer-songwriter Saffron Summerfield was a frequent visitor to the Baldry house in Muswell Hill during this period. To her, Baldry often appeared "troubled in mind."

"The '70s was not a good time to be a fantastic blues singer who also happened to be openly gay," says Summerfield today. "John was a sweetie who was totally misunderstood by the British music scene. His hit records didn't help him either, but we knew he was a truly fantastic blues singer, and everyone respected him. It was also common knowledge, however, that John had been ripped off so many times, by various managers. John's boyfriend at the time, an Austrian guy named Inga, who only weighed around ninety-five pounds, once managed to shut one manager's arm in a door and then proceed to punch him in the face." According to Summerfield, the manager in question, George Webb, had been taking what Baldry's closest friends felt was far too great a cut of Long John's income.

Looking back, Rod Stewart says that if Baldry was depressed at this time, he was far too proud to let on. Like all good Englishmen, he kept a stiff upper lip around his friends.

"There was a time when I didn't get to see him in person a lot," remembers Stewart, "but we would talk over the phone every couple of months, and he always put on a brave front. So I never knew anything about any depression, although he might have been depressed. There was probably a point in his life where he must have thought, 'Fuck it. Everybody and everything has left me behind.'"

In an interview with music journalist Chris Salewicz in March of 1973, Baldry spoke enthusiastically about his American success and his plans for the future. "I've got a feeling that between now and 1980 there's going to be a lot happening for me," he said. "In the States last summer, there was a lot of the spirit of the old Steampacket on stage."

Despite the spin, however, Salewicz followed a line of questioning that alluded to Baldry's ongoing management woes and made vague references to a "disastrous" concert with Lesley Duncan from the previous fall. Baldry appeared to let down his guard, temporarily. "I found myself just sitting at home looking at my four walls," he confessed, before regaining his composure and adding, "I feel very confident about my future recording career. I've got so many, I think, great ideas in my head. I haven't got a current backing group except for Ian Armitt who's been with me since creation. I think most of them will probably be Americans."

Baldry's agenda for the entire Salewicz interview seemed to have been to wag his finger at a judgmental English music press, which he felt had deserted him. His message was simple: England Bad, America Good. Years later, he became fond of saying that April 1, 1971, the day his plane first touched down at New York's Kennedy Airport, had been one of the happiest days of his life. Even in 1973, Baldry was telling Salewicz, "I love America," adding, "I can't wait to get back. In fact, I really don't know if I will ever play this country [England] again or whether people will welcome my presence."

A year earlier, in his interview with Roy Hollingworth, Baldry had intimated that home was where "the Heartaches" were. "I can see that I'm not going to be doing much more in England, ever again," he had said. "People's memories are sharp... they have never forgiven me for singing pop tunes."

He was still fuming, too, over his 1972 return to *Top of the Pops*, when Rod and Elton had walked him onto the stage. It was a bold PR move, but what should have been a hero's welcome, reinstating him as a serious rock figure, had backfired with the press, who accused him of name-dropping and coat-tailing his superstar friends.

"There appears to be so much enmity and animosity around with the people in control of the English rock scene," he had told Hollingworth. "For instance, when I did *Top of the Pops*... everybody was screaming 'hype, hype.' So what do you do? I know for a fact that both Rod and Elton said that they never enjoyed themselves so much for years."

To break up the boredom of watching TV at home in Muswell Hill, Baldry accepted the invitation of his friend, director Joan Littlewood, to make his West End debut in the rural blues-themed stage musical *Big Rock Candy Mountain*. The show had been written by musicologist Alan Lomax—the son of John Lomax, the man who discovered Lead Belly—and for Baldry, going to work every night at the Joan Littlewood Theatre to celebrate the music he loved seemed like a holiday. The gig was challenging for him, though, as he told Chris Salewicz: "I've played the Palladium in front of the Queen, but I was shitting myself going out in front of five hundred children."

Baldry had always been a theatrical performer, and he was more than happy to act like somebody else from time to time. He'd expressed his interest in movies and TV to interviewer George Tremlett in 1968, and since then he had made his screen debut as "Little John" in comedian Frankie Howerd's Robin Hood farce, *Up the Chastity Belt*. Although he was eager to act in more movies, he told *Melody Maker*'s Roy Hollingworth that he didn't much care for the hours.

"Great fun, but you have get up early," said Baldry. "One morning I had to be up at *six*, and doing a fight scene with John Gorman. Wow!"

Andrew Loog Oldham says he always felt that Baldry was first and foremost an actor. "John could have done any kind of theatrical thing," he suggests, "but he happened to have adopted the blues idiom because he loved it."

In 1972, Baldry had said much the same thing in the *Melody Maker*. "Theatre and rock is something I've always believed in," he told Roy Hollingworth. "At heart, I'm an actor, far more than anything else. No matter where I've sung throughout the world, when I get on the wooden boards… the pressing of two thousand people against you, and the smell of those old, old boards. It's then that I'm at home."

In 1974, foreshadowing the vocation he would take up in his later years, Baldry lent his (singing) voice to the animated feature film *Dick Deadeye*, produced by *Peanuts* animator Bill Melendez and based upon the drawings of Ronald Searle.

In the spring of '73, however, Jimmy Horowitz managed to pull Long John Baldry away from "the old boards" long enough to put him in front of a soundboard at IBC studios. *Good to Be Alive*, the third album in Baldry's back-to-his-roots trilogy, would allow him to delve deeply into his rural folk beginnings. This time, he was without the support of a major label or superstar producers. Horowitz, by now a trusted friend, gladly moved into the producer's chair.

"Rod and Elton were both busy," Horowitz remembers, "so John asked me if I would do it on my own, and I said sure. Everything just kind of fell into place. We had good musicians, and everybody played well. IBC wasn't really a high-tech studio, but it had a nice big room and excellent acoustics and a good control room. They were actually the most comfortable, and fun, sessions we ever did."

Baldry would remark on the laid-back vibe of those sessions in a later interview with journalist Steve Peacock. "We took it at a much easier pace than the ones I did with Rod and Elton," he said, "where [it was] bash, bash, bash, for a couple of weeks simply because they didn't have much time to spare. I think the main fault of those two albums is that they sound as if we rushed through them like a dose of salts, whereas the *Good to Be Alive* album has a much more relaxed atmosphere about it. I do think atmosphere is of as much importance on albums as musical content and musical performance."

The album displayed a convincing merger of blues-rock and folk, and it benefited from a more cohesive production. Horowitz re-enlisted Sam Mitchell and Lesley Duncan and added a powerful new female foil in singer Liza Strike, who joined Baldry on a duet of the Gram Parsons composition "She."

"I don't know where Sam Mitchell is now," says Horowitz today, "but he did some great playing on *Good to Be Alive*."

Baldry and Horowitz selected a fine assortment of songs for the album. The title song, by Colin Allen and Zoot Money, rocked with the best of them, while Baldry demonstrated his twelve-string prowess and added an autobiographical subtext to the traditional "Rake and a Rambling Boy."

This time around, Baldry brought a pair of rare self-written songs to the table as well. "Maggie Bell" celebrated the Scottish firebrand who had sung on his previous two albums, and his impassioned "Song for Martin Luther King" pays tribute to the fallen civil rights leader.

Looking back today, Margaret Baldry feels it's a shame her brother John didn't write down more of his thoughts and feelings in song. "John had an IQ of about 156," she asserts, "but he was very lazy. He was so articulate, and yet it was very hard to even get him to talk about what he felt inside. I think it was the way we were brought up."

Elsewhere on the album, Baldry, the master interpreter, tackles Rod Stewart's "Gasoline Alley" and the Bo Diddley classic "Let Me Pass."

"I remember Roddy turning up one night when we were recording the backing vocals to 'Gasoline Alley,'" recalls Horowitz, "and he was fucking blown away by them. Lesley was on form that night, and she kept coming up with all these Gladys Knight and the Pips–style backing vocal ideas."

Horowitz and Baldry both lived close to IBC, which Horowitz says lent the sessions a communal, neighbourhood feel. He adds that the album's cover photograph—a bearded Baldry tending to his goat—perfectly sums up the singer's life at that time.

"We used to call the album '*Goat* to Be Alive,'" laughs Horowitz. "There were a lot of funny things that happened on Muswell Hill. John was kind of well-known in the area, and because he never drove, people would see him as he walked the goat to the local post office, or up the hill to get his cigarettes and the morning paper. Here was this tall, elegant fellow out walking with a white goat on a leash. It got attention."

Horowitz does admit that occasionally the convivial atmosphere in the studio was threatened by Baldry's inexplicable mood swings. He maintains nonetheless that Baldry's propensity to enjoy a drink rarely got in the way of the music. "It was hard to get him out of those moods," says Horowitz, "but he was usually very professional when he worked with me. He did enjoy his vodka, that's true. But I suspect that, a lot of the time, he was just self-medicating his depressions. Of course we didn't realize that at the time."

Loitering at IBC during the *Good to Be Alive* sessions was a struggling twenty-two-year-old Canadian guitarist named Al Harlow. Harlow had packed off to London, from Vancouver, seeking fame and fortune, at the suggestion of a friend. He had then been introduced to Baldry, who invited him to watch the album's progress.

"We were in the big, double, high-ceilinged room, which had a grand old fireplace," recalls Harlow today. "I was there when a lot of the vocal tracks went down. John always knew what to say or where to go, but he'd stand out of the way and let Jimmy produce, although Jimmy still deferred to him. John created an atmosphere where people could show their stuff and flourish, you know?"

For Harlow, who would later come to prominence in Canada with his own band, Prism, the experience was invaluable. "Vancouver was still a backwater then, but this was the big time," he says. "To be in London, with all of this is happening around me, was very cool. After each session, we would all go out to the Speakeasy, the Marquee, the Ship Pub or the Bag O' Nails. And I got to see what the U.K. music scene was really like."

Speculation about oil shortages was creating a climate of doom in the recording business at the time, according to Harlow.

"The big scare," he recalls, "was that the entire record industry, so dependent on oil to make vinyl, was going to collapse and fold because of the [1973 Arab oil] embargo. No new artists would get signed because of the scarcity of vinyl. So I wasn't having a great year, and sometimes, when I was down and out, I had no place to stay. John told me jump in a cab and stay at his place for free. 'Young Alan,' he said, 'I'm not going to bugger you, you know.' He really just wanted to help. He showed me this great unconditional friendship, right off the bat."

Harlow fell in with Baldry's revolving entourage, which sometimes included Tony Macaulay's ex-fiancée, Anya Wilson, as they hit the popular bohemian spots on the Baldry tour of London.

"The Speakeasy was a great experience," Wilson recalls. "It was *our* club. I'd go there with John, and then we'd separate and we'd talk to various friends. Ginger Baker often used to drive me home, in one of his big old cars. Marc Bolan from T. Rex and John Wetton from King Crimson used to go there a lot, and members of the Bonzo Dog Doo-Dah Band. It was definitely like a circus, and I always felt that John was the ringmaster. He attracted all kinds of characters, and not in a bad way. It was one of the most colourful times that I've had in my life."

Roy Young, formerly of Hamburg's Star Club, was by now the Speakeasy's house piano player. "My role," says Young, "was to go down and do my rock 'n' roll thing, Ray Charles and Little Richard stuff, which became very popular amongst all of the people in the music industry. They would all get there 'round midnight, and the place was a ball of fire until about four in the morning, with a line of chauffeur-driven cars waiting outside… It was, without a doubt, the 'in' club of England, and people like Long John, Rod Stewart, Elton John, Eric Clapton and some of the Beatles and the Stones found it was a place that they could unwind and relax without being mobbed by onlookers."

According to Eric Clapton, the club's name perfectly described the nature of the place. "It was exactly that," he says, "a *speakeasy*. A place where you could go and meet your own kind after hours. There was a fair amount of imbibing and substance abuse going on, and also good food and some fairly loose women, too, you know? I mean, it was hot stuff for that time, but it was definitely for musicians. It wasn't just a celebrity thing."

Roy Young recalls that, most nights, his friend Baldry would be at a front table, holding court. "John Baldry really was a mountain, and not just for his height. It was partly his association with Rod and Mick and Elton, but everyone in the business had respect for him as a specialist in the blues. It was the place to be, so Baldry, Clapton and guys like Jeff Beck would all come to the club after their own gigs."

Besides experiencing Baldry's social scene, Al Harlow witnessed a musical climate change in London.

"There was Roxy Music," Harlow recalls, "Gary Glitter, who was at the height of his fame, and Marc Bolan, who was championing 'glam rock,' as was David Bowie, who had just released *Aladdin Sane*. There was a great big pink vertical cutout billboard of Bowie right in the middle of Leicester Square.'"

In a 1973 interview, Baldry spoke with journalist Steve Peacock about his affinity for the glitter and platform shoes look.

"I don't think I'm the glitter face of the year, that's for sure," he said, "but I'm not against dressing up in bizarre costumes. I think harder things might suit me better—various leathers and more rustic things, perhaps—I don't think satins and sequins are really *me*. In fact I've only just started wearing stack-heeled boots, and that wasn't because I was being a follower of fashion. It's just that I found that half the nation's youth was walking around looking taller than me, and they had no right to. Can't have that!"

Good to Be Alive was released in the U.K. only, by Gaff's GM Records label. Although the single "She" garnered some airplay, Baldry didn't do much promotion for it, leading some on the scene to believe he had gone into semi-retirement. In a prelude to an interview for *Sounds*, Steve Peacock set the scene with a dismal snapshot of the singer's newfound domesticity.

"Eleven on a wet and cold morning in Muswell Hill," Peacock began, "and John Baldry, attired in red-and-blue dressing gown and stack-heeled shoes, makes his way into the garden to feed chopped cabbage to his goats... These days Rod Stewart is his landlord, but the fact that vast riches have so far eluded him despite his seventeen years as a working musician doesn't seem to worry him."

In the interview, Baldry went to great lengths to appear blasé about the distance between his income and that of his well-to-do peers. "I don't think I'd really like to have loads and loads of bread," he told Peacock. "Of course, I'd like not to have to worry about money, but then even when I have had financial problems they haven't really worried me that much, I just push them to the back of my mind. These things have a habit of sorting themselves out. Friends of mine who've made lots of money seem to become very neurotic—but then it seems that the Seventies is a very neurotic era. People are getting very peculiar... I don't know whether it's the silver spoon and the nosebag that's doing it."

When asked by Peacock to account for his diminished visibility of late, Baldry blamed himself.

"It's my own fault really," he confessed. "There's hundreds of things I could have been doing but I seem to have developed an extreme form of lazy-itis. It wasn't drink or drug-induced, although I am a bit of a piss-artist as you know; it was just simply that I was going through an extremely lethargic period and I spent most of my time sitting here looking at the wall or at the television. I really don't know why it was, but of course now that I've done the new album I feel quite eager to get up and go again."

In a rare, unguarded interview with Roy Hollingworth in *Melody Maker* around the time of *Good to Be Alive*'s release, Baldry admitted publicly, for the first time, to lingering regrets over abandoning his blues vision during the Pye years.

"What killed me in England," he told Hollingworth, "was the impatience of people surrounding me... in 1966. I allowed myself to be swayed. I began to think that what I did was acceptable. And then, when I was nestled in the charts, there suddenly came respect for people like Mayall, and the old bluesers suddenly became enormous... and I missed out. If I'd waited another six months, then I really could have happened."

Despite the enthusiasm Baldry expressed for his new album, it never took off. He played tour dates with Rod and the Faces in Germany, plus a few slots opening for both Kevin Ayers and David Bowie. But by 1974, the major touring had stopped. According to Jeff Edmunds, a Toronto fan and collector who eventually became a personal friend of Baldry's and the unofficial Baldry archivist, there were too many factors in the way for *Good to Be Alive* to really take off back in 1973. "John's career was already dead in the U.K.," say Edmunds today, "and as a result, the album didn't do anything when it was released there." He contends that if a major label like Warner Bros. had released the album internationally, Baldry's career would have "skyrocketed."

"It would've been the third, in three years in a row, of good solid releases," says Edmunds. "John often said it was his favourite, because it was really the first album where he'd truly merged his folk, blues and roots-rock sides. It would be nice if it was someday recognized for its greatness by a proper CD reissue."

Baldry's spirits, already low, plunged even further with the failure of *Good to Be Alive*. Like many around the singer, Jimmy Horowitz says he was unaware that his friend was having problems with depression at this time.

"We both had the same doctor," Horowitz recalls. "I expect he prescribed him the same tri-cyclic that he gave me, Tofranil. As you know, there was a lot of cocaine about in the '70s through the '80s, but John was not a big fan of cocaine and usually went to bed before most of the rest of his musicians when he toured. He always seemed happiest in his own home listening to music or watching TV."

A reprieve of sorts came in 1975, in the form of a U.S. record deal with Neil Bogart's famously extravagant label, Casablanca.

"Jeff Franklin," Jimmy Horowitz recalls, "was president of an agency in New York called ATI, who represented both Rod Stewart and John. Franklin was very close with Neil Bogart. Billy Gaff came to me one day and said that Neil was going to release John in the States. Neil was a real record man. I was a little in awe of him, because he had this reputation of being a very innovative and visionary record guy."

Casablanca Records gave a belated North American release to *Good to Be Alive* that year and also commissioned the recording of a new album, *Welcome to Club Casablanca,* to be released in 1976. With the stroke of a pen, Long John Baldry was now labelmate not only to the likes of Donna Summer and KISS but also to George Clinton's progressive funkateers, Parliament, and the flamboyant Village People.

The cover photograph chosen in advance for *Club Casablanca* depicted a white-suited, fedora-topped Baldry singing in what appeared to be an exotic desert-oasis nightclub. In truth, the shot was taken in Neil Bogart's outlandishly decked-out office.

"He was a very colourful character," says Horowitz of Bogart. "I remember his strange office, which was not at all like a business office. It was very over-decorated and looked like a set out of the movies. There was a fountain in the reception area."

Before he began work on his own album, Baldry took time to contribute to a couple of small side projects. One was a bizarre Billy Russell and Harold Pendleton–backed project called *Boys in the Band,* in which he merely replaced the lead vocals of singer Tom Brown on an album's worth of finished tracks. Then there was a curious trip to Reykjavík to record an album with the Studdmen, sung in phonetic Icelandic. Those odd projects completed, Baldry rejoined Horowitz in Los Angeles to commence recording on his Casablanca debut. He and Horowitz had intended to do the whole thing in the States, using only American musicians. But an incredible set of circumstances put an end to that plan.

Horowitz had enlisted top session players like guitarist Jesse Ed Davis, who had worked with everyone from Conway Twitty to David Cassidy, plus drummers Jim Keltner and Pete Gavin. Guitarist Sam Mitchell rejoined the team, as did Klaus Voormann on bass. Then there was guitarist Alan Murphy, Baldry's most recent discovery, who had been playing in Long John's live band.

"John would always find wonderful guitar players from nowhere," Horowitz recalls. "And he was very enamoured of Alan, both for his guitar playing and I think he was attracted to him physically as well."

Things had gotten off to a great start when the project ran into the first of several unexpected obstacles.

"We had started cutting the album in Los Angeles when I started feeling sick," Horowitz explains today. "I didn't know why I was so sick, but I was just so tired all the time. I had gone over to Rod's place to talk with him about another project. Rod looked at me and said, 'My God, you're sick. Have you seen your eyes?' So I went over to the mirror and sure enough my eyes were glowing bright yellow."

A visit to his doctor confirmed that Horowitz had contracted hepatitis.

"We somehow managed to finish cutting John's basic tracks," says Horowitz, "but then we had to stop, because I just got too sick. I was told I had to stay in bed for three months, so we shut the album down for a while, and John went back to England."

Baldry's visits to Iceland and Los Angeles had distracted him from some of the pain and anxiety in his life. Back in the relative quiet of his Muswell Hill home, his feelings caught up with him. He had seen shots at the big time crumble twice in his career, and he was left with nothing, financially, to show for it. His Austrian boyfriend, Inga, had reluctantly left the U.K. when his visitor visa expired. Baldry increasingly turned to alcohol and whatever else he could get from his physicians. He was tired, sad and lonely. The trouble was, he still needed to work.

Ben Mattijssen, now managing director for the Dutch-based Munich Records, was working for Holland's Flying Dutchman Promotion agency when he booked Baldry to play a show at Dordrecht in 1973. Mattijssen says he noticed something was amiss from the minute he picked Baldry up at Rotterdam airport.

"John had nothing but a guitar case, a zippered clothing bag and a big duty-free bottle of cognac," remembers Mattijssen. "It was only a thirty-minute drive from the airport to the venue but, sitting in the passenger seat, he had already started drinking straight out of the bottle. At 8:15 PM, he changed into his flashy suit and went on, with this huge glass of cognac, which he proceeded to finish off before the end of his first forty-five-minute set. The second set was more of the same.

"He was becoming increasingly drunk, yet I noticed that his singing and playing remained outstanding. He finished his set with great success around 10 PM and asked me if I could pay him immediately and give him a ride to the Dordrecht train station, as he wanted to see his friends in Amsterdam. By now, he was stumbling while continuing to drink right out of bottle. I was very nervous about him travelling in that state, so I offered to let him sleep it off at my house and promised to drive him all the way to Amsterdam the next day. But there was no use in talking to him, so I drove him to the station, and I bought him a ticket. He was staggering with his guitar case, so I helped him to the platform and waited until the train arrived, at which point I put him on a seat opposite a friendly-looking middle-aged man who promised that he would wake John up at the point where he had to change trains. Then I put John's guitar case and clothing bag up in the overhead bins, thanked the guy opposite John after he promised me again that he would look after him, and jumped out of the train. I was still not sure John would make it all the way to Amsterdam."

Mattijssen recalled rumours he had heard that during the "Heartaches" years, a certain unscrupulous manager of Baldry's (Mattijssen was never told which one) had swindled him out of thousands of pounds and paid only in shirts, making sure the singer had "just enough booze to stay drunk all the time." Months later, he received a call from another musician telling him that the Amsterdam authorities had found Baldry lying in the gutter.

"He had been completely robbed," says Mattijssen, "and everything he had was gone. Later I heard other stories in bit and pieces, and from these stories I have reason to believe that after this Amsterdam incident John went straight into an asylum somewhere in the U.K."

The truth, however, was slightly more complicated.

Margaret Baldry, who was still living with her brother in Muswell Hill, explains exactly what happened next.

"John was despondent after he had split up with his boyfriend," Margaret remembers. "One evening, I had come home from work and found him still in bed at six o'clock in the evening. I said, 'What have you done?' and he said, sleepily, 'Ohhh, I've taken pills.'"

As it turned out, Baldry had taken an overdose of prescription Valium, which he had washed down with excessive amounts of alcohol.

"I mean," says Margaret, "he just wasn't himself at that time. And it wasn't just the boyfriend. He had been depressed about a few other things that were going on. You've got to remember he'd had a very successful period in the late '60s and had got a taste of the rock star bit. He'd been treated like a king, and I think he thought he could continue to live the style that was almost within his grasp in the '60s. I'd been with him at a club, and it was nothing to get twenty people drinking and there's John footing the bill for everybody."

Now the party was coming to an end. In what seemed one long morning after, the gloom-filled singer just wanted to go to sleep. Forever, if he could arrange it.

"He was very sleepy, but he was still conscious. When somebody does something like that, you don't take risks with it, so I immediately phoned the GP. I think I said, 'Really, John, I'm not putting up with this any more.' I felt as if I was always there, standing him up. 'You'll have to go and check into a hospital. I can't take this on as a responsibility.'"

Unaware that Baldry had been hospitalized, Jimmy Horowitz returned to London after his three-month recovery, in Los Angeles, from hepatitis.

"Casablanca was waiting for the album," recalls Horowitz, "so we decided I should go back to London and finish recording it there. When I got there, though, I found that John was in a mental hospital. I was told he had attempted suicide. I remember John telling me about how he woke up in the psych ward. He said there was this strange German doctor who'd said, 'Good morning, Mr. Baldry. My name is Dr. Boctor.' He said she was like Nurse Ratched, out of *One Flew over the Cuckoo's Nest.* I told John to get well and that I would be going back into the studio to finish the instrumental tracks for the album."

Baldry was only institutionalized for a brief period, but it was still a difficult time for him, stepping cold turkey off the alcohol and pills and experiencing symptoms of withdrawal.

"He was in there for less than a week," says Margaret Baldry, "in a ward with psychiatric patients. But it was there that he had his first epileptic fit. I'm not sure if it was epilepsy, though; it was never proved. He had quite a few fits over the years, but I'm sure a lot of it had to do with his drinking. I've done a lot of work with drug addicts, and if they've taken an overdose of Valium, you have to be very, very careful with them. If it's withdrawn too suddenly, they will start fitting. And John had taken a lot of Valium, which he'd gotten by prescription from his doctor."

She says that her brother loved getting exotic new medications because, she suspects, it made him feel special.

"He'd say, 'I've just got this new consultant, and she's getting this special medication all the way from America, 'specially for me.' And I'd say to John, 'Don't you actually question, you know, why you want to keep taking pills? They'll harm your body so much in the end, especially when you drink on top of them.' He had an addictive personality, and I suppose we're just very lucky that he was so anti-heroin or cocaine, thank God."

Anya Wilson remembers that, years later, Baldry would often share tales from the institution with her.

"He spoke of it being a bizarre experience," Wilson recalls, "and there was a bizarre cast of characters. John had a way of attracting strange people. He would say, 'They find me, Anya, they come out of the walls and they find me.' Margaret told him at the time, 'Don't worry, John. There are more *out* than *in*.'

Meaning that there were more mad people out than in the hospital. That really seemed to turn him around a lot."

Looking back, Margaret feels that her brother was merely paying the price for trusting the wrong people.

"I mean," she says, "as usual, he was 'down on his uppers.' Broke, you know? And there really was no reason for him to be in that situation. But John believed in people, and a lot of them really did relieve him of a lot of money. He had been shafted, to the hilt, by a lot of his managers."

As Ben Mattijssen had heard, Margaret believes that one of John's managers (she won't say which one) was robbing him blind while making sure that he never ran out of vodka. "These people were just stealing it off of him, taking their wives on free trips to Hawaii and Bermuda, all on John's account. It was common knowledge."

Margaret was puzzled by her brother's inability to realize that his entourage was rife with "sycophantic" hangers-on. "His IQ was verging on genius level," she says, "but he didn't have an ounce of common sense. Out of all these so-called friends, the only one who actually came to see him at the hospital was Alan Murphy."

According to Jimmy Horowitz, that wasn't the full story. Unbeknownst to Margaret, Horowitz had been sneaking Baldry out to the studio.

"Working on my own in London," he recalls, "I had to recut some of the bed tracks that we'd done in L.A., when I was getting sick. They just weren't as good as I felt they could have been. When that was done, I thought, 'I've got to get the vocals in now.' So I would go to the hospital and tell the staff that I was going to take John out for a drive in the country. But we'd actually drive down to Marquee Studios and spend three or four hours doing vocals. Then I'd take him back to the hospital and they'd say, 'Did you enjoy your drive into the country, Mr. Baldry?' and he'd say, 'Oh yes, it was very nice.'"

Horowitz flew back to Los Angeles to play the finished masters of *Welcome to Club Casablanca* for Neil Bogart. Going into Bogart's rococo offices, he says he wasn't sure the final album was any good. What had been planned as a focussed celebration of all-American music had mutated into a schizophrenic, bicoastal affair. "I was a little nervous about it," says Horowitz, "because I was very unhappy with the album. I was not convinced I'd done a good job, and I wasn't sure what Neil was going to say about it."

Horowitz, Lesley Duncan and ATI's Jeff Franklin entered Bogart's office oasis, passing the fountain and the stuffed camel on the way. Then Horowitz previewed the album for the legendary record mogul.

"He liked to listen to things really loud," says Horowitz today, "and he had this huge playback system in his office. He didn't say anything until he had heard the entire album. At the end of it I was prepared to go out and say, 'Well, sorry about the record,' but to my surprise he stood up, shook my hand, hugged me and said 'This is brilliant. This is going to be a number one. I'm so excited.' I was stunned, because I didn't think it was that good, but he absolutely fell in love with it, particularly with the Billy Nicholls song 'This Boy's in Love Again.'"

Horowitz disputes the suggestion that Bogart's enthusiasm was chemically assisted.

"No, I think this was genuine," he insists. "I don't think he was high on blow and, frankly, no record company executive ever did cocaine in front of me. Even in those crazy times, there was some kind of feeling that we didn't do it in the office."

Despite Bogart's all-natural enthusiasm for the album, however, business was business. When the album didn't catch on immediately with the general public, Baldry was suddenly on the back burner at the label whose priority releases—Donna Summer's "Last Dance," Meco's disco-fied "Star Wars Theme" and the Village People's "Macho Man"—bubbled to the top of the charts.

Nevertheless, Casablanca committed to back a tour behind the album. Perhaps, it was felt, Baldry could better promote the release by doing what he did best: assembling a top-notch touring band and taking his music to the people. Excited about giving it a go, Baldry returned to Los Angeles—closer to Casablanca and to Rod Stewart, now living there with his wife, actress Britt Ekland—to audition a new band.

As he left England for America, he had a feeling that he wouldn't be back for a while. His brief time in the asylum had taught him two valuable lessons. For one thing, Margaret was right: there were more "crazy" people out of the asylum than in. Better to just accept one's eccentricities and get on with it. Most significantly however, Baldry was now certain that, in order to truly embrace his inner outrageousness, he would need to heed the Village People's musical suggestion to "Go West." In America, perhaps, there would be an opportunity to reinvent the Baldry persona, far from the parochial judgments of British eyes.

a thrill's a thrill

As 1976 drew to a close, Long John Baldry returned to the Casablanca studios in Los Angeles to audition a new band to help promote *Welcome to Club Casablanca*.

Baldry had always been backed, on stage and on record, by strong female foils, women like Julie Driscoll, Madeline Bell and the fire-breathing Scottish singer Maggie Bell. In L.A., his lucky streak continued when he met a Janis Joplin-esque belter from the Seattle area named Kathi McDonald.

Even on paper, McDonald's pedigree was a perfect match for Baldry's. A veteran of Joe Cocker's *Mad Dogs and Englishmen* and the Rolling Stones' *Exile on Main St.*, she had also sung with Freddie King and Leon Russell and had done time, briefly, as an "Ikette" in the Ike and Tina Turner Revue—a rarity for a white performer. McDonald happened upon the Baldry gig after another singer backed out over a scheduling conflict.

"I was living in L.A.," says McDonald today, "and my friend Lea Santos was one of two backup singers for John Baldry. The other girl, Karen Friedman, had quit. She had a great gig backing Lou Reed on this big tour… So I went to try out, joined up and the rest was history. I never left."

Baldry's latest band also featured his new favourite lead guitarist, Alan Murphy, whom he'd met in Iceland during the Studdmen sessions. (Over the year, Murphy would be joined by guitarists Mark Habib and Phil Lithman). Keyboardist Bennett Salvay, drummer Paul Brown and bassist Jim Fish filled out the rest of the band. To prepare for the tour, Kathi McDonald recalls, the band was assigned to one of Casablanca's rehearsal studios.

"Donna Summer was their big act," says McDonald, "and our room featured this crazy, huge papier-mâché egg, the one she used to come down from the ceiling inside of, when she came on stage. This egg was huge, and the label didn't know where to put it, so it was stored in our rehearsal room. We used to joke about who was going to get in the egg."

On the road, however, Baldry and McDonald were definitely out of their shells, proving to be a dangerous combination on stage and off.

"We were *hellions*," laughs McDonald. "Yes, that's a lovely way to put it. John would usually instigate the insanity and, since he was my boss, I'd be agreeable. We could make fun out of nothing; we'd just grab it out of the air."

At the tail end of 1976, having left Billy Gaff after *Good to Be Alive* underperformed, Baldry had begun entrusting his career decisions to a husband-and-wife team professionally known as Piranha Productions (sometimes referred to as Piranha Promotions). Originally from England, the Piranha team represented some Toronto acts as well as the affairs of Angie Bowie, David Bowie's ex-wife. According to Baldry expert Jeff Edmunds, Baldry hadn't been especially impressed with the Piranha duo; seeing as no one else was offering, he had signed with the company out of necessity.

"Things always happened haphazardly to John," Edmunds says today, "and since he was spending more time in North America, he figured it would be convenient to have representation there. John still had an official mailing address in England—15A Ellington Road, London—but he was basically floating around North America, going wherever the work was. New York, Toronto, Los Angeles. He was like a pinball, just bouncing from thing to thing."

Many of Baldry's other associates at the time profess to having found the Piranha team distasteful. Kathi McDonald blames the team for souring Neil Bogart's enthusiasm for Long John Baldry. Casablanca quietly dropped Baldry from their roster in 1978, as he and his band continued to play dates around North America. "I guess there was some sort of falling-out with John's management at the time," she says today. "Their company was called Piranha Productions; the name says it all. I don't think the Piranhas and Mr. Bogart got along too well, so there wasn't much push on the record. Which was a shame, because it was a very good record."

Jimmy Horowitz confirms there was a problem between the Casablanca brass and what he calls Baldry's "tacky" management. "I'm not sure exactly what happened," he says, "but they managed to alienate the whole record company. They really offended Neil Bogart, who got very angry and soon lost interest."

Strictly adhering to the entertainer's motto, "the show must go on," Baldry's travelling circus, with minor lineup changes from time to time, continued a steady stream of consistent, if unconnected, shows.

"John's shows were always amazing," says his friend and colleague Holger Petersen today. "He had this ability to bring out the best in the musicians in his bands, just by his presence. He inspired people to play better. He also had a great sense of improvisation. In the middle of a show with the full band, he could suddenly pull out his twelve-string guitar and do a few Lead Belly tunes. And there was a genuine chemistry between John and Kathi, and what they did with their voices. Everybody realized that they were seeing some greatness there."

Baldry entered a Nashville studio in 1977 to cut both an ill-advised disco version of "On Broadway" for GM Records and a country music renovation of "Don't Try to Lay No Boogie Woogie on the King of Rock 'n' Roll" for Atlantic. In September of that year, he asked Anya Wilson, the woman who had helped get him on *Top of the Pops* ten years earlier, to come over and assist his managers with promotional activities.

"John had come back to London for a few days," Wilson recalls, "and he invited me out to dinner to meet the Piranha team. We went out to the Sombrero afterwards, and John said, 'You know, I would love you to consider moving to Canada, because I'd like somebody that I trust to handle the publicity, promotion, and these people need somebody.' His managers said, 'Yeah, we'd like you to come.' At that time I had nothing else going on. I'd just finished a relationship, and I had no ties. They promised me all kinds of money and things, so I came over, and of course none of that ever happened."

Having been promised lavish accommodations, Wilson was crestfallen to find she was being put up in the same communal house, in the Toronto suburb of York Mills, where Kathi McDonald and Baldry stayed when they were in town.

"When Anya came on board," McDonald recalls, "poor thing, she was the whipping post for those people, the managers, who worked down in the basement. If they would have taken that energy and put it to a more honest use, we'd be fat and rich right now. But it was all wickedness."

"Then [the Piranhas] went off to L.A.," says Wilson, "so it was just the rest of us. While we didn't have much money, it was actually a lot of fun. But it wasn't at all what I had imagined it would be like. I thought, oh, great, there'll be all these people handling everything else, and I'll just be doing promotion and publicity. But it was nothing like that. I was tormented day and night. I had to do everything, including learn how to be a tour manager. And I used to do the settlements, go and get the money after shows, the whole thing. So it was a great experience, mainly due to living with John and knowing him as practically a sibling."

In fact, says Wilson, she began to fill some of the roles that Baldry's actual sibling, Margaret, had played back in Muswell Hill, watching over Baldry with a similarly protective eye.

"I saw the advantage people took of him," remembers Wilson, "although he really wasn't that easy to walk all over. He had a kind of radar for the 'crazies,' and he tried to avoid them."

By now, Baldry had a long history of ill-fated alliances with ill-suited managers and hangers-on who would bleed him for his income without providing any sort of career game plan. Anya Wilson says today the real problem in Baldry's career was that he never had a manager who really took care of him. There was probably "no cut-and-dried route for his type of music," though, she admits. "John just wanted to continue to make a living, doing what he loved. So if somebody could give him a corporate gig for fifteen grand or something, you know, that'd keep him for months. But he was a survivor; he'd been around the block a few times."

Elton John also believes that Baldry never had what Elton would call a "proper, kosher" manager. "John was always surrounded by second-raters," he says today, "and he never had the representation he should have had. It was always chums and close associates. He had his own ring, a circle of friends that he would always see. And they were all nuts."

As his live band continued to evolve, Baldry was reunited with his old friend from Hamburg, Roy Young, the piano player from the Speakeasy. Young, who had relocated to Toronto at the time, agrees with many others that Baldry suffered from a lack of career vision, combined with a propensity to put faith in the wrong people.

"John was kind of a Jekyll and Hyde figure," says Young, "and would sometimes give you the impression that he wasn't quite sure what he wanted to do. Consequently, ideas from various people would creep in, *telling* him what he should do. He was totally influenced by some people who guided him to the wrong things. On the other hand, he would tell these managers what to do and demand total control. To be honest, I don't think even *John* knew exactly where he should go, even if he'd had Brian Epstein, Colonel Tom Parker or Robert Stigwood managing his career."

Kathi McDonald blames the Piranhas. "He put his entire life, trust, heart, soul and spiritual being into them," says McDonald with more than a hint of bitterness, "and they screwed him. They would lie with smiles on their faces. This house we lived in had paper-thin walls, so you could hear them in meetings. I'd hear them lying to him, so I'd tell him later, 'John, that's not true, I heard them on the phone, that's not true.' John would insist, 'Oh, they wouldn't lie to me, they're my management.' When he put his faith into somebody it was 101 per cent."

In between sporadic gigs, Anya Wilson helped Baldry get involved in a memorable side project. He was hired to write and narrate a four-hour syndicated radio documentary series, *The History of British Rock,* which allowed him to cross the ocean again to interview a number of rock legends, including Paul McCartney, Ginger Baker, Keith Moon and T. Rex singer Marc Bolan.

The Bolan interview, conducted on September 16, 1977, was unfortunately marred by tragedy. After leaving his interview with Baldry, Bolan, his wife, Gloria, and Gloria's brother had

gone out for drinks. On their way home, they got into a car accident. Gloria and her brother were badly injured, and Bolan was
killed instantly.

"After finishing up with John," Anya Wilson recalls, "Marc
and his entourage had all gone on to Tramps nightclub for
drinks. It was a terrible loss, and John was just devastated by
it; we all were. John's interview was the last one Marc ever gave.
Oddly enough, Rod was supposed to be in the series, and John
even went out to stay with Rod and Britt in L.A. for three weeks.
But Rod would never get around to it. He'd say, 'Ah, I'm not in
the mood now.' So of all the people, Rod never did the series."

Baldry was spending a lot of time in Toronto, but he made
frequent trips to New York City, staying up all night in the city
that famously never sleeps. In 1978, the year after the "Summer
of Sam," he was a regular fixture at the notorious Studio 54 and
also made occasional appearances at the Bottom Line. Away
from the U.K., he began to live out his post-asylum credo: he
would allow himself to become as outrageous as he wanted.
Baldry cultivated friendships with famous and infamous Man-
hattanites such as guitarist Sylvain Sylvain, of the New York
Dolls, and former Ten Wheel Drive singer Genya Ravan, who
had just produced the debut album for New York–based, Cleve-
land-expat punk rockers the Dead Boys.

Today, Ravan recalls Baldry affectionately. "His memory
makes me smile," she says. "He stayed in my apartment on
57th Street for a few days. His deep raspy voice was unmistak-
able, even when he spoke. He was always up and funny. Nothing
about him was a put-on. We hung out in Greenwich Village at
the 9th Circle Restaurant Bar. We ate there and listened to the
DJs playing music. We laughed and hit lots of clubs."

It was during one of his frequent nights at Studio 54 that
Baldry was enthralled by the vision of a slightly built, spandex-
clad boy he had spied across the dance floor. His given name

was Felix Rexach, but everyone knew him as "Oz." Rexach had moved to New York from Puerto Rico in 1975 to study ecology and was by 1978 completing his master's degree at NYU.

"I used to work in a boutique down in Soho called Havona," Rexach explains today. "The shop was run by a designer named Karen Davies, and I used to go to Studio 54 and showcase some of her spandex outfits. I just had to wear the clothes, and people would say, 'Hey, where did you get that?' So, I would tell them, and they'd say, 'Hey, can we get an order for ten thousand dollars' worth?' So she ended up going from retail to wholesale. That night, February 15, 1978, I was introduced to John, who was hanging out with a whole bunch of his friends. I didn't really know who he was at that point. "

Remarkably, Elton John swears he was also there that momentous evening. "When I first met Oz," he remembers, "he had a television aerial on his head. That was a perfect attraction for John. He was always attracted to people who were as eccentric and funny as himself."

Kathi McDonald, who was also in Baldry's party that night, recalls seeing Rexach in action, as an ace spandex salesman.

"Oz could sell stripes to a zebra," laughs McDonald. "He was so lighthearted, so lovely, with all this wonderful hair and this Puerto Rican accent. He didn't really *walk* so much as he *danced*. He was a delightful, chatty person with the most positive, white-light energy around him. He was fond of smoking the herb, although John never liked it. Still, when John fell hard in love, he'd do almost anything."

Baldry and Oz remained at the club with a few others until four in the morning, when they decamped for breakfast.

"I found out that he was playing soon at the Bottom Line," remembers Rexach, "so I told him to come down to the boutique to get some clothes. I ended up dressing the whole band for the performance. It's funny; there are pictures of them all dressed up in crazy spandex. It was amazing."

A few nights later Baldry and crew took to the stage at the Bottom Line. The celebrated *New York Times* critic Robert Palmer attended the show, but he left unimpressed with what he felt was an inauthentic appropriation of American blues by an out-of-his-depth English poseur. In the March 23 edition of the paper, Palmer began his screed with an ominous dig: "Long John Baldry was a power in English rock in the 1960s... but despite some American exposure, culminating in a Warner Brothers album in the early '70s, Mr. Baldry never caught on here."

The critic then got to the crux of his problem with Baldry, whose treatment of blues and rhythm and blues, he suggested, was perhaps "just too English for American audiences."

"He phrases his blues lines right on the beat," Palmer wrote, "without any real feeling for the playful rushing, delaying, and other tension-producing devices that better singers, black and white, bring to such material. When he delves into erotica, the music comes out sounding more tawdry than sexy, as if it has not been entirely divested of that old Puritan guilt."

On the positive side, Palmer gave credit to Baldry for consistently assembling what he termed "first-class touring bands." Writing about Kathi McDonald, he declared, "If her gospel frenzy was a little too rote, at least she livened things up."

In truth, Palmer's review epitomized the kind of snobbery that most British blues-rock acts endured daily from protectionist American critics. In 1972, celebrated rock critic Lester Bangs had had this to say about Baldry's friends, Savoy Brown, in the pages of *Creem* magazine: "It's easy to get down on British proto- or crypto-blues bands. After all, why should a bunch of Limeys forsake their roots in favor of painstaking note-for-note imitations of old rot-gutted black guys when the only reason they can sell it some times is because they have the flair to sing about being down and out in Dallas while dressed like absolute 'Yellow Book' fops."

It is unlikely Baldry was much affected by the lukewarm notice in the *Times,* for he was now head over stacked heels in love with a spandex-clad boy named Oz. Smitten, he began a long-distance relationship with Rexach, commuting constantly between Toronto and New York.

"At one point," Rexach recalls, "John came down and lived with me and my mother for six months in this place on Bleecker Street in the Village. John loved it in New York. He had many friends there. He even had connections with the whole Andy Warhol scene and people like Jane Friedman, who used to manage her husband, John Cale, from the Velvet Underground and, I think, Patti Smith."

Back in Toronto, Anya Wilson was helping to get John Baldry to another career milestone. This time, it was a new record deal with Capitol-EMI Canada.

"I was the one that instigated the deal with EMI," says Wilson today. "The Piranha team was in L.A., so I set up dinner with Deane Cameron, then EMI's director of talent acquisition."

Cameron, who is now the president of EMI Music Canada, had known of Baldry since his own high school days, when a girlfriend had introduced him to *It Ain't Easy.* Wilson says she put "all the heavy artillery on" when she invited Cameron down to a Toronto club to see the band perform.

"I was loaded for bear," she remembers. "John was playing at the Colonial on Yonge Street. Deane was a big fan, but he had concerns about John's reputation with the drinking and Kathi's supposed reputation for being unstable, whether it was true or not. So I said to John and the whole band, 'Look. You've all gotta behave tonight.' And they did. John was actually not drinking at all in the time leading up to the EMI deal. He had this whole routine where he would have tea and biscuits, or whatever like that, in the dressing room."

Wilson says the band put on an "exceptional show" that

night—so much so that Cameron gave her a gentleman's agreement on the spot to sign Baldry, pending negotiations.

"I called the Piranhas in L.A.," says Wilson. "They couldn't believe it. I said, 'Well, it's up to you guys to nail down the details,' and they did."

Around this time, Baldry's friend from London in 1973, Al Harlow, had himself returned to Canada, where his band, Prism, was also signed to Capitol [EMI] Records. "One day I was sitting in Deane's office at Capitol," Harlow recalls, "when his intercom buzzed. Deane said, 'Let Mr. Baldry in.' I'll never forget John's entrance, in the middle of the afternoon, dressed in a skin-tight green leather suit and a long, flowing white scarf."

In that meeting, Cameron and Baldry planned out his Canadian recording debut.

"I worked with John on the A&R process," explains Cameron today, "[in which] we discussed what kinds of songs would be on the record that would eventually become *Baldry's Out!* This was late '78, and by the time we did the deal and made the record, it came out in mid-'79. He was a true gentleman, and it was always a pleasant experience dealing with John in the studio and within the label. He was kind of shy and hesitant to speak up until you really got to know him. The real John Baldry, I learned, could be very funny and sarcastic, yet he was also very British and quite restrained."

Diplomatically, Cameron categorizes Baldry's management team at the time as "very interesting people" to deal with. As usual with Baldry, there were lingering questions about prior contracts and territorial agreements, such as his recording deal with Billy Gaff's GM Records. Even Long John wasn't sure who owed what to whom.

"The Piranha team were promising me that all of the old issues with Billy Gaff were resolved," Cameron recalls. "It was my impression that John wasn't really watching his own business."

Neither Wilson nor Cameron can comment directly on the well-circulated rumour that the two managers then proceeded to make off with Baldry's entire six-digit advance, paid out of Capitol-EMI's L.A. branch.

"They certainly didn't pay *me*, though," says Wilson. "I think I had $500 in traveller's cheques. I had to borrow some money from a friend to move into an apartment."

Jimmy Horowitz says today that he would dearly love to have a word with the Piranha team—if anyone could track them down, that is.

"They were the oddest people in the world," he says. "They're probably in jail somewhere. John was such a respectable person, and these people—they were just the tackiest people in the world. Supposedly, they ran off with most of the money. Some of that money was mine. I never got paid for any of the albums I did for them."

On the musical side, work on the album continued, with sessions in Toronto, Miami, London and L.A. The album opener, "Baldry's Out," featured a spoken-word introduction over a boogie-woogie piano vamp deliberately reminiscent of the first bars of the *It Ain't Easy* album. This time, rather than a busted-for-busking diatribe, Baldry riffed on his short stay in the asylum.

"Whenever something would happen," recalls Horowitz, "we always used to say, 'Oh yeah? Why don't you write a song about it?' So he and I just sat down and wrote together. We decided that we'd do it as a kind of reprise of 'Don't Try to Lay No Boogie Woogie... ' Then we'd reintroduce people to John as we knew him. "

Everyone at EMI, Deane Cameron recalls, was also excited about a couple of great young English guitarists in Baldry's band, Alan Murphy and Mick Clarke. "Alan eventually went on to work with Kate Bush," says Cameron. "He was an important element to John's band. He was a rock player, he was young, good-looking, and he took a real front-and-centre stage. And Mick Clarke provided a whole sort of hope that a new, youthful rock direction might be in the cards."

Today, Clarke recalls fondly the two years he spent playing with Baldry's band.

"Being a fellow Londoner, of course," says Clarke, "John was something of a legendary figure to me before I played with him, and the late Alan Murphy was also a good friend of mine many years beforehand. John lived up to his reputation with that amazing voice and soulful, bluesy acoustic guitar, night after night. Nevertheless, he was a very sensitive man and always found time for the small details, making sure everyone was okay and happy. He was someone you could trust."

As a title, *Baldry's Out!* was a playful warning to the world at large that Long John had been released from the asylum. Quite possibly, it was also a sly allusion to the singer's increasingly open, or "out," lifestyle. Jimmy Horowitz doubts that this secondary meaning was intentional on Baldry's part, however.

The centrepiece of the album was Baldry's recording, for the second time in his career, of the Righteous Brothers' classic "You've Lost That Lovin' Feelin'." This time, the song was recast as an urgent boy/girl duet between Baldry and Kathi McDonald. Released as a single, it was a hit in Canada and reached the top five in Australia, and it briefly returned Baldry to the lower reaches of the U.S. *Billboard* chart.

"Everybody who heard it just fell in love with it," says Horowitz today. "All kinds of places and people picked it up. But again, because of the Piranha team, I guess, it didn't happen in the U.S.A. They seemed to have a technique for pissing everyone off."

Horowitz remembers that, after tracking some string parts in London, he took the project to the swamplands of Orlando, Florida, where the band overdubbed all the vocal and guitar parts at the unfortunately named BJ Studios. "The place was a Christian recording studio," recalls Kathi McDonald, "so we used to joke that BJ stood for 'blow job.' We had been on the road for months. We probably had one day off a week. We were touring machines. But Jimmy, what a producer! The sessions went really well, and every day we knocked down at least two complete songs. 'You've Lost That Lovin' Feelin'' was one of the last."

Apparently even Bill Medley, of the Righteous Brothers, was enamoured of the Baldry and McDonald version.

"John actually met Bill," McDonald recalls, "when we played at the Whiskey A Go Go, in L.A. He came up to John, who was thinking, 'Uh oh, I probably spoiled their song,' but Bill actually said he liked our version more than his. That was the hugest, fattest, most wonderful compliment ever."

Keyboard player Roy Young witnessed the "real chemistry" between McDonald and Baldry in the studio. "Once their voices started to blend," he recalls, "we realized that there was something magical between the two of them."

McDonald says she was moved nearly to tears during the one-take performance of the song.

"We sang it facing each other," she says, "surrounded by Plexiglas, with headphones on. We did one practice run, and then we cut the song in one take. It was one of those very rare moments where you're both smiling and just speechless. Then you hear the playback and you're screaming 'Yeah!' and jumping up and down. So of course we had cocktails that night. But we worked very hard. We complied with their rules, no drinking in the studio. Although we actually we did sneak a little bit of wine in now and again. John would always say, 'As the last note is struck, prepare me a cocktail!' Then we'd go out and about on the town."

The track that garnered the most attention for the album, however, was "A Thrill's a Thrill," an emotionally charged paean to sexual experimentation and alternative lifestyles. Controversial for its time, the song—also released as a single—helped make *Baldry's Out!* the singer's best-selling album in the Canadian market.

"Oh God, yes, it was a big record," confirms EMI's Cameron. "It went double platinum in Canada, which is 200,000 units. We went platinum based on 'You've Lost That Loving Feelin',' but it was 'A Thrill's a Thrill' that really drove it home to double platinum. Other than *It Ain't Easy,* I'm guessing *Baldry's Out!* was one of the high points of his career."

Although he hadn't written it himself, Baldry imbued "A Thrill's a Thrill" so deeply with his own personality that it came off as a memoir, pitched emotionally somewhere between Lou Reed's revelatory "Walk on the Wild Side" and Frank Sinatra's "My Way."

Barbra Amesbury had penned the song back when she was known legally as the male songwriter Bill Amesbury, whose recording career peaked in 1974 with a Canadian top-ten single called "Virginia (Touch Me Like You Do)." Picked up, ironically, by Casablanca for the U.S., the single had stalled at number fifty-nine on the *Billboard* charts.

"A Thrill's a Thrill," written two years later, was a snapshot of a specific time in New York City when Amesbury lived in the notorious Chelsea Hotel, in an atmosphere of sexual and chemical experimentation and as part of a social scene that at one time included Andy Warhol, Patti Smith and Robert Mapplethorpe.

Amesbury's lyrics left little room for misinterpretation:

> *"The gays are straight, And the straights are queer*
> *And the bi's just call everybody dear; they know a*
> *thrill's a thrill*
> *...even in paradise."*

"It was never a song about me," Amesbury would later tell Richard Flohil in the liner notes for an EMI compilation. "It was a song about the place and the time."

The song became something of a cult anthem in the gay community, with bawdy couplets like *"leather whips and fingertips, I know a boy who's growing tits."* Yet Baldry refused to exploit his deeply personal identity for the sake of promoting a record. Gentlemen, after all, did not discuss their private affairs in public. According to Oz Rexach, Baldry was fond of quoting another, much older song: "It ain't nobody's business if I do."

"That was one of his signature closing numbers, or encores," says Rexach. "He'd even mimic Billie Holiday singing it. But you know, when he did 'A Thrill's a Thrill,' we had just met, and I always felt I was a fresh inspiration to all this. But John was always out. People knew. You can be out, but you don't have to be flamboyant, you know? He didn't like flamboyancy."

EMI took the precautionary step of releasing a special version of the single to radio.

"We just edited some of the lyrics," Deane Cameron acknowledges today, "but that's what we have always done in this industry. It happens to hip-hop music every other day. I don't even think, for back then, that it was that much of an issue. In my seventeen and a half years here as president of EMI, there have been some controversial records, but really, that wasn't one of them."

"They had to re-record it," Rexach recalls, "with clean lyrics like 'I know a boy who is now a girl,' or something. I think Barbra had a big fit about them changing the words."

Not all radio stations picked up the bowdlerized version of the song, though. Baldry's friend David Marsden was by this time breaking new ground at a cutting-edge Toronto radio station called CFNY. The station's progressive and relaxed FM format was perfectly suited to Baldry's "underground" anthem.

"I loved it," says Marsden. "I knew Bill Amesbury—she was Bill then—quite well, and we always played the album version with the actual words."

Marsden also remembers that a light went on in his head one night when Baldry brought Oz with him to the CFNY studios.

"Oz, of course, is quite flamboyant," says Marsden, "and they'd spend the night hanging out in the radio station. John was playing music, and Oz was with him. I suppose my gaydar hadn't been working, but I was totally and utterly oblivious, which was kind of odd, if you know me. I think it took me until 1999 to even realize what 'Baldry's Out' could also mean. But, you know, my viewpoint is this: John was a singer and a great performer who happened to be gay—he wasn't a gay performer. So we played his record, and if people wanted to connect the dots, he didn't care. If they didn't, that was just fine. I mean, back in the early '80s that song was considered quite risky. 'Oh my God,' you'd think, 'are we gonna get in trouble?' John was addressing topics in that song that people hadn't quite yet come to discuss openly. Twenty-odd years ago, 'Now that the young boys are all hanging out in bars, old men don't have to cruise all night in cars' was an extremely controversial line. People were somewhat open about the concept that there were people around who liked their own sex, but to put it out—bam—just like that.

"When I look back on it now, knowing John as well as I came to, I'm shocked at his bravery, because it was unlike him. The song was so advanced, so in front of everything we're doing today. And when I say 'we,' I'm referring to Canada, where we recognize gay marriage. There was John, twenty-five years ago, putting this song out, and then putting out an album called *Baldry's Out!* It was a double-header. I'm sure he was chuckling to himself, thinking, 'I'm getting away with this. I'm actually teaching people something, I'm putting new words into their vocabularies and no one has figured it out yet.' But I would hazard to guess that if you were to speak to people inside the gay community who used to listen to John on my show back then, most of them still don't know that he was a gay man. I would bet on it. Although the two big Toronto gay publications ran large notices when he died."

To this day, Barbra Amesbury says she regrets allowing EMI change the lyrics for the radio version of "A Thrill's a Thrill." She also recalls how Baldry was cautious, in its wake, about tipping his hand too much with regard to his sexuality.

"After 'A Thrill' became a hit for John," says Amesbury, looking back, "I gave him another song called 'Christopher Street,' which took the genre one step further. John was worried that if he stayed in that direction his audience might think he was gay. Not to mention what Capitol thought. The music biz has always been homophobic, and John knew that."

Roy Young agrees Baldry was reticent to become a gay-identified entertainer.

"At that time, he had asked me to manage him," says Young. "So I suggested that it might be a good idea to explain to the world just who John Baldry really was. But something in him wouldn't go the whole way. It was absolutely his choice, but I happen to think that it was also his downfall."

With a strong-selling album in the stores, Baldry was back in a familiar position. After all the false starts and dead stops in his career, *Baldry's Out!* gave him another kick at the can. And John Baldry, the private gentleman, had also found his thrill. For the first time in his adult life, he was in a serious relationship. There was little time for domestic bliss, though. Long John Baldry's more public persona, the entertainer, had work to do.

this could be home

HIS PROFILE rising once again, thanks to the buzz surrounding his EMI debut, Long John Baldry felt poised to recapture a little of his former glory. Unfortunately, fresh new problems lay on the road ahead.

Shortly before another tour promoting *Baldry's Out!*, Kathi McDonald moved in with Baldry in New York, where he had staying much of the time.

"It was almost funny," she recalls. "John, Alan Murphy and I, plus Pat McDonald, our road manager, were in this third-floor apartment up on 105th. We had no money and nothing to eat, while the Piranhas would be ordering room service for themselves over at the Waldorf Astoria."

The situation couldn't have been good for Baldry's health, which was once again suffering. It was a sad foreshadowing of the frailty he would exhibit on and off for the rest of his life.

"He had decided, no more meds," McDonald remembers, "so he got rid of the Dilantin, which he'd been prescribed after his epileptic seizures back in Britain. John was just living in this vomit-stained robe. He called it 'The Orange Robe of Putrescence' because he threw up all over it."

Baldry had been on a slow burn over the injustices of his management team. Eventually, in the words of Kathi McDonald, he "flipped out."

"He was getting angrier and angrier about the Piranhas," she says, "until one day he'd had enough and started freaking out, especially since they were no longer returning his phone calls. Then our phone was cut off. So John flipped out and pulled out a rifle. He had no ammunition, mind you, but he held it up and said, 'I want you guys to go get my management.' He was livid. I've never seen anybody so mad. So we just ran out of there, hauling butt down the street."

McDonald says that she and Alan Murphy went to the Waldorf Astoria to confront the Piranha duo on Baldry's behalf. "We said, 'You've got to come and get John. Something's really wrong.' They said, 'Oh no, John can't possibly be ill. We start touring in a couple of days.' What assholes. They treated him like a product; he was the goose that laid the golden egg. There wasn't time for firing and arguing. They had this tour all lined up."

McDonald recalls that everyone in the band literally prayed for tour dates, though; they were starving, and the road meant they would get regular meals and slightly better accommodation.

"Once we got on the road," she says, "everything made more sense, because we had our own rooms, we had food, we had drink, we had our own space, we could clean our own clothes, go for a walk. We were excited about getting back to the Boarding House in San Francisco and the Bottom Line in New York. The BBC filmed us there, singing 'You've Lost That Lovin' Feelin',' walking down the streets of New York, for *The Old Grey Whistle Test*. Anyway, we eventually got the Piranhas to give us some comforts, although it's a shame that you have to fake that you're going to pull a gun war on somebody to get them on your side. They were gone at the end of that tour. John had wanted to get rid of them before, but somehow they would always chill him out. I heard they were wiping out John's bank account and had even spent his British income tax cheque. They were fucked-up people with no hearts and souls."

Jeff Edmunds recalls flying to L.A. in the summer of 1979 to see Baldry's show at the Whiskey and then back to New York for the Bottom Line show. "I remember Genya Ravan," he says, "walking around the stage throwing flowers."

Ravan, pleading pharmacological amnesia, isn't sure about this. "I don't recall if I appeared and he threw roses, or he appeared and I threw roses. I mean... I was quite high in those days, so if there were roses, I probably snorted them."

Unfortunately, critic Robert Palmer was also at the New York show, and he expressed his displeasure in another nasty review, which ran in the August 29 issue of the *New York Times*.

"The distinction of having been a founding father of British blues-rock," Palmer began, "[is] roughly comparable to having introduced a particularly unpleasant new strain of influenza. But Long John Baldry's show at the Bottom Line on Monday evening wasn't simply unpleasant. It was a nightmare from which this listener emerged fairly horror-stricken."

This time, even Baldry's bandmates felt the sting of Palmer's poison pen.

"The show began with Roy Young," he continued, "a venerable English Little Richard imitator, who sang tunelessly from atop his electric piano while holding a leather hat firmly in place atop his head. At least he involved the audience. Mr. Young then introduced Cathy [sic] McDonald, a singer whose histrionics are so extreme one fears she is about to have a nervous breakdown every time she opens her mouth."

The review ended by dismissing Long John Baldry himself.

"Finally," Palmer wrote, "Mr. Baldry appeared, looking vaguely reptilian in his clinging, sharkskin-like clothing. Mr. Baldry has a curious voice that ranges from fog-horn bottom to a high insect chirruping, and his Anglo-American backing band was decently solid. The music he performed had its occasional charms, mostly when the material veered away from pseudo-blues and pseudo-gospel in the direction of mainstream rock. But England has produced plenty of authentically soulful rock singers by this time, and there's no longer any real percentage (if ever there was) in suffering through the sort of overkill that remains Mr. Baldry's stock in trade."

Perhaps, Baldry came to think, it was best to stay out of New York for a while. In 1980, Oz Rexach decided to leave Manhattan to be with him in Toronto.

"New York," says Rexach today, "just wasn't a healthy place to live then. It seemed like people that stayed there would get messed up. There were suddenly harder drugs, like cocaine, which was the big recreational drug of the time."

Baldry had recently parted with the Piranha Productions team but continued to be hamstrung by unresolved financial matters from their tenure as his managers. Unsure of his future, he was having difficulty finding a place to live in Toronto while he ironed out a new management deal with Neill Dixon and Steve Propas. They were the owners of a management company called Dixon-Propas Management and a record label called Solid Gold, which had enjoyed moderate successes with a variety of Canadian pop and metal acts. Baldry was about to record his second EMI album in a new studio in Hamilton, Ontario, so somebody suggested that he and Oz and the band move into a farmhouse in nearby Dundas. Kenn-Wynn Farm was a rustic retreat far from the madness of the previous ten years.

"It was this big old Victorian mansion," remembers Rexach, "about a hundred years old. John met this lady from Hamilton named Marianne Heatherington, who had a little antique shop, and we started furnishing the place with couches, chairs and other pieces. John loved animals, and we had a lot of them, including these two cats, Punky and Junky. We also had rabbits, which John liked because they are very independent and very cute."

"Kenn-Wynn was a funky, palatial kind of place," remembers Kathi McDonald. "We all moved in there together, even our road manager and tech, Marshall Paul, from Toronto. John could *decorate*. He painted all the walls so beautifully. He would go around and find accessories and trimmings and stuff. We'd be on our way to a gig, and he'd have us pull over because we'd have to pick up a big clay bust or some antique mirrors. I remember getting all scratched up with these rose bushes that he just *had* to buy. It was before cable, so we only picked up three television channels, but this was where John's love of soaps developed. We had no car, and the driveway was about a quarter of a mile long. We'd have to get people to come and fetch us to do the liquor store run or to go to the Safeway for groceries. The only nightlife was the Collins Hotel or going over to the nearby farm of Kelly Jay, from [the band] Crowbar. But it was quite fun, actually."

Kelly Jay, who'd met Baldry back in 1973 when Crowbar were in London to tape *The Old Grey Whistle Test,* was the proud owner of a nearby home and biker hang-out that he called "Bad Manors."

"John had just moved to Kenn-Wynn Farm," Jay recalls, "and it was a gorgeous place, too, a beautiful Victorian with huge rooms in it. At Christmas, the place reeked of evergreens. Oz would do these elaborate displays. I would invite them over to Bad Manors, and we had some really good parties."

Baldry also spent some time with another legendary rock 'n' roll exile living the farm life in Ontario: Arkansas-born rockabilly singer Ronnie Hawkins. Known to many as the man who gave Robbie Robertson's crew their first gig as the Hawks, before they became the Band and backed Bob Dylan, Hawkins was the squire of his own manor in Stony Lake, near Peterborough.

· "Long John Baldry had one hell of a voice," says Hawkins today, "and he always put on a good show. That Kathi McDonald could really sing, too. And they were really good together. I only know of two English cats that had a throat like that, him and Joe Cocker. I mean, Mick Jagger shouldn't even be allowed to sing. If he'd had a voice like Long John Baldry, boy, the Rolling Stones might be in the big time!"

While living at Kenn-Wynn, Baldry found a new person to take on the role in his life first played by Baldry's mother, then by his sister, Margaret, and his friend Anya Wilson. He had met Evelyn Muncaster earlier in the year, when he was flying first-class from Toronto to Regina to do a show. Always an anxious flyer, Baldry was into his first cognac of the morning when he began chatting with Muncaster, who was at the time married to a senior executive of the successful automotive supply chain, Canadian Tire.

"I looked over across the aisle," Muncaster recalls, "and rec-ognized Long John Baldry, scrunched up and with a drink in his hand. I acknowledged that I knew who he was, and we just talked about things. He said, 'Will you join me in a cognac?' I had a long day ahead of me, but I thought, what the hell. We had a very interesting conversation and, after we landed, exchanged numbers. A few months later, I went to see him at a little club on Merton Street in Toronto. Then a month or so after that, I got a call from Doug McQuigg [a friend of Baldry's who had helped him get settled in Toronto and adjust to his new management deal with Dixon and Propas]. Doug asked me to come and help John because he was going to be doing this album. He had just signed this management thing with Neill and Steve—or 'Deal and Steal,' as John nicknamed them, although they weren't really bad. Doug said that John was going to need help sorting out his administration. He suggested we visit John at Kenn-Wynn. So I thought, I've got nothing better to do other than play squash at the Granite Club; why not? It was kind of an adventure."

Former David Bowie sideman Stacey Heydon was chosen to produce the second EMI album, *Long John Baldry,* and sessions commenced in Hamilton at Grant Avenue, a new studio owned and operated by Bob and Daniel Lanois (the latter of whom would subsequently collaborate with Brian Eno and produce records for U2 and Bob Dylan).

Kathi McDonald says that the sessions with Heydon went smoothly, although Baldry regretted having agreed to let the band rehearse at his Dundas residence. "We pushed the stuff back in one of the big living rooms," she remembers. "John didn't like to rehearse where he lived; he liked his home to be his little castle. He was very into being homey, relaxed and comfortable."

But despite presenting a great selection of tunes, including the Burt Bacharach and Bob Hilliard chestnut "Any Day Now," Bonnie Dobson's arrangement of the traditional song "Morning Dew" (which Baldry had learned from the Grateful Dead's version) and the best efforts of some of Canada's best hit songwriters, the new album failed to excite critics or get much radio play. (Curiously, "Morning Dew" was released as a single in Holland, where it entered the top ten for a time.)

EMI was not happy. Unless Baldry could connect with the mainstream on a third album, the business relationship would be over. Deane Cameron and his team felt that the best way to do it was to get Long John Baldry onto rock radio.

Out in Vancouver, British Columbia, a group named Chilliwack had been racking up Canadian successes for years, and they had recently scored a huge North American hit with "My Girl (Gone, Gone, Gone)." With its Beach Boys–styled harmony chorus, the song remains a staple of classic rock radio to this day. So in 1982 Cameron brought in Chilliwack's mainstays, Bill Henderson and Brian McLeod, to produce Baldry's third EMI album, *Rock with the Best.*

"I hadn't met John before," says Henderson, "but we were with the same company, and Steve and Neill were getting Brian and me to do a number of projects for them. We had sort of become staff producers. When we were asked to produce Long John Baldry, I was very excited about it, because I had really liked *It Ain't Easy*. He was great."

Evelyn Muncaster, who had taken on the task of sorting out Baldry's finances, began to question his idyllic retreat at Kenn-Wynn from a business standpoint.

"He didn't have a car," recalls Muncaster, "and didn't drive, so he was stuck on this bloody farm. If you needed a package of cigarettes at three o'clock in the morning, you're taking a cab for twenty bucks. Nothing about it made any logical sense from a business point of view. So we started to think it was no longer feasible for John to live out at the farm. He couldn't really afford it. We told him it wasn't working and that he should be in Toronto, where it was happening."

Any moves, however, would have to wait until after the band had finished the new album. Henderson concedes today that, going into the sessions, he wondered if perhaps he and McLeod were too hard-rock for Baldry.

"I always thought there was bit of mismatch in the whole thing," says Henderson, "because Brian and I pursued a particular kind of sound we had, which involved a high degree of accuracy in the performance of the players' parts in the studio. We liked to record everything very precisely. Of course, that's just not what John did! We had actually had lots of experience with looseness in our own past, but at the time we got together with Baldry, Brian and I had perfected this really tight sound. I thought John was wonderfully tolerant of our approach. He wanted a hit just like anybody else, and he figured maybe we could do it because we were creating hits. We rehearsed with the band John had put together. John would sit there at the microphone, have a few drinks and just fall asleep during rehearsal."

Henderson and McLeod had written some material specifically for Baldry's album, under the pseudonyms Willie Short and Ralph Long.

"We wrote him this song, 'Twenty-Five Years of Pain,' because he was celebrating twenty-five years in the music industry," remembers Henderson. "John said, 'Bill, I like your song, but it wasn't twenty-five years of pain. I enjoyed every moment of it.'" The two also provided *Rock with the Best*'s title track, along with an answer song to Baldry's pop albatross entitled "Let the Heartaches Stop."

"He sang the way he wanted to sing, and he wasn't into tidying things up too much," Henderson recalls. "And, you know, good for him, for hanging on to his character all the way through."

Coming from the blues tradition, not to mention the booze tradition of some of Rod Stewart's sessions for *It Ain't Easy*, Baldry found the clockwork precision of "the Chilly Wacks" unusual. After recording basic tracks at Grant Avenue, the whole team flew out to Vancouver's Mushroom Studios, where Henderson happily enlisted the house engineer, Rolf Hennemann.

"He's a great guy," says Henderson, "and he'd worked on a lot of big records, like Heart's *Dreamboat Annie*. Rolf likes to tell a story about John sleeping on the couch while the tracks were being done and saying, 'Wake me up when we have a hit!' He was very good about it. John knew the music business does what it does. You've got to work with the times. He was trying to do that. He didn't let it get on his tits."

Kathi McDonald did not appear on *Rock with the Best*, owing to a major falling out she and Baldry had had during a U.S. tour. It was her first absence from a Baldry album since she'd begun working with him.

"In any long musical relationship," says McDonald today, "there are always one or two musical divorces. We just had a falling out—one of those arguments that you say, 'Years from now, we'll look back on this and laugh.' Only thing is, I look back now and can't remember exactly what it was about. I think it was in Texas, and I think he pissed me off or went too far, but honestly I can't recall what it was. So I didn't work with him for quite a while after that."

In place of McDonald, Henderson and McLeod had brought in their own belter, Darby Mills, who was the singer in McLeod's heavy rock project, Headpins. Mills played the role of Baldry's female foil on record only; a succession of different singers would be brought in for live shows.

Evelyn Muncaster recalls that Dixon and Propas would drop by the studio after the production had moved back to Toronto's Phase One Studios for final overdubs and mixing. "Neill and Steve used walk to into the recording studio," she recalls, "carrying a stack of papers and record reviews. They would check on what the Chilliwack guys were doing, then walk right out again."

Deane Cameron remembers some of his own visits to the studio. "I walked in," he says, "and John was on the phone with Paul McCartney. Certainly Rod and Elton were more frequent callers." Yet Cameron was still not sure the music was heading in the right direction.

"Brian and Bill had enormous respect and roots themselves," he says, "so it all sort of worked on paper. But the problem, in hindsight, I guess, was that they ended up making a straight-up, Canadian rock–sounding album."

By this time, Baldry and Oz were back in Toronto, living in a more affordable apartment at the Village by the Grange.

"He used to call it the Village by the *Deranged*," says Muncaster, "but he and Oz liked it, because it was close to the trendy Queen Street West strip, with shops, restaurants and clubs. John could sit in with Tony Flaim and the Downchild Blues Band, or go over and drop in at the Jarvis House and pick up a couple hundred bucks playing a solo folkie gig."

Muncaster wasn't actually managing Baldry's career, she

says, but she provided guidance. "I was just a Rosedale house-wife," she declares, "so I wasn't making any management decisions. But the most important thing was that I was nurturing, and that's what John needed."

"We got him into more mainstream gigs, like voice-overs, and more commercials," says Muncaster. "My ultimate musical plan was for him to go to Vegas, where he could make lots of money and then do whatever the hell he wanted. I mean, God knows John was already theatrical."

"Voice work was like 'falling off a log' money for John, although at first he didn't even want to put together a voice audition tape. He'd say, 'Who the hell do they think I am? I don't have to do any damn audition tape. I've got records, I've got history!' So he wouldn't do it. But Doug used to be in the advertising business, and he knew this man, Morgan Earl, who had a little studio in Yorkville. Of course it was easy for John, so he just aced it. He was quite pleased with himself after that, and it opened up the commercial world for him."

Baldry's deep, well-travelled voice lent gravity to any product he pitched. And voice work was, after all, acting. Instead of assuming the character of a Delta sharecropper, he'd be telling the story of Levi's jeans or explaining the engineering behind a Kawasaki motorcycle.

"You can go into the studio," Baldry told the BBC's Spencer Leigh, "read your lines, leave, and wait for the cheques to come in the mail. You don't have to travel very much, and you don't need a band."

"It certainly did supplement John's income," says Muncaster today, "so he wouldn't be beating his brains out on the road. Mind you, he would not give up the musical dream. And we didn't really want him to."

Although his voice work provided him with an easy revenue stream, Muncaster says that Baldry was still plagued by money problems.

"He had, like, three bank accounts, and [we were still] trying to pay all the people in England. British Telecom hadn't been paid thousands and thousands of pounds, and [John] still owed money for his tax bills. At one point we even suggested that he should file for bankruptcy, but he refused to do that, because of the stigma associated with it. He was a gentleman, and a gentleman does not go bankrupt."

Baldry was also resistant to the suggestion that he curtail his practice of keeping his band on a full-time retainer.

"We told him that he could not keep a band on a weekly salary," remembers Muncaster. "He was paying them all something like three hundred and fifty bucks a week, whether they were working or not. It just wasn't feasible. He was very upset about all that. But he knew he had no money. Eventually, a lot of them went off and did their own thing."

Once work was finished on *Rock with the Best*, Baldry was ready to tour in support of the album. He held auditions in Toronto for a new, pared-down version of the band.

"He settled on four people," remembers Muncaster, "including a drummer, Charlie Cooley, fresh out of Humber College's music program. He was somebody John could mould. Then we had keyboardist Gary Breit, who now plays with Bryan Adams. John immediately recognized his potential. They also picked George Ford, who was an older player John knew from England, back in the Beatles days. He was the veteran who looked after the rookies in the group. It was pretty rough going for a while, because they were so new and green. But they started getting better on the road."

Baldry played the larger clubs with his fresh, compact band while keeping up a schedule of intimate solo shows at festivals and smaller events. But the new album was, as industry insiders say, "underperforming at retail." Despite Baldry's great start with EMI, the law of diminishing returns caught up with him.

"What happened," Deane Cameron explains, "was that the first release ended up being the biggest hit. The follow-up album did okay, but it didn't have the sensational hits. And we threw everybody off with [the mainstream rock of] *Rock with the Best*. So we came to a parting of the ways. We were out of ideas. It wasn't an unpleasant parting, and I always talked to John, but you just get to the point sometimes where a partnership runs out of ideas."

As EMI prepared a "best of" compilation to recoup on their three-album investment, Baldry flew out to Montreal with Evelyn Muncaster to resume the tour. "The shows went well," Muncaster remembers. "He missed his Kathi, though. He'd call her in when he had enough money."

Oz Rexach says that, volatile as Baldry's relationship with McDonald could be, she was nevertheless the singer with whom he most enjoyed working.

"There was a lot of drama between them," says Rexach. "Kathi was like a Janis Joplin. As a matter of fact, when Janis died, Kathi was the lead singer for Big Brother and the Holding Company for years. Believe me, if anyone could raise Janis from the grave, it would be Kathi. But she followed the lifestyle, too, with the parties."

From time to time, Evelyn Muncaster recalled, they would hire other female singers. But Baldry would sulk that they "just weren't Kathi."

"Sometimes," she says, "after a show with one of these other singers, I'd turn to John and say, 'She sounded okay tonight, John,' and he'd just say, 'Aaargh, she's a cow!' It wasn't really their singing; it was that he missed Kathi. And he missed Oz on the road, too. Every night that he'd be away, he was on that phone to Oz. Every single night, no matter where he was."

On a western swing, Muncaster recalls, some of Baldry's old demons surfaced.

"Sometimes John would drink too much," she says, "and he'd come on late. I had to actually ask Doug to fly out west one time, because John was in a bloody rage about things. He went over the deep end, and nobody knew what he was mad about. I guess it must have been one of his bouts of depression, but nobody could do anything with him. So Doug had to fly out to straighten everything out. He got John calmed down, but I think he'd had a bad fit of depression, which manifested itself into a big 'Fuck off and die, all of you.'"

On the road and off, Baldry's health was faltering. Lack of exercise, a bad diet, and indulgences in drinking and smoking played havoc with his overall well-being.

"John's health was always up and down," says Oz Rexach today. "He liked to drink, although he didn't like to smoke marijuana, because he said it was bad for his epilepsy. I actually thought it would be good for him, but he was old-fashioned and didn't want to smoke it. I saw a lot of his seizures. They were infrequent, and sometimes he would go seven years without having one. He avoided strobe lights, anything that was too flashy, because it would sometimes trigger a seizure. He still smoked cigarettes, though. Then he developed an ulcer. Plus the stress, travelling and all that just got to him. He liked vodka in his earlier days, but in the latter part he just drank a little bit of wine. Beer wasn't that good, because it affected his gout. Gout is a chemical thing where your blood makes more uric acid. The uric acid builds up in your joints, and it's like crystals. It's very painful. He would get a flare-up in his knee or his toes. His toes would swell up, and he couldn't get his shoes on. His hands would sometimes suffer. His whole body was affected by it."

Kathi McDonald witnessed Baldry's gout with alarming frequency on the road.

"He'd get up on stage with the gout, and it was so painful," McDonald remembers. "It's terrible, but I used to tease him about it and call him a 'man a-gout town.' Of course, he didn't find that very funny. I once saw him hauled over the road cases backstage. But I tell you what, when that first note struck for him to sing, there would be a smile on that face and he'd be back up on that stage. He would tell the audience all about the gout in painful medical detail and make jokes about it."

After the EMI deal lapsed, Baldry parted with Dixon and Propas. Evelyn Muncaster, citing personal reasons, also left Baldry's employ.

"You know, I loved John," says Muncaster today, "but he was hard. I mean, when it was time to go on the road for a month or two months, everything would be left until the eleventh hour. I felt sorry for Oz sometimes, because on the last day he would be given the task of washing all the clothes and ironing all the shirts and dragging all the suitcases out, while John would be hollering at him, 'Where's my this?' or 'Where's my that?' But Oz would just laugh and say 'I'll get it, John, don't worry, it's coming.' Oz stayed cool. He knew how to humour him."

Adrift again, Baldry continued to do sporadic live shows and occasional voice work. His early training in coffee-house gigs came in handy, and he found he could put together a solo set, when he needed to, on his trusty twelve-string. After a successful stint at Toronto's Café in the Park, Baldry approached the club's manager, Ron Scribner, about running his career. It was a typical Baldry move. Scribner was genial and seemed to know what he was doing, so why not?

Jeff Edmunds remembers speaking with Scribner about Baldry at the time.

"They were working on trying to get John a new record deal," he says. "I even wrote letters to a few labels myself. John had done a recording of Creedence Clearwater Revival's 'Run through the Jungle' and a demo of the old Walker Brothers hit 'The Sun Ain't Gonna Shine Anymore,' but nothing came of those, and he and Scribner soon went their separate ways."

After five years of riding out career highs and lows in Toronto, Baldry realized he couldn't bear the thought of another freezing Ontario winter. On August 23, 1985, he and Oz moved to Vancouver.

Baldry had visited the West Coast regularly since the *It Ain't Easy* days. In 1984, he'd flown to British Columbia to play at a mountaintop benefit for the endangered Stein Valley, appearing alongside John Denver and noted environmentalist David Suzuki. He'd taken out Canadian citizenship in 1980.

"I liked Canada," he would later tell publicist Richard Flohil. "It had a lot of the energy of the United States without the downsides. I seemed to earn a degree of respect, and Canadian audiences liked my music. I thought, 'This could be home,' and I have never regretted that decision."

The next phase of Long John Baldry's life would bring a mixed bounty of domestic stability and ill health. But after years of being rock's nomadic Hamlet—dodging the slings and arrows of outrageously dwindled fortunes—he was ready to take a stab at peace and contentment.

. . .

it still ain't easy

Long John Baldry and his constant companion, Felix "Oz" Rexach, were the very picture of domesticity as they settled into a cozy two-bedroom apartment near Kitsilano Beach in Vancouver. Their spacious sundeck afforded them thrilling views of both the majestic Coast Mountains and the cool, blue-green waters of the Strait of Georgia. It still wasn't easy—Baldry wasn't getting rich, but at least he was breaking even in paradise.

The city of Vancouver was abuzz with preparations for the upcoming world's fair, Expo 86. Space-age structures and a new civic monorail system were transforming the sleepy, post-hippie town into a green-glass city of the future. In a one-page bio from that year, Baldry expressed boundless optimism for his adoptive hometown: "My fondness for Vancouver is well known, and I've long been regarded as part of the furnishings of the city anyway. I expect to be very involved with the goings-on of Expo."

By the time he moved west, Baldry had not recorded or released an album in over three years.

"John always had these long periods," says Baldry archivist Jeff Edmunds, "where nothing was happening musically. When he got to Vancouver, he did a lot of voice work. Without that work, he would've really been sunk."

Then a nightclub impresario named Gary Taylor made Baldry an offer: he would help launch a Baldry "comeback" album, via his independent label Musicline Records, and a cross-country tour to support it.

Oz Rexach was wary of Baldry's enthusiasm for the Taylor enterprise. "Long John was about to sign a management deal with him," says Rexach today. "John always seemed to have bad management, and after the Piranha Productions people screwed him, he really should have known better."

Nonetheless, Taylor and Baldry hatched a plan to record what would become the *Silent Treatment* album. The idea was to synchronize the album's release date with both the opening of Expo 86 and Baldry's thirtieth anniversary in show business. The project would also reunite Baldry with two old colleagues, Kathi McDonald and producer Jimmy Horowitz. Horowitz had been driven off by, among other things, Baldry's former managers, and he was equally leery about the new one, whom he called "another tacky individual."

"Despite that," says Horowitz, "I agreed to come out to Vancouver, and we started recording at Mushroom Studios with Rolf Hennemann engineering. John had enjoyed working there, on *Rock with the Best,* and I really loved it, too. It was the closest in feel to working back at IBC in London, so I was very comfortable there." Additional recording was done at Vancouver's Blue Wave Studios and at Cherokee Studios in Los Angeles.

In the short bio for *Silent Treatment,* Baldry boasted that his album was the real deal, with all the blood, sweat and guts that other records of the day lacked. "A lot of the L.A. stuff, these days, is often too fluffy," he said, "but these songs have got guts.

They are ultimately fabulous songs. They are danceable tunes, with *real* drums and *real* human noises."

In addition to Baldry's cover version of the Walker Brothers' "The Sun Ain't Gonna Shine Anymore," the album included Jack Green's "Life in Japan," Bobby "Blue" Bland's "Ain't No Love in the Heart of the City" and the self-explanatory finale, "A Life of Blues," in which Baldry coyly alluded to his standing as an "unmarried man" in couplets like, "The blues have been my total life / Meant more to me than any wife." He and Kathi McDonald reunited for a smoking version of Smokey Robinson's "Ain't That Peculiar," and Baldry once again demonstrated his uncanny ability to find great musicians with the addition of guitarist Papa John King and harmonica player Butch Coulter. Both musicians would remain in his bands for the rest of his career.

Baldry's first-ever rock video, produced by Frank Garcia and directed by Frank Anzalone, was created for the title song. Garcia recalls how he ended up producing the clip.

"I had just finished up the Fabulous Thunderbirds' break-out video for 'Tuff Enuff,'" he says, "when Papa John King contacted me. He knew that I was a big fan of LJB's music, and he told me that they were still mixing the *Silent Treatment* album and wanted a music video made for the title song."

Garcia noticed the on-set reverence for Baldry, who inspired the crew with what Garcia called his high degree of professionalism.

"He'd never made a music video before," says Garcia, "but you would never know it. The thing that summed up the shoot for me was the first take, the performance master shot. LJB and the band mimed the song to camera perfectly, and after the take, the whole crew stood up and gave Long John and the band a standing ovation."

Jeff Edmunds volunteered to do a "guerilla marketing" campaign for the album. "It was an independent release," says

Edmunds, "so I was phoning colleges and universities across Canada to get them to play it, and we actually got it added on some college and university charts."

As Frank Garcia completed a rough cut of the "Silent Treatment" video, he received word that his "Tuff Enuff" video was to receive the best video award at the Blues Foundation's W.C. Handy Awards, held in Memphis, Tennessee. Garcia asked Baldry to accompany him to the ceremony, which was hosted by B.B. King and Carl Perkins.

"It didn't take LJB very long to say yes," Garcia recalls, "and the Blues Foundation's director, Joe Savarin, quickly made arrangements to accommodate him and include him in the star-studded blues lineup."

On the morning of the show, Garcia and Baldry were invited to a formal breakfast attended by the Blues Foundation's board of directors and various music and media executives. "A huge video screen was brought into the conference room," Garcia recalls, "so we could debut the 'Silent Treatment' video."

Joe Savarin asked Baldry to come up on stage to explain just what the blues meant to him.

"John didn't go up to the podium," says Garcia. "He just stood up at our table, without a microphone, and in his perfect English, told the room of about a hundred plus people about his passion and love for Big Bill Broonzy, Muddy Waters and his close friend Willie Dixon. I had not seen Baldry's public-speaker side before. Everyone was in awe of his amazing presence, powerful voice and heartfelt words. When he finished, the room erupted with applause and a standing ovation. Then they played the 'Silent Treatment' video. The room went wild, like it was Saturday night. When the video finished, he got *another* standing ovation. I was truly honoured to receive my own award from the Blues Foundation that evening, but the real honour was spending those moments with LJB in Memphis."

While in Memphis, Baldry ran into legendary music manager Chesley Millikin, an Irish-born former head of Epic Records in London, who had worked magic in the careers of Jackson Browne, Charlie Sexton and Stevie Ray Vaughan. Baldry told Millikin all about his bad luck with managers. Millikin, at that point based in Austin, Texas, responded by saying that he would like to manage Baldry internationally.

"John was thrilled about that," remembers Jeff Edmunds, "but then Gary Taylor came and demanded that he retain John for North America. So Chesley backed off. John stayed with Taylor for a couple of years more, and I helped out as they launched the *Silent Treatment* tour."

Drummer Vince Ditrich, who now lives on Vancouver Island, recalls how he came to join John Baldry's merry band around this time.

"I auditioned for John in the spring of 1987," says Ditrich, "and stayed until around 1991. Like any musician, I had been well aware of John for years and years; I'd worked clubs where we opened for him, or where we helped set up the band's equipment. I was quite awed at the thought that I might be able to work with him. In the band, among others, were George Ford and Jimmy Horowitz, both long-time Baldry cohorts. Kathi McDonald was not singing with him at the time, and in her stead was Kirsten Nash, who also played tenor sax."

McDonald was once again absent from a John Baldry tour, only this time it was not her choice or Baldry's. McDonald, it transpired, was locked away in the Skagit County jail, in her native Washington State, on what she still insists was a "trumped-up" misdemeanour drug charge.

"I know," laughs McDonald, "everyone always says, 'It wasn't my pot, officer!' but really, I had nothing to do with it. What happened was that I had bought this house back in my hometown, Mount Vernon. My dad had helped me with the down payment.

I was away in Canada playing with John, and my ex-husband, who was a bit of a drinker and a pothead, had been living in my house. Unbeknownst to me, he'd been growing marijuana plants on my land. Well, he'd gone out to some bar and shot his mouth off to another guy he'd just met about how he had this incredibly high-grade marijuana growing in his home. He invited the guy to the house to see the stuff. And, naturally, [the guy from the bar] turned out to be a DEA agent. The house was in my name, so they waited for me to come home weeks later. I'll never forget it. I was sitting in my front room at 1:34 PM watching *One Life to Live* with my new kitty-cat on my lap when all of sudden this SWAT team stormed into the house. They said I could either co-operate with the search or they'd rip up the place with crowbars. They found all this pot. The cops said it was either me or my dad who was going to jail, since his name was also on the mortgage."

McDonald took the rap herself and was sentenced to six months and seven days. That meant she would have to sit out the *Silent Treatment* tour.

"I was pissed," says McDonald, "because it was a good tour, where everyone was gonna get paid for once. They had even borrowed a proper tour bus from Ronnie Hawkins. But John, God bless him, was great. He told everyone I'd gone off to 'charm school,' and he visited me every week, signing autographs for all the staff and inmates. I was actually treated well inside, and I even got to go out on a work release program. My lawyer drove me back to Canada, if you can believe it, to do the video for 'Ain't That Peculiar.' John had threatened that if I couldn't make it to the shoot, he'd use a ventriloquist's dummy to represent me in the video." Soon after her release, McDonald was back on the road with the band.

By now, Baldry was entering the "legacy" phase of his career, and Canada afforded him a chance to be a kind of rock star emeritus. Vince Ditrich, the neophyte in the band, says that Baldry was generous about sharing his rich history in rock.

"I was only twenty-three at the time," says Ditrich, "wet behind the ears and lily-white in behaviour. John never claimed to be a great musician, but he took great pride in what he saw as a special and acute ability to recognize nascent talent. He put increasing stock in his capacity to recognize talent early. I think it was a natural way to elegantly channel the weight Canadians assigned him. John was a raconteur of unsurpassed ability, and I learned much about telling a story from this master. He would often tell us about how he discovered Rod or Reg and charming little vignettes of drinking and carousing, which we gobbled up with laughter and enthusiasm. He was quite avuncular with me, and seemed very much to appreciate how seriously I took the gig, while at the same time snickering about how much of a choirboy I was, comparatively, amongst that gaggle of loony partying machines. He often, very generously, made reference to my falling into the category of talents he had discovered, which meant a great deal to me. I was one degree of separation from the Beatles, the Stones, Clapton, Elton John, Jimmy Page and the rest."

Oz Rexach, however, notes that Baldry's legendary status sometimes threatened to overwhelm their Kitsilano home.

"That was the hardest part of it all, for John," says Rexach. "It was always 'Legendry John Baldry,' and it was tough to live with that. Sure, it was true, John had been there way back when— John Lee Hooker always remembered John as 'the white kid with the blues voice'—and he really did command that respect. He knew he was unique, people who knew music knew him, but on the other hand, he never really got the recognition that he thought he rightly deserved. So I think it became a source of frustration. Why did all these other people he helped make it so big, and not him? After a while, it was like a curse."

The *Silent Treatment* tour was mostly well attended, and the reviews were politely positive. According to a Musicline tour report provided by Jeff Edmunds, attendance figures from May to June 1987 ranged from approximately three hundred people at Montreal's Club Soda to over ten thousand patrons for a three-night stand at the Ontario Place Forum in Toronto.

"The record was doing all right as an independent," says Edmunds, "and then EMI picked it up for distribution. Ultimately, though, it was another in a series of false starts for John. Something good would happen, then nothing got built on it."

Baldry confessed to the *Toronto Sun*'s Bob Thompson that the album had been "a slow mover" at retail. "It has taken people a while to realize its existence," he said, "and then when they do realize, it takes a little while for them to like it."

He was guardedly optimistic, if perhaps a little too frank, about the *Silent Treatment* tour in an interview with Stephen Godfrey of the *Globe and Mail*.

"No, no, it's great," he told Godfrey, "I really do enjoy performing. It's just been... a rocky start. The band has only been together ten days, you know? But I think the tour will be excellent. It's an extremely well-played album. But people have been saying it isn't *bluesy* enough. How was I supposed to know that just after we finished it, blues would come back into fashion, through people like Robert Cray or TV stars like Bruce Willis? My timing seems to be perverse. I have always been terrified of cashing in on... things which I helped start, like the blues thing in England and its influence on America."

Baldry also resisted the suggestion that the new album was any sort of a comeback. "I hate the word 'comeback,'" he scoffed to journalist Joel Rubinoff of the *London* [Ontario] *Free Press*. "It's an awful word. It's horrid. Use *renaissance* if you like."

On the topic of his health, he was candid with reporters about the crippling effects of his gout—making reference to his "special gout shoes," of which he had several pairs—and to continuing bronchial and sinus problems. His brother, Roger, recalls that around this time he and others, including Gary Taylor, had tried in vain to get John to eat better, drink less and take up an exercise regimen.

Man and his goat: Mayley dances to her master's voice, Muswell Hill,
October 31, 1973.

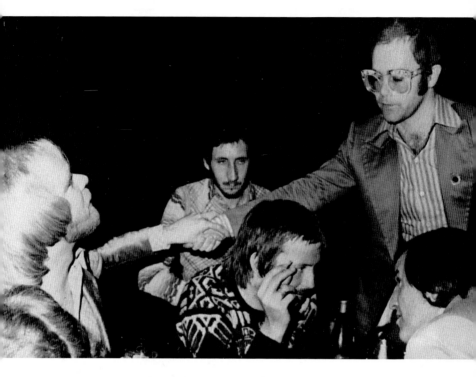

above: Holding court at the Speakeasy, London, 1973. *Left to right:* Baldry, Pete Townshend, Eric Clapton, Elton John and Alan Price (The Animals). UNATTRIBUTED MAGAZINE PHOTO / COURTESY PERSONAL COLLECTION OF JOHN BALDRY

facing page, top: Elton John and Rod Stewart, Baldry's star pupils, produced a side each of his 1971 U.S. debut, *It Ain't Easy.* © 1971 WARNER BROS. RECORDS

facing page, bottom: Ron Wood's Lewis Carroll–inspired drawing of John as the Mad Hatter adorns the cover of *Everything Stops for Tea*, once again produced by Baldry protégés Elton and Rod. © 1972 WARNER BROS. RECORDS

above: Welcome to Club Casablanca, 1976. What appeared to be an exotic desert oasis nightclub was actually label boss Neil Bogart's extravagantly themed office. CASABLANCA RECORDS / COURTESY JEFF EDMUNDS COLLECTION

facing page: A cheery Baldry doffs his cap for a 1976 Casablanca Records promotional photo. COURTESY PERSONAL COLLECTION OF JOHN BALDRY

above: Baldry puts a spell on Canada, Commodore Ballroom, Vancouver, 1979. © DEE LIPPINGWELL / DEE LIPPINGWELL PHOTOGRAPHY

facing page: Baldry and "Roddy" camp it up for Stewart's then wife Britt Ekland in Stewart's home, Los Angeles, 1978. COURTESY PERSONAL COLLECTION OF JOHN BALDRY

below: Faux zebra–clad Baldry celebrates his outrageousness in America, 1979. "In England," he later said, "I was stifled…Here you can do what you like." COURTESY PERSONAL COLLECTION OF JOHN BALDRY

facing page: Spandex and leather: Baldry squares off with Kathi McDonald, Bottom Line, New York City, August 27, 1979. COURTESY JEFF EDMUNDS COLLECTION

above: Proud partners John and Oz (Felix Rexach) celebrate happier times.
COURTESY PERSONAL COLLECTION OF JOHN BALDRY

facing page, top: EMI Canada gold record ceremony for *Baldry's Out*, 1981.
Left to right: Don Grierson, Kathi McDonald, Baldry, Jim Mazza, Gary Gersh
and unidentified. EMI PHOTO / COURTESY PERSONAL COLLECTION OF JOHN BALDRY

facing page, bottom: Backstage with the Moody Blues, Toronto, 1980. *Left
to right:* Patrick Moraz, John Lodge, Baldry, Ray Thomas, Justin Hayward
and Graeme Edge. COURTESY PERSONAL COLLECTION OF JOHN BALDRY

above: Charity event, Vancouver, 1995. *Left to right:*
Baldry, Kirsten Nash, Doc Fingers, Tom Jones. Old
pals, Baldry and Jones jammed well into the morning.

facing page: "John," says Eric Clapton today,
"was actually more powerful to me when he was
on his own, just playing acoustic." © PETER DONISH /

above: Roddy gives a brotherly hug to his mentor on Baldry's sixtieth birthday, Vancouver. COURTESY PERSONAL COLLECTION OF JOHN BALDRY

facing page: Never-before-published outtake from promotional shoot for Stony Plain Records' *Right to Sing the Blues.* Edmonton, October 29, 1996. © RICHARD SIEMENS PHOTOGRAPHY

top: Baldry with Mike McCartney. "My wife, Ro, took this at the Royal Alberta Museum," adds McCartney, "when I brought my *Liverpool Life* exhibition to Edmonton in 2001." © MIKE MCCARTNEY

bottom: Barrister Hall, Columbus, Ohio, July 19, 2004, believed to be Baldry's final U.S. performance. © ANDREW MYERS, ANDREW MYERS PHOTOGRAPHY / RANDY WEIDENBUSCH, FLASHBACK PHOTOGRAPHY

Vince Ditrich noticed in 1987 that Baldry's health seemed "precarious."

"John was a heavy drinker," said Ditrich, "and it was not uncommon for him to drift off to sleep in a chair after the show, from fatigue and far, far too many drinks. He also ate things like lobster, caviar, curry and exotic cheeses. Gout, of course, was an unwelcome companion on a number of tours, and he'd hobble around, with often much hand-wringing before the show, about whether or not he could go on. There were some notably disastrous dismounts from stages as he became less and less steady on his pins. I felt that he was becoming prematurely old, but I also thought he might be able to reverse this trend if he just laid off the booze a bit."

Ditrich also recalls that the roadhouses he played with Baldry were often somewhat beneath an artist of legendary stature.

"I don't think John had much patience for the shitty gigs that he was often dealt," says Ditrich. "I can only imagine the thoughts running through his head about the grand theatres he'd performed or the greater success of his many protégés as he played to drunken hooligans in a godforsaken beer parlour in the middle of nowhere. I remember playing to a room full of ungrateful drunks in Kamloops, B.C. They were mostly uninterested except to heckle until we finished the last song of the set. Then they went apeshit, presumably because the end of the show proclaimed that last call was nigh. John was totally disgusted, and after what must have been three solid minutes of foot-stomping and screaming, he turned to us and spat out, 'Oh, very well... Let's give them cunting 'Loving Feeling.'"

According to Jeff Edmunds, who saw the damage reports, the sheer scale of the *Silent Treatment* tour doomed it to hemorrhage cash. "John had an eight- or nine-person band with him," he says. "I'm not sure who was financing the tour, but I know it wasn't Taylor."

As usual, Baldry's management at the time had proved ineffectual as far as career direction was concerned. Ditrich speculates that Baldry's bad luck with managers may have had something to do with his tendency to place social interaction above business sense.

"John had difficulty in separating the hangers-on from the real movers and shakers," Ditrich observed. "Management issues, accounting issues, booking issues all got very clouded and disorganized as unqualified persons interfered, often in order to make their groupie-dom appear more legit. I don't suppose the various management organizations in Canada that he worked with were ever particularly stellar in their effect, but they must have been seriously impeded by the halo of interference that seemed to follow John. He would have benefited from a solid team of pros who insulated him from unwelcome distractions."

One welcome distraction from the road came in late 1987, when Baldry was coaxed back into musical theatre. A Vancouver secretary-turned–stage producer named Pat Waldron hired him to play Captain Hook in a big-budget theatrical production of *Peter Pan* that featured U.S. Olympic gymnast Cathy Rigby in the title role. Jeff Hyslop, who would go on to fame for his performances in *Phantom of the Opera* and *Kiss of the Spider Woman,* was hired to direct. In his red velvet pirate costume, Baldry's Hook bore an uncanny resemblance to Captain Morgan from the rum bottles.

"He could play it very funny," says Waldron, "and the comparison between five-foot-tall Cathy Rigby and six-foot-seven John was very funny, visually. There was some flying on wires involved, and John didn't like heights. When the pirates went to hoist him up one day he said, 'Cease and desist! Put me down!'"

In an interview with the *Hamilton Spectator*'s Nick Krewen, Baldry admitted that the role allowed him to even be more outrageous than usual.

"It helps me get rid of a lot of my inhibitions," he told Krewen. "There's a lot of things you can get away with while hiding in a costume. I can be a lot more daring than Mr. Baldry, blues singer, onstage."

He also told Krewen he enjoyed the responsibility of a nightly production. "The discipline involved is very good. There's little room for ad-libbing, and you have to be there on time. You daren't be late because you have a family of thirty-five [depending] on you."

Peter Pan opened at Vancouver's Queen Elizabeth Theatre for a three-week run and was remounted for a few more weeks in Seattle and Spokane, Washington. The show won four local Jessie Awards, and the *Globe and Mail*'s Stephen Godfrey was among the critics who raved about the "colourful, thoroughly professional affair." His otherwise glowing review was marred by two negatives, however: Hyslop's choreography, which he found "stale," and Baldry's performance, which he felt was too camp.

"The other chief weakness," Godfrey wrote, "is in Baldry's Captain Hook. It seems like perfect casting: Baldry has a nicely insinuating speaking voice, a feline purr with a dash of gravel. But he doesn't sing particularly well here, and his acting, both as Mr. Darling and Hook, is awkward and insincere. The Captain and his campy pirates are too bland to be worthy foes for a gang of lost boys looking for adventure."

Baldry was greatly moved when his old comrade from the London days, Lionel Bart, made the trip over to Vancouver for the opening of *Peter Pan*.

"He was thrilled," says Waldron, "that Lionel came out from England. He was definitely quite a crazy man and had lived quite the wild life from what I gather. John told me that apparently Lionel had been ripped off terribly for his royalties from *Oliver!* He had struggled for years until he finally ended up getting his full fee paid to him."

Another figure from '60s London, Andrew Loog Oldham, was also living part-time in Vancouver by then.

"John told me Lionel came over to see him," says Oldham, "but he turned up here a month early by mistake. John said that Lionel had only said to him, 'Find me an A.A. meeting, but one with pretty boys.'"

Sadly, and perhaps inevitably, even Baldry's triumphant return to the stage was marred by unfortunate business dealings.

"Gary McAvay of Columbia Artists had offered our production a U.S. tour," Pat Waldron recalls. "John was thrilled, of course, to get a chance to be on Broadway and take the show on a long tour all through the States. But Cathy Rigby's manager-husband, Tom McCoy, told them, 'If you want Cathy Rigby in the show, you have to let me produce it.' They did, and so he scooped the touring rights from under us. It was two years of heartbreak. We went bankrupt, and he made seven million bucks."

Evelyn Muncaster also flew in for the show. Baldry was in his element, she says, in the musical theatre setting. "I never saw John look better, or look as fit. I had always thought he should do a one-man oral history of the blues, where he could tell stories and then play a few songs in between on his twelve-string. Of course he never got to do it."

Pat Waldron actually recalls discussing such a project with Baldry immediately after *Peter Pan* closed.

"It was to do with this guitar," she explains. "It starts out in slavery, and it's about this guitar passing from person to person. It's this one guitar, a metaphor for the evolution of the music. Every person had a different approach to playing this guitar. It was an excellent concept, because it gave you a real history of the beginnings of jazz. They went to New Orleans, to Chicago, to the '20s, over to Britain, the first rock 'n' roll stuff, and then to New York. It was an interesting script, and it promised to be a fascinating project, but we never had the money, the time or the focus."

By 1989, guitarist Al Harlow was back in Vancouver, where he continued his music career while also teaching at North Vancouver's Capilano College. He invited Baldry to give a lecture in his music history class.

"I just asked John, as a favour, if he would produce a history of British blues," says Harlow. "He immediately replied, 'Why, of course, young Alan, I'd be delighted.' So he took his guitars in, and not only did he tell the entire history of the British blues and his own role in it, including lots of modest anecdotes, but he also delivered an incredible one-man concert. We're talking noon here on a November afternoon. The whole thing was taped, and I have to say, it's as good a documentary of the blues as you would ever hear on the BBC."

Baldry split with Gary Taylor that year, but unfinished business, as usual, remained. In a handwritten accounting request from 2001, he spelled out his allegations, vis-à-vis the *Silent Treatment* album.

"Most musicians, studios, etc. were not fully paid by Mr. Taylor for this project," Baldry accused, in bold calligraphic strokes, "although he has made a lot of money selling copyrights to the recordings, territory by territory. He has not paid any royalty for this... or any kind of advance. Is regarded by Vancouver legal profession as ultra-slippery or 'litigation-proof.'"

Jeff Edmunds speculates that Baldry's dealings with Taylor were the straw that broke the camel's back. "John never really had a manager after that," he says. "He never trusted anyone enough."

Baldry did establish himself firmly as a local fixture in Vancouver, freelancing and doing more voice work, performing one-off gigs at the famous Commodore Ballroom and turning out for benefit concerts for local charities. David Marsden, who lived in Vancouver for ten years, remembers that "whenever there was money to be raised, or performers needed, John Baldry was always the first one in line. Whether it was raising money for AIDS, starving children or animals, there was no differential for him."

Al Harlow recalls one charity event in which Baldry teamed up with a celebrated Welsh friend.

"Tom Jones had come to Vancouver to do a fundraiser for [local entrepreneur and philanthropist] Jacqui Cohen," says Harlow. "There was an all-nighter afterwards at her restaurant. Tom and John were very good friends, so the liquor and the cigars flowed that night. Jones turned around to John, with his cigar, his stem glass and the microphone all in one hand, and said, 'John, do you remember 'Bring 'Em Down?' John said, 'Of course I do. Shall we?' It was great. They played till five o'clock in the morning."

Throughout the '90s, Baldry was also a regular performer at the many prestigious folk and blues festivals across western Canada and the Pacific Northwest States. Years earlier, he had formed a solid friendship with the Edmonton Folk Festival's artistic director, Holger Petersen. Petersen, who also presides over the roots music label Stony Plain Records, remembers well meeting Baldry for the first time.

"I was already aware of John through R&B *Live from the Marquee*," he says, "and I think John should have received more credit on the cover of that album. I'd also heard the United Artists release, *Long John's Blues*, as early as about 1969, when it came out in Canada. So I was aware of his blues roots. I think it was shortly after he moved to Canada that he started coming through Edmonton with any regularity. The very first show he did in Edmonton was at the Highwayman, which was a very large tavern where they used to do concerts. I had, and still have, a blues show on radio station CKUA, and as I interviewed him, I found that I really enjoyed talking to him. I especially liked his clear devotion to the blues and the fact that he really was just a great storyteller, so informative and so passionate about what he was talking about. I wound up meeting the rest of the band and hanging out with them most of the night. So every time John would come through, with all these wonderful people, I would end up partying with them and leaving at daylight with a huge smile on my face."

The two formed a lasting personal and professional relationship, Petersen says. "It got to the point where we'd just end up hanging out all the time. Going out for Indian food in Edmonton was a ritual."

In the summer of 1989, Baldry played as a member of his good friend Willie Dixon's Dream Band. He told Holger Petersen about it on his *Natch'l Blues* program.

"It was a wonderful lineup," Baldry enthused, "possibly one of the finest I've ever been in. There was Mose Alison on piano, Al Duncan on drums and, on bass, the very fine jazz bassist Rob Wasserman. There was Cash McCall on guitar—great guitar player, you don't hear enough of the guy these days—Cary Bell on harmonica and myself on guitar."

Baldry noted with sadness that Dixon did not get to perform with his own Dream Band.

"We were booked to play the Benson & Hedges Blues Festival in Atlanta," Baldry explained, "and that was the first time that Willie ended up in hospital, in the last few months before he died. He had had a really bad fall down the stairs, and couldn't travel at that time, so the organizers of the festival were disappointed, naturally. But they said, 'Well, even though Willie can't come, can we have the band anyway?'—which was a nice gesture."

At the festival, the Willie Dixon Dream Band joined an all-star bill that included B.B. King, Johnny Winter and Ruth Brown, among others. After the show, Baldry wanted to tell Dixon in person what a great gig it had been. So rather than fly directly home to Vancouver, he stopped in to visit Dixon in Los Angeles.

"He was back at home and recovering," Baldry told Petersen, "at his beautiful home in Glendale. He was telling me his plans for a recording studio when, unfortunately, he started having a stroke in the garden."

Baldry called out to Dixon's wife, who phoned for an ambulance while Baldry tried his best to prop up his three-hundred-pound friend.

"The last time I saw him alive," Baldry recalled, "he sort of gave me a little wave from the ambulance as it took off."

In the coming year, Baldry would also grieve the deaths of both his parents. It was a devastating blow, as he had remained very close with them, particularly his doting mother. He later described the worst moment of his life as "losing my mother and father, in 1989 and '90, within four weeks of each other."

A happier moment came in 1991, however, when Baldry was hired to voice the title character in the CBC animated series *Nilus the Sandman*. The role was perfect for his baritone voice, which by now had attained a paternal grain in the lower frequencies. He was thrilled to play Nilus, a witty and whimsical guide to a world of music, dreams and imagination. Fellow musicians Don Francks and Holly Cole also lent their voices to the series, which ran on Canadian television for over six years.

"The feel I was giving the character," Baldry explained to Les Wiseman in *TV Guide*, "was slightly eccentric, Peter O'Toolish. Authoritative, but still the kind of person kids can relate to, a father figure who growls and purrs."

Holger Petersen had made it clear that he would love to do a blues record with Baldry, and between voice work sessions, the two began discussing Baldry's Stony Plain debut. The recording would be called *It Still Ain't Easy*, to commemorate the twentieth anniversary of the release of *It Ain't Easy*. "There are a couple of tunes on it," says Petersen today, "like 'The Busker,' that carried on that theme, with the narrated introductions and that sort of thing."

Baldry and Petersen hired Tom Lavin, from Vancouver's Powder Blues Band, to produce the album and enlisted players from the Vancouver scene, such as Amos Garrett and Colin James. Garrett was especially appreciated on one of the album's jazzier numbers, "Midnight in New Orleans" (he also appeared in the video) and on the title cut. James played for no fee, according to Petersen, on "You Wanna Dance."

Some other great guitarists were featured as well, including Papa John King, Gaye Delorme and Alligator recording artist Lucky Peterson, the latter joining B.B. King's former rhythm section, Tony Coleman and Russell Jackson, on "One Step Ahead" and "Shake That Thang." Baldry also brought in Bobby King and Terry Evans, backup singers who had worked with Ry Cooder, to lend their voices to "Get It while the Gettin's Good." He showed off his own "folkie" side on "Can't Keep from Cryin'."

"I really enjoyed doing that album," says Petersen. "I helped select a lot of the material, and John really nailed it. I love the way he combines his acoustic and electric sides."

A territorial deal with Germany's Hypertension Records had kept Baldry connected to his German fan base, an audience he had nurtured since the early days of his career in Hamburg. In April of 1993, he returned to Hamburg's Club Fabrik, assisted by a full band, to make a live recording that became Baldry's second Stony Plain release, *On Stage Tonight, Baldry's Out!—Live in Germany.*

Baldry explained his love of Germany, and of continental Europe in general, in Stony Plain press materials of the time. "I think the most satisfying thing about playing in Europe," he said, "is the enthusiasm of the audiences... who seem to respect us as musicians and who love the music. And during the day, we get to be rock 'n' roll travellers amid wonderful scenery, wining and dining well as we go."

Kathi McDonald was generally right by Baldry's side on these day trips, sightseeing and partaking of the local delicacies.

"Once, we went up to Neuschwanstein Castle," recalls McDonald, "the royal palace in the Bavarian Alps. We just had a really great time, and they served drinks and cake afterwards. John spoke fluent German, and he used to say that whenever he crossed over that border, it clicked in like a computer. 'It's all in German,' he'd say, 'I think in German and I dream in German.' And it was true; he totally turned into a German-speaking person. Germans would tell him, 'What an amazing accent you have.' He was terrible sometimes, though, doing imitations of Adolph Hitler on stage. Probably some kind of subconscious thing; remember, he was born in the Blitz and put underground. He said he'd never forget the sound, the mood and the darkness of it all. How could a kid forget something like that?"

Back in Vancouver, Baldry continued to work on the *Nilus* series while picking up commercial work. In 1993, he lent his voice to the character Dr. Ivo Robotnik in the animated television series *Adventures of Sonic the Hedgehog.* Despite these projects, Baldry's life in Vancouver was a far cry from the life he'd known in London. Geographically and metaphorically, he'd come a long way from rocking out at Eel Pie Island or walking the goat on Hampstead Heath. Vince Ditrich would often see Baldry, with Oz, out and about in the city. He appeared, to Ditrich's eyes, to be content.

"Vancouver was loosey-goosey, socially," says Ditrich. "The open and liberal atmosphere in the city must have been a soothing and secure place for a same-sex couple to live. Although I should point out their comfortable penthouse apartment on Maple Street was the scene of a lot of madness, and if there is ever a need for a new sitcom premise, one could look no further. I think he also enjoyed that he could walk to many of the places he needed to go, since he never got a driving licence—he was the most neurotic passenger I have ever witnessed. His collection of friends and acquaintances was large and exceptionally varied.

He almost always acted as if he were a member of the nobility, but he adored nothing more than 'madness,' which was his code for an environment of chaotic excesses—which in his Baldry-esque way would always be viewed through the lens of comedy of errors, or farce, later recounted with a large helping of caricature and mimicry to make his stories more colourful."

Bill Henderson recalls that Baldry had become a valued member of the Vancouver music community, and a generous one.

"One year I was hosting the West Coast Music Awards," Henderson says, "and the first thing I did was come out and sing my song 'Raino,' with my acoustic guitar. At the end I did this little bit of vocal embroidery, a little bit of fancy stuff. John came on right after me and said, 'Whoa, did you hear that beautiful sound—it was like birds fluttering down.' It was such a sweet and wonderful thing to say, and I was quite touched."

In 1995, EMI released another "Best of" album, this time a two-disc retrospective called *Long John Baldry: A Thrill's a Thrill—The Canadian Years*. The respectfully packaged set came with detailed liner notes by Baldry's friend and publicist Richard Flohil and photographs from the 1979 era up to 1995.

Later that year, Baldry and Rexach moved out of the penthouse to a second-storey condo above a futon shop on 4th Avenue, still within walking distance of the beach. Entering the compact apartment, visitors were struck by the books, CDs, guitars and antique furnishings packed into every corner. Baldry's library was stacked high with hardback biographies and history books on subjects ranging from Alexander the Great and the Roman Empire to the Battle of Hastings, along with a dog-eared edition of *The Diary of Samuel Pepys*.

"Long John loved history," says Rexach. "He would just sit here, in the light, reading and listening to music. And he was also an avid collector of antiques, particularly Victorian Eastlake furniture. I remember once he did an interview with

Pamela Wallin for CTV where he talked quite candidly about the furniture, all his hobbies, his collecting. I lived with him for twenty-seven years and for about twenty-five of them, we collected and accumulated a lot of stuff."

Shortly after they moved, Baldry had a significant health scare. The episode would signal the beginning of his slow physical decline over the next decade.

"John had a bleeding ulcer," Rexach recalls, "and we had to rush him to the emergency. I thought he was just not feeling well, because we had had some curry earlier and he had said his stomach was hurting. But at the hospital they had to do a major operation to prevent the bleeding. That was his wake-up call. I remember Margaret came over and looked after him, nursed him back to health. He quit smoking after that. He never had another cigarette for the rest of his life. But when you are in a blues bar or club, everyone is smoking. Even if you are not smoking you're breathing it in. He wouldn't play certain clubs because people smoked there. He made a point, even in Germany, where people liked to just sit around and smoke sometimes, he wouldn't play in theatres that had smoking. I couldn't smoke around the house. I had to go outside."

As was par for the course in Baldry's life, this terrible incident was followed by a career highlight, his next recording for Stony Plain, 1996's *Right to Sing the Blues*. Baldry's most authentically bluesy release since he had moved to Canada, the album would go on to win the 1997 Juno Award, the Canadian industry's highest honour, for Blues Album of the Year.

Papa John King once again provided some dominant guitar work, while Kathi McDonald sang her heart out with Baldry on "Midnight Hour Blues." The album's title track was written by Daryl Burgess and guitar ace Colin James, who also provided the track's wailing guitar solo. Baldry also tackled old favourites like Little Willie John's "I'm Shakin'," another version of Bonnie

Dobson's "Morning Dew," and two songs from his earliest influences, Lead Belly and Big Bill Broonzy, on "East Virginia Blues" and "Whoa Back Buck." Holger Petersen joined the chorus on the rowdy sing-along "They Raided the Joint."

"We recorded *Right to Sing the Blues* in Edmonton," says Petersen today, "and used different combinations of people. Some from John's band, like Kathi and Papa John, along with some Edmonton players like Bodhan Hluszko or Rusty Reed from Jann Arden's band. It was always fun in the recording studio, and I thought he was very focussed. By then, he'd had a lot of experience doing jingles and voiceovers, so he was very professional when he did his parts. Even at the session for the album photographs—John with this great smile and his Panama hat, or sitting in a chair playing a twelve-string... you could tell he really knew what he was doing."

In 1998, Baldry was nominated for another award, this time a Grammy for Best Children's Spoken Word Album for his narration on Disney's *The Original Story of Winnie the Pooh*, a project he'd secured through Anya Wilson and her husband, *Billboard* magazine columnist Larry Le Blanc. The category featured narrations by the likes of Gabriel Byrne and Eric Idle. In what can only be termed a comical irony, Baldry lost out to yet another *Winnie the Pooh* recording, this one read by beloved former CBS newsman Charles Kuralt, who had passed away the previous year.

On the music front, Baldry formed an economical three-piece band, featuring new find Matt Taylor on guitar and Butch Coulter on harmonica, to take to Europe for a mini-tour. In Hamburg, the trio touched down at the Downtown Blues Club, where on September 21, 1999, they recorded a second live album: *Live, Long John Baldry Trio*. Baldry gushed about Taylor in the liner notes to the Stony Plain release, predicting the young guitarist would become "one of the great leading virtuosi of this new millennium."

Baldry had planned to visit with his sister and brother before continuing the European tour with some small British dates. One night, though, just before showtime in Oxford, his precarious health took a turn for the worse.

"He had actually been here visiting me," recalls Margaret Baldry. "I said to John, 'You really, really do not look well enough to be doing these tours.' He moaned, 'I have to do it, though. I need the money.'... His first gig was at Banbury, in Oxfordshire. He did the first set of the gig and just started kicking everything over and called out, 'Somebody, can you please take me to hospital?'"

"I'd had a slow bleeding ulcer that I didn't know even existed," Baldry would explain in a 2001 interview with *The New Breed* magazine. "Then suddenly on this night, all hell broke loose. It went bang, just like in *Alien*... I was taking some medication for my arthritis, called Indomethacin, which has a very bad side effect for some users causing stomach problems. The trouble is that because it is a pain-killer, you don't sense that you're in pain!"

Margaret rushed to her brother's bedside at Oxford's Horton Hospital, staying with John as he was transferred to the intensive care ward. "They were giving him blood transfusions," she recalls. "He was having fits, and he was very, very ill. He wouldn't eat a thing."

When he was discharged from Horton Hospital, Baldry was moved to his brother's home in Hampshire, where, says Roger, "after two or three days, his condition deteriorated."

"He developed gout all over his body, in every single joint," explains Margaret. "I think it was a reaction to everything that had happened to him, the illness, having a transfusion, not eating anything. He was screaming in pain."

Just as Margaret and Roger were discussing what to do, Baldry's old protégé, Rod Stewart, stepped in to save the day.

"Rod apparently arranged for the ambulance to collect John and take him to the London Clinic," says Roger. "I remember it was late on a very frosty Saturday evening when the ambulance arrived."

"He was in the clinic for about three weeks," adds Margaret. "Rod said, 'I don't care what it costs,' although Roger had offered to pay, and John's medical insurance ended up paying for it."

Anya Wilson phoned her old friend Baldry while he was recuperating at the posh London clinic. "He said, 'Rod's put me in here now,'" remembers Wilson. "I think Rod was just so distressed to see John in agony... without anyone seeming to know what was wrong, or what the correct treatment should be."

Baldry recovered, but he was never the same again. In 2001, he celebrated his sixtieth birthday with an extravaganza at Vancouver's Commodore Ballroom, taped for a later television broadcast. Although he was able to perform and to enjoy the party, he was not in the best shape physically.

Evelyn Muncaster had flown out for the party, and she noticed the stress in his voice and facial expressions. "It was so hard for him," she recalls. "I had been to a number of his birthdays at the Commodore, and that year he was just in so much pain."

True-life stories, unlike movies and novels, rarely resolve with the main character coming full circle. Yet, for Long John Baldry, that is exactly what happened. In 2001, on what would be his last recording project, *Remembering Lead Belly,* he paid tribute to the man who had inspired him to make his own music.

The album's producer, Andreas Schuld, approached the recording in much the same way John Lomax had conducted the field recordings he had made of Huddie Ledbetter in the late '30s and early '40s, for the U.S. Library of Congress.

"Instead of a wire recorder, as used originally by Lomax," Schuld explained in the liner notes, "we used a hard-disk recorder and—as Lomax—one cheap mike for most of it." Since the digital recording gear was extremely portable, Schuld found it easy to bring the studio to Baldry, who recorded his performances in his own bedroom. Having played Lead Belly's songs since his earliest days, he was usually able to record his vocal and guitar tracks in one take.

Baldry explained to journalist Martin Dunphy, in a 2002 interview for Vancouver's *Georgia Straight*, that the original intention had been to release the disc in 1999, to commemorate the fiftieth anniversary of Lead Belly's death.

"But the whole project never got off the ground until Easter of 2000," he told Dunphy. "We had to do it on the odd weekend, as available. In essence, we recorded in the afternoon, either in my place, in my bedroom, or over at Andreas's. So it's really a home-made album."

From the most famous Ledbetter song, "Rock Island Line," which Baldry had first learned from the Lonnie Donegan recording, to songs like "John Hardy" or "Gallows Pole," which featured a soul-disturbing screech from Kathi McDonald, the album ran like the one-man blues road show that Baldry never managed to mount. "Good Morning Blues" opened with an excerpt from a kitchen recording Baldry had made in Cornwall, in 1958, which was edited neatly into the 2001 Vancouver bedroom session and augmented by Butch Coulter's overdubbed harmonica part, "flown in" from Germany.

The project's sense of history, both personal and musical, was reinforced by the inclusion of two spoken-word "bonus tracks." The first featured Baldry discussing Lead Belly with Holger Petersen. At one point, Petersen asked Baldry to put into words just what it was about Lead Belly's music that had left such a lasting impression on him.

"I think it's safe to say," Baldry asserted, "that if there'd been no Lead Belly... Big Bill Broonzy... Muddy Waters... there wouldn't have been that initial thing to capture us and drag us in, which happened with so many of the people that I was grow-ing up with and, of course, the people that came a little later, like Keith Richards, Mick Jagger and the Davies brothers from the Kinks and, oh, the list just goes on and on. But Lead Belly and Bill Broonzy were the major catalysts for us."

The second bonus track on the disc features Petersen in conversation with Alan Lomax, the son of the man who had recorded Lead Belly in the first place.

"John was so pleased about including that Alan Lomax inter-view," says Petersen today, "which I think really gives the project so much depth. Lomax talking about discovering Lead Belly, I mean, God, the guy was there when it happened. [He] and his father, you know, discovered Lead Belly and brought him to Washington, and here we have this actual interview with him, talking about what happened."

Shortly after the release of this labour of love, Baldry cel-ebrated his sixty-first birthday with another huge party at the Commodore. He promoted the album on the festival circuit in the months that followed, and later that year he did a short tour of the U.K. with Manfred Mann. When his old friend, the BBC's Spencer Leigh, met up with him, however, it was clear that Baldry was a shadow of his former self.

"Sadly," Baldry told Leigh, "I'm shrinking, as I have osteopo-rosis of the spine and I'm getting a buffalo hump. I have to be very careful about getting out of the bath, as if I broke my hip it might take forever to repair. I'm *shrinking* John Baldry now."

As his osteoporosis worsened, Baldry underwent hip replace-ment surgery to treat it. "I think that was probably the last time I saw him," remembers Andrew Loog Oldham, "just after his hip replacement. These tall geezers tend to have a problem with that, you know?"

Roger Baldry remembers his brother's last U.K. tour, this time with Dave Kelly and Butch Coulter, in the final months of 2004.

"John had a few days' break at my place on Dartmoor in Devon," says Roger. "I felt that there was a deterioration in him. He was not exactly unkempt, but he was not his normal sartorial elegance... His voice, I thought, was weak, and he sat through much of his performance, like an old man."

Hard living, most of it fun, had taken its toll on Long John Baldry, and the next few months of his incredible life would be his last.

i'll be seeing you

B ALDRY ONCE told a friend that he was terrified of hospitals. If he went in, he feared,
he would never come out.

By late 2004, although he had sworn off smoking for good,
Baldry was suffering from a persistent hacking cough and
chronic wheezing. He resisted Oz Rexach's attempts to get him
some medical attention until March 2005, when he was simply
too sick to fight it. Two weeks after being admitted to hospital,
Baldry was moved to a rehabilitation clinic. Once again, Rod
Stewart came to his mentor's side.

"Rod visited him at the rehab clinic," remembers Jeff
Edmunds. "It was really hard there for John; everybody there
was ninety years old, and people were throwing up all over the
place. He just wasn't very happy. In early April, he took a turn
for the worse and wound up in the intensive care ward, from
then onwards."

Margaret and Roger Baldry had been following their brother's decline since the previous Christmas, communicating with
him regularly via long-distance telephone calls.

"When John's condition dramatically deteriorated," Roger recalls, "he had a tracheotomy fitted and obviously couldn't communicate, but staff would take the phone to John so he could hear our voices. Over a period of weeks John had exploratory operations on his lung, and we were kept fully informed of his deterioration by [his doctor], who said that the prognosis was not good and [that he] would advise us when he thought it would be appropriate to visit John, as he believed he was unlikely to survive."

By late April, he and Margaret were on a plane bound for Vancouver and, quite possibly, for a good-bye.

Roger Baldry, seeing his "skeletal" brother through the windows of the intensive care unit, was reminded of their father's wasting death a decade and a half before. Jim Baldry, also a big man, had been similarly reduced, said Roger, "to a pathetic shell."

"John's feet and knee joints looked enormous," he remembers, "because his leg bones had no flesh on them. Although in obvious pain, when he saw Margaret and myself arriving, his face broke into the biggest, brightest, happiest smile. John's condition and his obvious joy to see us moved us to tears. Sadly, financial constraints meant we could only stay for two weeks. His doctor gave John's chance of survival as being the spin of a coin. Even if he did survive, it was most unlikely that he would ever perform again, because of the damage to his lungs."

In July, Evelyn Muncaster rushed out to Vancouver and accompanied Rexach to visit Baldry at the hospital.

"I was told that he'd just had a transfusion the day before," Muncaster recalls. "So when we walked in and saw him, he had an amazingly good colour… He looked really quite well, save for the fact that he had lost a tremendous amount of weight. He couldn't speak, because of the tube, and that seemed like an extremely sad thing to do to such an eloquent man. It was heartbreaking. Oz was there every single day, being very positive."

Word went out to Baldry's many friends and former band-mates around the world that he was extremely ill. Brian Auger received an urgent call at his home in California from a tearful Kathi McDonald.

"Kathi said, 'John's very ill,'" remembers Auger, "'I think you'd better call him. He'd love to hear from you; it would really buck him up.' I called the hospital, but they told me he was unable to speak, so I called Oz, who told me that John had developed pneumonia, that he'd been in the hospital for four months and that he couldn't speak because he was on a ventilator. At that point, I realized just how ill John was, and so I said to Oz, 'If you're going up to the hospital today, please send him our love, from all of us in the family, and tell him to get well soon, man.' I was just glad that he knew that we all cared for him and we were pulling for him. That's all we could do, really."

On July 1, Rexach was given the grim prognosis that Baldry's condition was beyond treatment. Although Baldry had been admitted to the hospital to treat a lung infection, his immune system was so depleted that he had fallen victim to so-called sick air syndrome, medically known as Methicillin Resistant Staphylococcus Aureus, or MRSA, an increasingly common condition affecting chronic care patients.

Jeff Edmunds says that he and Rexach did their best to make Baldry comfortable in his last days.

"Oz and I always tried to pick music that he liked," recalls Edmunds, "so the last music I played for him was 'Up above My Head,' a Sister Rosetta Tharpe song that he'd once recorded. I put it on, and he sort of raised his eyebrows and smiled at me. When I showed him this article in *Mojo* magazine that mentioned him, he perked up and put on his glasses so he could read it himself."

At 10:30 PM on July 21, 2005, surrounded by friends and loved ones, Long John Baldry was officially pronounced dead at the age of sixty-four.

The cause of death was listed as severe chest infection, although it may have been Baldry's appetite for living that ultimately killed him. It was of little matter now, anyway. All that was left was to mourn the passing of a legendary gentleman and to celebrate his roller-coaster ride of a life. It hadn't always been easy being Long John Baldry, but now he was, in the words of his hero Martin Luther King Jr., "free at last."

Memorials were held in Vancouver and Toronto, and fellow musicians and fans in each city showed up for a wake and jam session in Baldry's honour. In Vancouver, Kathi McDonald, Papa John King, Colin James and others performed, with Oz Rexach in attendance, at a loud yet reverent send-off at the Yale Tavern. In Toronto, Roy Young and members of the Mississippi Hippies, the backup band robbed of the chance to do a planned 2005 tour with Baldry, joined Anya Wilson, Evelyn Muncaster, Richard Flohil, Frank Garcia and Jeff Edmunds at a tribute held on a bluesy November evening at Hugh's Room.

Garcia, who had planned the aborted tour with Baldry (it was meant to celebrate the CD releases of *It Ain't Easy* and *Everything Stops for Tea*) converted the Baldry website he'd set up in 2001, www.longjohnbaldry.com, to a memorial site.

"Bringing Long John online," says Garcia today, "just like making his first video, was a high pleasure for me, and John's fans now have a place to go for LJB info and music. The guest book is a testament to the enormous love John gave to everyone who heard his music or [whom he] simply met shopping or while travelling the world. John Baldry was a messenger of love. He delivered and gave love generously. That was his high purpose here on earth."

A year after his brother's death, Roger Baldry would thank the many friends and fans who had sent their condolences to him and Margaret in a message posted at Garcia's site: "A memorial stone has been erected in the Churchyard of St. Lawrence's Church, Edgware, London. John spent his formative years in this area and was a choirboy at the Church. As a young man he practised his banjo and guitar in Canons Park nearby. John's love of baroque music was perhaps inspired at this church where Handel composed many of his works and played the organ there. A simple wooden cross, which had previously marked the family gravesite for sixty years, has now been relocated to Dartmoor and is placed alongside a red oak, which has been planted in lasting memory of John. John will be forever in our hearts."

He added that the oak "will grow to sixty feet and is a truly magnificent tree, a fitting memorial to John."

Baldry's long-time friend and protégé Rod Stewart said goodbye to his departed mentor onstage at the National Exhibition Centre in Birmingham on July 19, 2005. Against a series of projected photographs of his old mate, Stewart sang Sammy Kahn's sentimental standard "I'll Be Seeing You" in tribute to the man who gave him his start.

Stewart believes that Baldry will likely receive posthumously the kind of respect he rarely enjoyed in life. "At the time," Stewart says, "I don't think people realized that John Baldry, Alexis Korner and Cyril Davies were the guys who really fought to bring black blues to England. Along with Chris Barber, of course, they were instrumental in bringing Muddy Waters and Lead Belly and all those guys over to Britain. We owe them all a great debt, especially John. Not just myself but the Rolling Stones, Led Zeppelin, the Yardbirds, Eric Clapton and Jeff Beck. We all owe these guys something, because they laid the path and broke down the barriers for us. Long John Baldry is such a wonderful man. It's hard to say 'was,' because he's still a wonderful man, although he's gone from us."

Among the many things Stewart learned from Baldry, Jimmy Horowitz asserts, was great showmanship. "He taught Rod a lot about how to work with the crowd and how to stand on a rock stage. Consequently, Rod is a tremendous showman; most of his peers have no idea how to do it. John would play these blue-collar type clubs up in the north of England, and sometimes it didn't go down that well. But he knew how to milk an audience and, by the end of his set, he'd be back for three encores!"

Stony Plain's Holger Petersen agrees with Stewart, however, that John Baldry never got the credit he was due for introducing blues to so many people.

"Although many famous people recognized him," says Petersen today, "I fear the general public might have missed it. It's a shame that in Europe, for instance, when they think of Long John Baldry, they think of some lounge lizard on television singing 'Let the Heartaches Begin' or 'Mexico.' Those songs were so far removed from the soulful blues that John spent his life and career performing and promoting. History should remember him more for the amazing work that he did and the huge talent that he had for singing and performing the blues. Anybody who had a chance to see him live will never forget what a great performer he was, and what a funny comedian he could be. He was just a consummate entertainer."

Likewise, Eric Clapton regrets that Baldry's British legacy remains slightly tarnished.

"I think he probably did some of that damage himself," says Clapton, "with his career choices, you know? Those records he made in '67 got him pigeonholed with a lot of people who don't really know very much about the history of English R&B. They probably think that's all he did. There's a thing about pop music that it tends to kind of smear over the surface so that you don't look very deep. So anyone who knew John from those records would automatically assume that there wasn't anything else to the guy's repertoire. But John was a butterfly, you know? He would float around, and that's the way he wanted it to be. I don't think he really liked being pigeonholed in any way, so maybe he *deliberately* made those records, so that, you know, no one could really pin him down. That's another way of looking at it."

Guitarist Geoff Bradford, too, remembers Baldry as a trailblazing blues explorer who never truly got the respect he deserved. "When you think of people like Van Morrison," says Bradford, "he gets up there [nowadays] with B.B. King, and I think, 'Christ, what's he doing?' There's people like that have come and gone since John, but John was head and shoulders above them."

Baldry's friend and former road manager John Peters feels that Baldry's genius was his gift of insight: "To be able to take the right musicians and put them in his bands and let great music happen. His soul resonated with those of Lead Belly and Wilson Pickett."

Mick Fleetwood, for his part, recalls Baldry as a great entertainer.

"You know," says Fleetwood, "even when all the shit hit the fan, Long John Baldry could walk on the stage, just him and a guitar, and turn out an hour's worth of music. I would venture to say that you wouldn't take your eye off him. That, I think, should be his final legacy. I guess all that's missing is that he wasn't like this huge international star. He was like Joe Cocker, in that he owned the songs he sang. That, in itself, is an art form. If you mess with a Rolling Stones song, you'd better know how to do it, and make it your own. In the wrong hands, it's a dangerous domain to get into. He was very lucid, very dry onstage, and he could deal out these little dry witticisms in interviews or in the clubs and always had an incredible command of the situation. When Baldry sang, even in the noisiest, booziest pubs in the land, you could hear a pin drop. The punters realized that something was going on. A singer either has that command or he doesn't, and John never lost it. He was such a unique character, in my opinion, and had he been a huge megastar, I'm sure the world would have loved his eccentricities."

Giorgio Gomelsky calls Baldry a true "servant" of the music: "Like all people who have a passion for music, nothing else mattered."

Vancouver-based broadcaster Terry David Mulligan, who witnessed Baldry's last twenty years, recalls that the singer's deep historical roots had a huge impact on the musical community there.

"For us," says Mulligan, "John was the living link between his own heroes—blues greats he knew personally like Muddy Waters, Willie Dixon and Howlin' Wolf—and the musicians he discovered and inspired. He was from a magic time in London, when blues ruled the British Isles. John had shared the stage and influenced all of the great blues and rock artists after him, the Rolling Stones, Led Zeppelin, Rod and Elton, just to name a few. Yet somehow John made his way to Vancouver, and we all were richer for it. He showed all of us, audiences and musicians alike, what a world-class musician looked and sounded like. Young musicians would leave his gigs saying to themselves, 'I've got a ways to go.' My favourite stage to see John on was the Commodore. He and the legendary old dance hall had something in common: they were both throwbacks to another time and another place, when gritty, honest music shone bright and true. A number of times, I got to watch John from the side of the stage at the Commodore, before he went on. He was always riveted on whoever was out there in the lights. He saw the power in the place and in the moment and was drawn to it, as sure as Elvis himself."

Songwriter Gary Osborne had known Baldry in the '60s but noted that as Baldry aged, his blues voice gained a startlingly authentic quality. "A year or so before he died," Osborne recalls, "I heard John Baldry singing live, with just a twelve-string guitar, on a radio show called *Loose Ends*. He was singing better than I'd ever heard him. It was as though over all those years

John had become the blues singer he always knew he could be. I was thrilled for him."

To many of the musicians who worked with him over the years, Baldry was more than just a formidable entertainer: he was a valued friend and an agreeable ally. Brian Auger says that he was happy that he and Baldry stayed in touch after their years in Steampacket.

"We played up in Vancouver, with Kathi," Auger recalled. "My son Karma was in the band, and John had known Karma since he was born and seen him grow up... So, he was very excited about coming down to the gig. He sat in with us, and we all had a great night. He was raving about Karma; he said, 'Oh my God, I had no idea. Karma's become such an incredible player.' My daughter Savannah was up doing some dates on that tour with us, and he just thought it was wonderful, as did I, to have this family connection between all of us. He was such a magnanimous gentleman, and one of the most genuine human beings that I've met in all my forty years in the music business."

Kathi McDonald recalls numerous examples of Baldry's generosity and humour.

"John totally made everybody laugh," she says, "and made everybody comfortable. He was never, ever intimidating to his band; what would be the point of that? You can't force talent out of someone, but you can guide them and be on their side and they're better. Unfortunately a lot of the people bypassed him and got really famous, because John was just like a dad: he brought out the best in everybody. I'll never forget one time, when we played the Winthrop Blues Festival in Washington State with Koko Taylor as the headliner. They had introduced her as 'Koko Taylor, Queen of the Blues.' Well, we were on stage, getting ready to do our second-to-last song, and I guess he'd had a few cocktails, because he suddenly bellows out, 'Koko Taylor, the Queen of the Blues? I thought *I* was the Queen of the Blues!'"

Guitarist Mick Clarke recalls Baldry as a "great showman" onstage, and a hilarious comic off. "I fondly remember his myriad of jokes, cartoon sketches and hilarious anecdotes on the tour bus. He kept all of us laughing, even on the incredibly boring twelve-hour trips."

Susan Lane, widow of Baldry's good friend from the Faces, Ronnie Lane, credits Baldry with getting her through the difficult days after her husband lost his twenty-year battle with multiple sclerosis.

"Ronnie played a double bill with Long John around the beginning of the '90s. When Long John took the stage, Ronnie pulled me close to him and faced me forward rather like a schoolchild and said, 'Look—the ultimate showman.' And indeed he was. Ronnie beamed with a look reserved for his favourites and the best, which usually coincided. Ronnie and Long John spent the evening amusing themselves in a private conversation. As we got ready to leave, heading towards our transport, Long John turned and looked at me, then he walked across the parking lot, he took my hand and placed a kiss upon my cheek. It was the most gentlemanly kiss. Not receiving a lot of emotional support in those days, it was more than appreciated. As the years passed, Long John would phone and check on Ronnie. Most importantly, the night just after Ronnie had passed, Long John called and allowed me to pour out my widow's grief. He tried very hard to console me with so many kind words in that beautiful English brogue. For a very long time after Ronnie died, a lot longer than I'm willing to admit, it was just Ronnie and Long John on the box."

Anya Wilson says that, despite all the ups and downs, Baldry had a great time on Earth.

"John treated his life like a big adventure," she says. "I don't think he particularly got hung up about making the wrong decisions and beating himself up. I think he took life as it came. And he experienced many weird and wonderful things. You know, John is a survivor. Yes, I'm deliberately speaking about him in the present tense, because in a way I think he's still here. If anyone's got a powerful spirit, and I've felt it several times, it's him."

"John had a sadness in him," remembers *Peter Pan* producer Pat Waldron. "Like any of us, I'm sure he would have been happier if he'd ridden higher on the wave. But he never complained. We were very close the last few years."

Many, like Cameron Crowe, recall Baldry as a musician of great significance whose passing heralds the end of a distinct era in rock music.

"I love the *world* of Baldry," says Crowe. "I'm telling ya—'Don't Try to Lay No Boogie Woogie' was a watershed live moment, a real moment in time. That sultry, British boogie blues period is virtually gone now."

Al Harlow remembers speaking with Baldry just after his sixty-fourth birthday.

"Noel Redding [from the Jimi Hendrix Experience] had just died, and we were talking about lives, the old days in London, and that kind of stuff. John kind of chuckled and said, 'Sometimes I wonder, have I done the right thing by carrying on with this music thing? Has it really benefited me?' And I told him, 'John, you're an international treasure. There've been ups and downs, ins and outs. I don't know how we all measure success, but, John, you've totally done the right thing. It's solid gold, man. Your artistry is beyond dispute. Don't overthink it.'"

Elton John, whose chosen last name pays perhaps the biggest tribute to Baldry of all, recalls the man he once called "the boss" as one of the great British eccentrics.

"He was many things to me," says Elton. "He was a dandy and a gentleman who liked a good time and loved his music. That, for me, when I was young, was all I needed to be influenced by him. He literally saved my life, and I loved knowing and working with him. It's extraordinary that people have to wait until they die to get mass recognition. Nina Simone, for example, was totally underrated until she died, and now it's wonderful to see she had a top ten album in England. Likewise, Johnny Cash had a number one album in America after he died. I don't know if that's going to be the case with John, because I don't think, in all honesty, that he ever recorded the one album that personified him. He should have done [his 2003 Lead Belly tribute, *Remembering Leadbelly*] in the mid-'60s. He was great live, and he never recorded the big blues album that he should have done at the time, which is a shame."

Late-period Baldry guitarist and friend Lindsay Mitchell was entrusted with the task of taking the urn containing Long John Baldry's ashes back to England. According to Holger Petersen, Mitchell was boarding a British Airways flight to London when he explained to the flight attendant that his carry-on luggage consisted of the legendary musician's ashes. Mitchell asked the flight attendant if such a music legend might be worthy of one last upgrade to first class. The flight attendants were happy to comply, and the urn was promptly moved up to the exclusive front cabin. Mitchell, however, was left in coach.

It was the kind of funny but sad story that would surely have made Long John Baldry laugh uproariously. Even in death, Baldry couldn't resist one more comic twist.

·
·
·

the essential long john baldry

A SELECTED DISCOGRAPHY *compiled by Jeff Edmunds*

ALEXIS KORNER'S BLUES INCORPORATED | *R&B from the Marquee* (1962)
U.K., Decca Records (ACL 1130)
Long John Baldry sang on only three songs on Blues Incorporated's debut, including one early self-penned tune, "I Thought I Heard That Train Whistle Blow." Released on CD in the early 1990s.

LONG JOHN BALDRY | *Long John's Blues* (1964)
U.K., United Artists (ULP 1081)
This album features many of the musicians from the Hoochie Coochie Men, Baldry's band at the time, although, for contractual reasons, Rod Stewart is notably absent. It includes songs such as "Got My Mojo Working," "Goin' Down Slow" and "Everyday I Have the Blues," which became staples of Baldry's live shows throughout his career. Released on CD in 2006.

LONG JOHN BALDRY | *Looking at Long John* (1966)
U.K., United Artists (ULP 1146)
Baldry's second United Artists album is a departure from the blues sound of the first album, with a hint of soul reflective of his year and a half in Steampacket. Highlights include Baldry's first recording of "You've Lost That Lovin' Feelin'," a song he would re-record as a duet later in his career.

In 2006, both of Baldry's UA albums were compiled, along with extra tracks and singles, into one double-CD set for EMI, *Looking at Long John Baldry (The UA Years 1964–1966)* (EMI 0946 3 50899).

LONG JOHN BALDRY | *Let The Heartaches Begin* (1968)
U.K., Pye Records (NPL 18208)
This album's release was timed to capitalize on the success of Baldry's single "Let the Heartaches Begin," which went to number one in England in November 1967. It includes many songs written by Tony Macaulay, who was one of the hottest songwriter-producers of the day, having written hits like "Build Me Up Buttercup" for the Foundations and "Love Grows (Where My Rosemary Goes)" for Edison Lighthouse.

LONG JOHN BALDRY | *Wait For Me* (1969)
U.K., Pye Records (NSPL 18366)
Baldry's next Pye album contains more soulful renditions of chestnuts like "River Deep, Mountain High" and "Cry Like a Baby." Another highlight from the Pye years was "Mexico," which was ITV's theme song for their coverage of the 1968 Olympics in Mexico. He ended his Pye contract in 1970.

LONG JOHN BALDRY | *It Ain't Easy* (1971)
U.S., Warner Brothers (WS 1921)
Elton John and Rod Stewart produced one side each of Baldry's North American debut, allowing him to adopt the blues-rock

sound that he continued to pursue for the remainder of his career. The album opener, "Don't Try to Lay No Boogie Woo-gie on the King of Rock 'n' Roll," presaged by his spoken-word busking-days diatribe, "Conditional Discharge," became Bald-ry's signature song. The album includes a great version of Willie Dixon's "I'm Ready." Released on CD in 2005.

LONG JOHN BALDRY | *Long John's Blues* (1971)
U.S., United Artists (UAS 5543)
Baldry's 1964 album for United Artists was reissued for America with a gatefold sleeve showing photos and clippings from the era. The bonus on this record is the inclusion of Baldry's duet with Rod Stewart on Sister Rosetta Thorpe's "Up above My Head," the B-side to Baldry's 1964 single "You'll Be Mine."

LONG JOHN BALDRY | *Everything Stops for Tea* (1972)
U.S., Warner Brothers (WB 46 160)
This follow-up to *It Ain't Easy*, once again produced half and half by Elton John and Rod Stewart, represents a slight move away from the blues-rock of its predecessors towards a more folk-rock sound. Baldry shines on great versions of Willie Dix-on's "Seventh Son" and "You Can't Judge a Book," plus a superb rendition of the Dixie Cups' "Iko Iko." Baldry and Stewart duet on the traditional folk song "Mother Ain't Dead." The album cover features a drawing by Ron Wood depicting Baldry as the Mad Hatter from *Alice in Wonderland*. Released on CD in 2005.

LONG JOHN BALDRY | *Good to Be Alive*
(1973 in the U.K.; 1975 in North America)
U.K., GM Records; North America,
Casablanca Records (GML 1005)
Good to Be Alive, along with *It Ain't Easy* and *Everything Stops for Tea*, completes the trio of Baldry's best recordings, as far as songs are concerned. The title song, "Good to Be Alive,"

showcases the essential Baldry: a folksy, bluesy troubadour harking back to his busking roots. Released in 1973 in the U.K. on the Gaff Management label, it was not released in North America until Casablanca Records put it out in 1975. Were it not for this delay, Baldry's stature in North America quite possibly would have been significantly elevated. Never released on CD.

LONG JOHN BALDRY | *Welcome to Club Casablanca* (1976)
U.S., Casablanca Records (NBLP 7035-V)
This is a great but forgotten Baldry record, in part because Casablanca, the label, was primarily known for disco artists like the Village People and Donna Summer. Recorded in 1976 in Los Angeles and London with crack session players, it features soulful versions of "Ain't No Love in the Heart of the City," "Had Enough" and "Easy Evil." The album cover photo was taken in label president Neil Bogart's office, which transformed into a nightclub for the occasion.

LONG JOHN BALDRY | *Baldry's Out!* (1979)
Canada, Capitol Records—EMI of Canada (ST 6459)
Highlights from Baldry's first album for Capitol EMI Canada include his duet with Kathi McDonald on "You've Lost That Lovin' Feelin'," which Bill Medley of the Righteous Brothers once declared his favourite version of the song. The album went double platinum in Canada after the release of the single "A Thrill's a Thrill," a beautiful and controversial song by Barbra Amesbury. Currently available on CD.

LONG JOHN BALDRY | *Boys in the Band* (1980)
Canada, Quality Records (SV 2068)
This album was released by Quality Records in Canada to capitalize on the success of *Baldry's Out!* The material was recorded

in the mid '70s, and producer Billy Russell replaced Tom Brown's vocals with Baldry's vocals. More than likely, Baldry agreed to this in an attempt to secure a record deal. The material is album-oriented rock highlighted by the title song and the work of Baldry's guitarist Alan Murphy, who later worked with Kate Bush. Not available on CD.

LONG JOHN BALDRY | *Long John Baldry* (1980)
Canada, Capitol Records—EMI Canada (SW 17038)
Baldry's second EMI release was produced by former Bowie sideman Stacey Heydon and recorded by Bob and Daniel Lanois at Grant Avenue Studios in Hamilton, Ontario, quite near Baldry's home, at the time, in Dundas, Ontario. Highlights include Bonnie Dobson's "Morning Dew," which became a top-ten hit in the Netherlands. Baldry also covers two Mink DeVille songs, "Savoir Faire" and "Mixed Up, Shook Up Girl." Capitol Records had Baldry record "Love Me Two Times" by the Doors after a computer program indicated that Baldry and the Doors shared the same fans.

LONG JOHN BALDRY | *Rock with the Best* (1982)
Canada, Capitol Records—EMI of Canada (ST 6490)
This album was recorded in Vancouver, British Columbia, and produced by Bill Henderson and Brian McLeod of the Canadian rock band Chilliwack. Henderson and McLeod also wrote some of the songs, including "Let the Heartaches Stop," a humorous response to "Let the Heartaches Begin."

LONG JOHN BALDRY | *Silent Treatment* (1986)
Canada, Musicline Records (ML 0001)
This mix of rock, blues and big ballads was released on the fledgling independent Musicline label. Baldry made his first-

ever rock video for the title song. A standout on the album is
Baldry and Kathi McDonald doing a great version of the Walker
Brothers' hit "The Sun Ain't Gonna Shine Anymore." "A Life of
Blues" is also great, a self-penned and very autobiographical
song. Available on CD.

LONG JOHN BALDRY | *It Still Ain't Easy* (1991)
Canada, Stony Plain Records (SPCD 1163)
This was Baldry's first record for the independent, Edmonton,
Alberta–based roots label Stony Plain Records. It is primarily a
blues-based record, with a wide variety of rockers and ballads,
folk material and blues. Baldry and McDonald do a great interpretation of Willie Dixon's "Insane Asylum," and Baldry also does
a beautiful a cappella rendition of a traditional song, "Do More."

LONG JOHN BALDRY | *Live, On Stage Tonight* (1993)
Canada, Stony Plain Records (SPCD 1192)
Baldry had a long history of leading great bands and putting on
incredible live shows. This was his first live recording, and it features long-time band members Butch Coulter, Papa John King
and Kathi McDonald performing great versions of live staples
like "I'm Ready," "It Ain't Easy," "Stormy Monday Blues" and
Baldry's signature song "Don't Try to Lay No Boogie Woogie on
the King of Rock 'n' Roll".

LONG JOHN BALDRY | *A Thrill's a Thrill—*
The Canadian Years (1995)
Canada, EMI Music Canada (S22Z 29609)
This double-CD retrospective of Baldry's Canadian recording
career includes material from Capitol Records and Stony Plain
Records. Richard Flohil's liner notes are quite informative and
cover many different periods of Baldry's career. The recording

provides an original overview of Baldry's blues-rock material from 1979 to 1995. Currently available on CD.

LONG JOHN BALDRY | *Right to Sing the Blues* (1996)
Canada, Stony Plain Records (SPCD 1232)
Baldry won the 1997 Juno Award (Canada) for the Best Blues Recording. The title song was written by and features the guitar work of Canadian blues ace Colin James. Baldry does excellent versions of traditional blues songs such as "East Virginia Blues" and "Whoa Back Buck." A bonus track contains a lengthy interview in which Baldry and label boss Holger Petersen discuss Baldry's early days and his friendship with Willie Dixon.

LONG JOHN BALDRY | *Live, Long John Baldry Trio* (2000)
Canada, Stony Plain Records (SPCD 1268)
Another live recording from Germany, this was recorded in September of 1999 and features Butch Coulter and young U.K. guitarist Matt Taylor. The recording is a replica of Baldry's acoustic shows, featuring blues material such as "Good Morning Blues," "Can't Keep from Crying Some Times" and "Back Water Blues."

LONG JOHN BALDRY | *Remembering Leadbelly* (2001)
Canada, Stony Plain Records (SPCD1275)
Lead Belly was Baldry's biggest musical influence, and here Long John pays tribute in an album that takes him from the 1950s, when he first heard Lead Belly's music, right up to the days he and Andreas Schuld recorded this album in Baldry's bedroom in Vancouver. In the extensive liner notes, Baldry writes about his history with each of the songs on the album. The first thirty seconds of "Good Morning Blues" are lifted from a recording that a seventeen-year-old Baldry made in a Cornwall, England, kitchen back in 1958.

OTHER NOTABLE LONG JOHN BALDRY
APPEARANCES ON RECORD

ROD STEWART | *Every Picture Tells a Story* (1971)
U.S. and U.K., Mercury Records (LP 609)
Long John Baldry sings background vocals, with Maggie Bell, on the title song.

VARIOUS ARTISTS | *Mar Y Sol* (1972)
U.S., Atco Records (SDE 2-705)
Baldry performs a live version of "Bring My Baby Back" at the First International Puerto Rico Pop Festival.

STUDDMEN | *Tivoli-Sumar A Syrlandi* (1974)
Iceland, Steinar Records (VR 21415)
The Icelandic band Studdmen included one-time Baldry sideman Jakob Magnusson. Baldry sings "She Broke My Heart" on the album.

acknowledgements

THANKS TO Barbara Pulling for her wise editorial suggestions and for calmly guiding the book into its present state, and to Rob Sanders for hiring me in the first place.

Since Long John Baldry was deceased by the time I began researching this book, it was necessary to pull together any first-person recollections from previously recorded interviews, periodicals and comments Baldry made in the biographies of his peers. I am most grateful to Nick Orchard and Holger Petersen, who generously shared their exclusive Baldry audio and video archives, and to Sid Griffin and the BBC's Spencer Leigh, who allowed me to borrow Baldry quotes from their interview texts. Thanks must go to Baldry archivist Jeff Edmunds, who was a valuable resource concerning the singer's life and career. Other Baldry quotes were drawn from a thorough, yet unaccredited, 2001 interview Mr. Baldry gave to a publication called *The New Breed*, a photocopy of which was provided to me by Jeff Edmunds. I was not able to track down the origins of this publication and would welcome the chance to give credit and thanks to those responsible. Special thanks to Ann Merchant who not only transcribed the lion's share of my interviews but also cheered me on to the finish line and made valuable suggestions along the way.

I am deeply indebted to the many key people in Long John Baldry's life who graciously agreed to be interviewed exclusively for this book: Elton John, Rod Stewart, Paul McCartney, Brian Auger, Mick Fleetwood, Eric Clapton, Chris Barber, Ian McLagan, Mike McCartney (thanks also for the "foties"), Giorgio Gomelsky, Andrew Loog Oldham, Ramblin' Jack Elliott, Cameron Crowe, Ronnie Hawkins, Kelly Jay, Geoff Bradford, John Mayall, Tony Macaulay, Jimmy Horowitz, Kathi McDonald, Felix "Oz" Rexach, Margaret Baldry, Roger Baldry, Anya Wilson, Evelyn Muncaster, Billy Gaff, Bill Henderson, Deane Cameron, Holger Petersen, Roy Young (thanks to Greg Godovitz and to Stella for the dinner with Roy), David Marsden, Terry David Mulligan, Vince Ditrich, Saffron Summerfield, Ben Mattijssen, Frank Garcia, Graham Wood, Barbra Amesbury, Al Harlow and Jim Byrnes.

Thank you to Pete Frame for granting permission to quote text from many of his excellent Rock Family Trees and to Beatles archivist extraordinaire Mark Lewisohn for help in sorting out the convergence between Baldry and the Beatles. Thanks to Andrew Darlington for the clippings. Lastly, thanks to Malcolm Gladwell, author of *The Tipping Point*, for actually responding to my email and confirming that Long John Baldry was what Gladwell called a classic Connector, "putting people from many disparate worlds in touch with each other and in touch with an idea."

This book includes brief passages from *Blowing the Blues* by Dick Heckstall-Smith and Pete Grant (Clear Books, 2004); *Sir Elton* by Philip Norman (Sidgwick & Jackson, 2000); *The Beatles and Some Other Guys* by Pete Frame (Omnibus Press,

1997); *Kink* by Dave Davies (Hyperion, 2000); *Rod Stewart: The New Biography* by Tim Ewbank and Stafford Hildred (Portrait Books, 2003); *Mods* by Richard Barnes (Plexus Publishing, 1994) and *My Music,* edited and compiled by Mark De Novellis (Orleans House Gallery, 2005). Certain quotes from the Rolling Stones appeared on a website called *Confessions of a Sixties Drummer,* a tribute to drummer Carlo Little. Some Keith Richards quotes are from Robert Greenfield's 1972 interview with Richards in *Rolling Stone* magazine. Baldry concert reviews by Robert Palmer originally appeared in the *New York Times.*

Certain lyrics from "A Thrill's a Thrill" by Barbra Amesbury, © 1975 Amesbury Music. Used by permission.

Lyrics from "A Life of Blues" By John Baldry, Jimmy Horowitz, and John King, © 1987 BMAR (copyright controlled).

index

P AUL MYERS is the author of *Barenaked Ladies: Public Stunts, Private Stories* (Simon & Schuster, 2003). As a broadcaster, he has appeared on CBC Radio and CTV Television and contributed to the U.S. music channel VH1. His writing has appeared in a wide variety of publications, including the *San Francisco Chronicle,* the *San Francisco Bay Guardian,* the *Globe and Mail,* the *Georgia Straight,* the *Vancouver Sun, Mix* magazine and *Electronic Musician.* Paul Myers is also an accomplished songwriter, guitarist and producer.